Algorithm Challenges
The Dojo Collection

Version 1.1.6
April 22, 2017

By Martin Puryear

Copyright © 2016, 2017 by Martin Puryear and Coding Dojo

All rights reserved. This book or any portion thereof may not be reproduced or used in any manner whatsoever without the express written permission of the publisher, except for the use of brief quotations in a book review or scholarly journal.

First Printing and eBook Release: 2016

Coding Dojo, Inc.
10777 Main Street, Suite 100
Bellevue, WA 98004

www.codingdojo.com

ISDN: 978-1-365-45721-0

Algorithms Course Summary

Every day for **at least one hour**, we will challenge you with algorithm problems from our sequential curriculum.

Daily Operation
Each onsite cohort will divide into groups, and groups will be tasked with solving algorithms on whiteboards. In the session's last 15 minutes, one group will present solutions, as will your instructor/TA. Online, challenges will be posted by the instructor at a common location.

Goals
One important goal of the course is to get you comfortable describing your code's functionality. This is important for technical interviews, where you are asked to demonstrate your knowledge using only whiteboards.

Another important goal is to familiarize yourself with algorithms and data structures that solve complex problems efficiently, even as they scale worldwide.

Rules
1. Show up – the only way to rewire your brain to think like a computer is *repetition*. Make sure you're on time for every session to get the challenge's introduction.

2. No Laptops – to simulate a technical interview, do not use laptop or refer to old code during challenges. Until directed otherwise, work problems on a whiteboard.

3. Be respectful – being able to walk others through your algorithm, explaining how it works, is as important as correctness. There will be many chances to discuss with peers or present to the class. All students should give the speaker full attention and respect. Public speaking is a common fear; we will learn to conquer our nerves. This only happens in a welcoming environment.

4. Work in groups – group work requires you to articulate your thoughts and describe your code, skills that are also useful when working in engineering teams more generally. Groups that are too large do not lead to participation by all group members. *Don't be just a spectator!* Unless otherwise directed, **solve algorithm challenges in groups of 2 or 3** – no smaller or larger.

Presenting
Every day, two groups present solutions. Make sure all group members have a chance to describe the algorithm; give presenting groups the proper respect.

Questions to ask about solutions
1. Is it clear and understandable?
Can you easily explain functionality and lead the listener through a T-diagram? Does the code self-describe effectively, or do you find yourself having to explain the meaning of the variables 'x' and 'i'?

2. Is the output correct?
Does your algorithm produce the required results? Is your algorithm resilient in the face of unexpected inputs or even intentional attempts to get it to crash?

3. Is it concise?
Remember the acronym DRY (Don't Repeat Yourself). Less code is better, so long as it is fully understandable. Pull any duplicate code into helper functions.

4. Is it efficient?
Does your function contain only necessary statements, and does it require only necessary memory? Does it stay efficient (in run time as well as memory usage), as the input size gets very large? Are you mindful of any intentional tradeoffs of time vs. space (improving run time by using more memory, or vice versa)?

Tips
- Think out loud, to provide a window to your thinking. You may even get help if you are on the wrong track!
- Describe assumptions. Clarify before writing code.
- List sample inputs, along with expected outputs. This validates your understanding of the problem.
- Don't bog down. Add a comment, then move on.
- Break big problems down into smaller problems.
- Focus on correct outputs, *then* on *'correct'* solutions.
- Don't stress! Algorithm challenges are brain cardio. This is not an evaluation of your abilities or expertise!
- Have fun! *Problem analysis* is a fundamental skill that makes you a more effective software engineer.

Table of Contents

CHAPTER 0 – FOUNDATION CONCEPTS 1
- Computers, Software, and Source Code 1
- Code Flow 2
- Variables 2
- Data Types 3
- Not All Equals Signs Are the Same! 4
- Printing to the Console 5
- Functions 6
- Conditionals 7
- Complex Conditionals 8
- Chaining and Nesting 9
- Loops 10
- FOR Loops 10
- WHILE Loops 11
- Other Loop Tips 12
- Loops and Code Flow 13
- Parameters 14
- Foundations Review 15

CHAPTER 1 – FUNDAMENTALS 16
- Return Values 17
- Arrays 18
- Writing Values into Arrays 19
- Combining Arrays and FOR Loops 21
- Using a T-Diagram 23
- Comments 25
- Fundamentals Review 26

THE "BASIC 13" 27

CHAPTER 2 – FUNDAMENTALS, PART II 28
- Modulo Operator 29
- Math Library 31
- Using Modulo to Extract a Digit 32
- Variables that Live Longer than a Single Function Call 33
- Fundamentals Part II Review 35

SOLVING WHITEBOARD PROBLEMS (RIOT WALK) 36

CHAPTER 3 – ARRAYS 37
- Array.length 39
- Passing By Reference 40
- Another T-Diagram (Loops) 41
- "Truthy" and "Falsey" 43

Arrays Review	44

"BASIC 13" REVIEW — 45

CHAPTER 4 – STRINGS AND ASSOCIATIVE ARRAYS — 49
More About Strings	49
Switch/case statements	51
Fast-Finish / Fast-Fail	53
Associative Arrays (Objects)	54
FOR ... IN Loops	55
Why Don't We Allow Built-In Functions?	56
Strings and Associative Arrays Review	57

DEBUGGING YOUR JAVASCRIPT CODE — 58

CHAPTER 5 – LINKED LISTS — 59
Objects and Classes	59
Linked Lists	60
Prompts	63
Alerts	64
Write Understandable Code!	67
Linked Lists Review	69

THE "BUGGY 13" (#1) — 70

CHAPTER 6 – QUEUES AND STACKS — 72
Queues	73
Stacks	74
Circular Queues	76
Queues and Stacks Review	79

CHAPTER 7 – ARRAYS, PART II — 80
Test-Driven Development	80
Divide and Conquer	81
Time-Space Tradeoff	83
Data Sufficiency	85

THE "BUGFUL 13" (#2) — 86

CHAPTER 8 – LINKED LISTS, PART II — 89
Runners and Linked List Iterators	90
Doubly Linked List	94

CHAPTER 9 – RECURSION — 96
Three requirements for effective recursion	96

    T-Diagrams and Recursion   98
    Dynamic Programming and Memoization   100

CHAPTER 10 – STRINGS, PART II   107

THE "BUG-LADEN 13" (#3)   113

CHAPTER 11 – TREES   116
    Binary Tree Depth   118
    Binary Search Tree Traversal   119
    Self-Instantiating Classes   120
    Making BST a Fully Navigable Data Structure   122

CHAPTER 12 – SORTS   124
    Big-O Notation   126
    Adaptivity   127
    Stability   128
    Memory Analysis   129
    Sorting Review   131

THE "BUG-INFESTED 13" (#4)   132

CHAPTER 13 – SETS AND PRIORITY QUEUES   135
    Sets and Multisets   135
    Set Operations   136
    Set Theory Recap   138
    Priority Queues   139
    Heap Data Structure   140

CHAPTER 14 – HASHES   144
    Hash Collisions   146

CHAPTER 15 – TREES, PART II   151
    Full Trees and Complete Trees   151
    Repairing a Binary Search Tree   152
    BST Partitioning   153
    Repairing a More Complex Binary Search Tree   154
    Breadth-First Search   155

CHAPTER 16 – TRIES   156
    Trie Data Structure   156
    Trie MultiSet   159
    Trie Map   159

CHAPTER 17 – GRAPHS   160

    Graph Terms — 161
    Representing Graphs — 162
    Edge List — 163
    Adjacency Map — 164
    Adjacency List — 165
    Directed and Undirected Graphs — 166
    Edges Have Weight — 166
    Depth-First Search — 167
    Breadth-First Search — 168
    Directed Acyclic Graphs — 169

CHAPTER 18 – BIT ARITHMETIC — 170
    Numerical Systems — 170
    Octal System — 171
    Hexadecimal System — 172
    Binary System — 173
    Bitwise Operators, Part 1 — 174
    Bitwise Operators, Part 2 — 175
    Bit Shifting and Masking — 176

CHAPTER 19 – TREES, PART III — 178
    AVL Trees — 178
    Rotation — 180
    Red-Black Trees — 183
    Splay Trees — 184

CHAPTER 20 – SPATIAL, LOGIC, ESTIMATION — 186
    Spatial Problems — 186
    Logic (Thought) Problems — 187
    Estimation — 190

CHAPTER 21 – OPTIMIZATION — 191
    The Performance Journey — 191
    Code Tuning — 211
    Optimization Review — 222

INDEX OF CHALLENGES — 223

INTERVIEW TIPS — 236

Chapter 0 – Foundation Concepts

Computers, Software, and Source Code

Computers are amazing. They rapidly perform complex calculations, store immense amounts of data, and almost instantly retrieve specific bits of information from mountains of data. In addition to being fast, they appear superhuman in their ability to use information to make decisions. How do they do it?

Simply put, computers are machines. We as humans are skilled at creating tools that perform *specific* tasks *very* well: a toaster, for example, or a lawn mower. Computers are tools built from components such as semiconductor *chips*, and ongoing advances in material science enable these pieces to get smaller and faster with every successive year (see *Moore's Law*). This is why computers have become so breathtakingly fast, but it only partially explains why they can seem so *smart*. It doesn't really tell us why they are so universally relied upon to solve such a diverse range of problems across today's world.

Computing is exciting because computing devices are flexible – they can be *taught* to do things not imagined when they were originally built. Science fiction may become science in the future, but for today they only know what we *tell* them; they only do as they are told. Who *teaches* them, who *tells* them what to do? Software engineers, developers, programmers! You are reading this, so you probably intend to be one too. From a computer's viewpoint, you are training to become an educator. (-:

How do programmers tell computers what to do? We create **Software**. Software is a sequence of instructions that we build and provide to a computer, which then "mindlessly" runs those instructions. Computers cannot natively understand human language, nor can humans read the language of semiconductor components. To talk with computers, we need a "go-between" format: something that software engineers can understand, yet can also be translated into machine language instructions.

Many of these "go-between" languages have been created: PHP, Python, Ruby, JavaScript, Swift, C#, Java, Perl, Erlang, Go, Rust, and others – even HTML and CSS! Each language has differing strengths and therefore is useful in different situations. Programming languages all do essentially the same things though: they read in a series of human-readable steps instructing a computer how to respond, and they translate the steps into a format the computer can understand and later execute.

All these sequences of instructions, written in programming languages like JavaScript, are what we call **Source Code**. How and when this source code is translated into *machine code* will depend on the language and the machine. *Interpreted languages* like PHP, Python and Ruby translate from source code into machine code "on the fly", immediately before a computer needs it. *Compiled languages* do some or all of this translation ahead of time. As we said earlier, a computer simply follows instructions it was given. More specifically, though, it executes (*runs*) machine code that was built (*translated*) from some piece of source code: code that was written by a software engineer.

Let's teach you how to think like a computer, so you can write effective source code. We have chosen to use JavaScript as the programming language for this book, so along the way you'll learn the specifics of that language. With very few exceptions, however, these concepts are universal.

Chapter 0 – Foundation Concepts

Code Flow

When a computer executes (runs) a piece of code, it simply reads each line from the beginning of the file, executing it in order. When the computer gets to the end of the lines to execute, it is finished with that program. There may be *other* programs running on that computer at the same time (e.g. pieces of the operating system that update the monitor screen), but as far as your program goes, when the computer's execution gets to the end of the source you've given it, the program is done and the computer has completed running your code.

It isn't necessary for your code to be purely linear from the top of the file to the end of the file, however. You can instruct the computer to execute the same section of code multiple times – this is called a program `LOOP`. Also, you can have the computer jump to a different section of your code, based on whether a certain condition is true or false – this is called an `IF-ELSE` statement (or a conditional). Finally, for code that you expect to use often, whether called by various places in your own code, or perhaps even called by others' code, you can separate this out and give it a specific label so that it can be called directly. This is called a `FUNCTION`. More on each of these later.

Variables

Imagine if you had two objects (a book and a ball) that you wanted to carry around in your hands. With two hands, it is easy enough to carry two objects. However, what if you also had a sandwich? You don't have enough hands, so you need one or more containers for each of the objects. What if you had a box with a label on it, inside which you can put one of your objects. The box is closed, so all you see is the label, but it is easy enough to open the box and look inside. This is essentially what a *variable* does.

A variable is a specific spot in memory, with a label that you give it. You can put anything you want into that memory location and later refer to the value of that memory, by using the label. The statement:

```
var myName = 'Martin';
```

creates a variable, gives it a label of `myName`, and puts a value of `"Martin"` into that memory location. Later, to reference or inspect the value that you stored there, you simply refer to the label `myName`. For example (jumping ahead to the upcoming Printing to the Console topic), to *display* the value in the variable `myName`, do this:

```
console.log(myName);
```

Chapter 0 – Foundation Concepts

Data Types

Containers exist to hold things. You would create a variable because you want it to store some value – some piece of information. A value could be a number, or a sentence made of text characters, or something else. Specifically, JavaScript has a few *data types*, and all values are one of those types. Of these six data types, three are important to mention right now. These are Number, String, and Boolean.

In JavaScript, a *Number* can store a huge range of numerical values from extremely large values to microscopically small ones, to incredibly negative values as well. If you know other programming languages, you might be accustomed to making a distinction between integers and floating-point numbers – JavaScript makes no such distinction.

A *String* is any sequence of characters, contained between quotation marks. In JavaScript, you can use either single-quotes or double-quotes. Either way, just make sure to close the string the same way you opened it. `'Word'` and `"wurd"` are both fine, but `'weird"` and `"whoa!'` are not.

Finally, a *Boolean* has only two possible values: `true` and `false`. You can think of a Boolean like a traditional light switch, or perhaps a yes/no question on a test. Just as a light switch can be either *on* or *off*, and just as a yes/no question can be answered with either *yes* or *no*, likewise a Boolean must have a value of either `true` or `false` – there is nothing in-between.

One of the main things we do with variables, once they contain information of a certain data type, is to compare them. This is our next section.

Chapter 0 – Foundation Concepts

Not All Equals Signs Are the Same!

In many programming languages, you see both = and ==. These mean different things! Code (X = Y) can be described as *"Set the value of X to become the value of Y"*, and you can describe (X == Y) as *"Is the value of X equivalent to the value of Y?"* It is more common – but less helpful right now while learning these concepts – verbalize these as *"Assign Y to X"* and *"Are X and Y equal?"*, respectively.

Use = to **set** things, == to **test** things. Single-equals is for assignment; double-equals is for comparison.

Many programming languages are extremely picky about data types. When asked to combine two values that have differing data types, some languages will halt with an error rather than do so. JavaScript, however, is not so strict. In fact, you could say that JavaScript is very *loosely* typed: it very willingly changes a variable's data type, whenever needed. Remember the == operator that we described previously? It *actually* means "after converting X and Y to the same data type, are their values equivalent?" If you want strict comparison without converting data types, use the === operator.

Generally, === is advised, unless you explicitly intend to equate values of differing types, such as `{1,true,"1"}` or `{0,false,"0"}`, etc. (If this last sentence doesn't make sense yet, don't worry.)

Quick quiz:
1. How many inputs are accepted by the == operator and the === operator, respectively?
2. Do inputs to == and === operators need to be the same data type, for the operators to function?
3. What is the data type of the output value produced by the == and === operators?

Hey! Don't just read on: *jot down answers* for those questions before moving on.

Done? OK, good....

Answers:
1. The == and === operators both accept *two* values (one before the operator, and one after).
2. *No*, two values need not be the same type for these operators. However, if they are not, === always returns `false`. The == internally converts values to the same type before comparing.
3. The == and === operators both return a *Boolean* value (`true` or `false`).

Now that you know just a little about Numbers, Strings and Booleans, let's start using them.

Chapter 0 – Foundation Concepts

Printing to the Console

Eventually, you will create fabulous web systems and/or applications that do very fancy things with graphical user interface. However, when we are first learning how to program, we start by having our programs write simple text messages (strings!) to the screen. In fact, the very first program that most people write in a new language is relatively well known as the "Hello World" program. In JavaScript, we can quickly send a text string to the *developer console*, which is where errors, warnings and other messages about our program go as well. This is not something that a normal user would ever look at, but it is the easiest way for us to print variables or other messages.

To log a message to the console, we use `console.log()`. Within the parentheses of this call, we put any message we want displayed. The `console.log` function always takes in a string. If we send it something that isn't a string, JavaScript will first convert it to a string that it can print. It's very obliging that way. So, our message to be logged could be a literal value (`42` or `"Hello"`), or a variable like this:

```
console.log("Hello World!");

var message = "Welcome to the Dojo";
console.log(message);
```

We can also combine literal strings and variables into a larger string for `console.log`, simply by adding them together. If you had a variable `numDays`, for example, you could log a message like this:

```
var numDays = 40;
console.log("It rained for " + numDays + " days and nights!");
```

Notice that we put a space at the end of our `"It rained for "` string, so that the console would log `"It rained for 40 days and nights!"` instead of `"It rained for40days and nights!"`

So, what would the following code print?

```
var greeting = "howdy";
console.log("greeting" + greeting);
```

It would print `"greetinghowdy"`, since we ask it to combine the literal string `"greeting"` with the value of the variable `greeting`, which is `"howdy"`. Make sense?

One last side note: if you *really insist* upon writing a string to the actual web page, you could use the old-fashioned function `document.write()`, such as `document.write("Day #" + numDays)`. However, you won't use this function when creating real web pages, so why get into that habit now?

Chapter 0 – Foundation Concepts

Functions

Let's say that you are writing a piece of code that has five different places where it needs to print your name. As mentioned above, for code that you expect to call often, separate this out into a different part of your file, so these lines of code don't need to be duplicated each time you print your name. This is called a `FUNCTION`. Creating (or *declaring*) a function could look like this:

```
function sayMyName( )
{
   console.log("My name is Martin");
}
```

By using the special `function` word, you tell JavaScript that what follows is a set of source code that can be called at any time by simply referring to the `sayMyName` label. Note: *the code above does not actually call the function immediately*; it sets the function up for other code to use (call) it later.

'Calling' the *function* is also referred to as 'running' or 'executing' the function. If the above is how you declare a function, then the below is how you actually *run* that function:

```
sayMyName();
```

That's it! All you need to do is call that label, followed by open and close parentheses. The parentheses are what tell the computer to execute the function with that label, so don't forget those.

One last thing: there is nothing stopping a function from calling other functions (or in certain special situations, even calling itself!). You can see above that the `sayMyName` function does, in fact, call the built-in `console.log` function. Naturally, you would not expect `console.log` to run *until* you actually called it; in the same way, any code that you write will only start running when some other code calls it (maybe part of the computer browser or the operating system). So, except for the very first piece of code that runs when a hardware device starts up, all other code runs only because other code called it.

To review: when we *declare* a function, it allows some other *caller* to execute our function from some other place in the code, at some other time. It does not run the function immediately. So, if your source code file contains this:

```
function sayMyName( )
{
   console.log("My name is Martin");
}
```

…and then you execute that source code file, nothing would actually appear in the developer console. This is because no code ever called `sayMyName()`. You set it up, but never used it.

Chapter 0 – Foundation Concepts

Conditionals

If you are driving and reach a fork in the road, you must decide which way to go. Most likely, you will decide based on some very good reason. In code, there is a similar mechanism. `IF` statements look at the value of a variable, or perhaps compare two variables, and then execute certain lines of code if the result is what you expect. If you wish, you can also execute *other* lines of code if the result goes the other way. The important point is that each decision has only two possible outcomes. You have a certain test or comparison to be done; `IF` the test passes, `THEN` you execute certain code. If you wish, you can execute other code in the "*test did not pass*" (`ELSE`) case. This code would look like this:

```
if (myName == "Martin")
{
   console.log("Hey there Martin, how's it going?");
}
```

The `IF` statement is followed by parentheses that contain our *test*. Remember that we need to use a double-equals to create a comparison, and here we compare the value of variable `myName` to the string `"Martin"`. If the comparison passes, then we execute the next section of code within the curly braces. Otherwise, we skip that code. What if we want to greet users with a cheerful comment, even if they are not Martin? You can execute other code in this case (called the `ELSE`). We might write code like this:

```
if (myName == "Martin")
{
   console.log("Hey there Martin, how's it going?");
}
else
{
   console.log("Greetings Earthling. Have a great day!");
}
```

Note: the "test" between the `IF`'s parentheses is an *expression* that results in a *Boolean* (a `true` or `false` value). This expression is evaluated when execution reaches the `IF`. If it evaluates to `true`, then your code enters the `IF` statement; if it evaluates to `false`, you enter the `ELSE` (if there is one).

Here is a brief code-based definition of how IF and ELSE statements operate:

```
if (EXPRESSION)     // EXPRESSION is evaluated upon reaching this line
{
   // body of 'IF': code runs only if EXPRESSION evaluates to true
}
else
{
   // body of 'ELSE': code runs only if EXPRESSION evaluates to false
}
```

Chapter 0 – Foundation Concepts

Complex Conditionals

The expression evaluated by an `IF` statement can be more than a simple comparison. It can perform multiple comparisons, combining or modifying these values with AND, OR and NOT connectors – as long as it eventually produces a Boolean that the `IF` can use to determine *which way to go at the 'Y'*.

In spoken language, we can create compound conditional statements such as *"If it is Friday and I'm in a good mood, then let's go out and have some fun!"* Hence we would *not* go out if *either* it is *not* Friday, *or* if I'm *not* in a good mood. There are symbols in JavaScript that represent these logical AND, OR and NOT concepts.

The **AND** operator combines two logical tests, requiring **both** inputs to be `true` for the result to be `true`. The symbol for logical AND is a double-**&**, located between the two logical conditions, like this:

```
if (today == "Friday" && moodLevel >= 100)
{
   goDancing();
}
```

The OR is just the flip side of the AND. As conveyed above, we need both expressions to be `true`, but this could also be accurately described by the converse statements – such as *"If it is not Friday, or if I'm not in a good mood, then let's not go out."* The **OR** operator combines two logical tests, evaluating to `true` if **either** input is `true`. Another example might be *"If it is raining or if it is too far to walk, then let's call Uber instead!"* The logical OR is double-|, located between two logical conditions, like this:

```
if (raining == true || distanceMiles > 3)
{
   callUber();
}
```

We run the `callUber()` function unless *both* tests are *not* true (i.e. not raining *and* distance is three or less). So, we have the AND operator and the OR operator. The **NOT** operator inverts a single boolean: what would have been `true` becomes `false`, and what would have been `false` becomes `true`. Logical NOT is an exclamation point !. *"If it isn't snowing, I'll wear shorts"* could become this code:

```
if (!snowing)
{
   bravelyDonSomeShorts();
}
```

The function would be called only when we enter the `IF` statement, which is when `!snowing` is equal to `true`, which (rephrased) is when `snowing` is equal to `false`. Make sense?

Chapter 0 – Foundation Concepts

Chaining and Nesting

So, we see that we can build complex expressions for a single IF statement. Why stop there? We can chain `IF..ELSE` statements with other `IF..ELSE` statements, like this:

```
if (myName == "Martin")
{
   console.log("Hey there Martin, how's it going?");
}
else if (myName == "Beth")
{
   console.log("You look fabulous today!");
}
else
{
   console.log("Greetings Earthling. Have a great day!");
}
```

We can also nest an `IF` statement within another (or within an `ELSE`). This chaining and nesting can go on indefinitely, as needed. Can you decipher the below? When would you walk/fly/swim?

```
if (weather != "rainy")
{
   if (distanceToStadium < 3)
   {
      console.log("I think I'll walk to the game.");
   }
   else
   {
      console.log("It's a bit far, so maybe I'll fly.");
   }
}
else
{
   console.log("Hey, I'm a duck! A little water is OK. I'll swim.");
}
```

If not rainy, and if distance to stadium is less than 3 (miles?), then we walk. If not rainy, and if distance is 3 or more, then we fly. If weather is rainy (regardless of distance), then we swim. What an odd duck!

Chapter 0 – Foundation Concepts

Loops

Sometimes you will have lines of code that you want to run more than once in succession. It would be very wasteful to simply copy-and-paste that code over and over. Plus, if you ever needed to change the code, you would need to change all those lines one by one. What a mess! Instead, you can indicate that a section of code should be executed some number of times. Consider the following: "Do the next thing I tell you *four* times: hop on one foot." That would be much better than "Hop on one foot. Hop on one foot. Hop on one foot. Hop on one foot." (even though it is just as silly) Programming languages have the concept of a *LOOP* that is essentially a section of code that will be executed a certain number of times. There are a few different types of loops. The most common are `FOR` and `WHILE` *loops*. Shall we explore each of them in turn? Yes, let's.

FOR Loops

`FOR` *loops* are useful when you know how many times those lines of code will run. `WHILE` *loops* are slightly better when you don't know how many times to loop, but you will loop *while* a certain test continues to be true. To create a `FOR` *loop*, in addition to the code to be looped, you specify three things within parentheses following the `FOR`: any initial setup, a test that must be true in order to start the loop, and any code to be run at end of each time through the loop. Here is an annotated example:

```
//       A     ;      B    ;        D
for (var num = 1; num < 6; num = num + 1)
{
   // C
   console.log("I'm counting! The number is ", num);
}
// E
console.log("We are done. Goodbye world!");
```

The above will execute in this sequence: A - B-C-D - B-C-D - B-C-D - B-C-D - B-C-D - B - E.

Let's walk through this `FOR` loop in detail. Up front, local variable `num` is created and set to a value of 1. This *step A* happens exactly once, then we start looping. *Step B*: we compare `num` to 6. If it is less than 6, then the code within curly braces (*step C*) is executed, and then 1 is added to `num` (*step D*). We then return to *step B*. When the test at *step B* fails, we immediately exit without executing *step C* or *step D*. At that point, execution continues from *step E*, following our closed-curly-brace.

Said another way, we INIT, then we [TEST? – BODY – INCREMENT] while TEST is true, then we exit.

```
for (INITIALIZATION; TEST; INCREMENT/DECREMENT)
{
   // BODY of the loop -
   // this runs repeatedly as long as TEST is true
}
```

Chapter 0 – Foundation Concepts

WHILE Loops

`WHILE` *loops* are similar to `FOR` *loops*, except with two pieces missing. First, there is no upfront setup like is built into a `FOR` loop. Also, unlike a `FOR` statement, a `WHILE` doesn't automatically include code that is executed at the end of each loop (our D above). `WHILE` *loops* are great when you don't know how many times (iterations) you will loop. Any `FOR` *loop* can be written as a `WHILE` *loop*. For example, the above `FOR` *loop* could be written instead as this `WHILE` *loop*, which would execute identically:

```
// A
var num = 1;
// B
while (num < 6)
{
   // C
   console.log("I'm counting! The number is " + num);
   // D
   num = num + 1;
}
// E
console.log("We are done. Goodbye world!");
```

Behaving identically with the above `FOR` loop, the `WHILE` code written immediately above will execute in this sequence: A - B-C-D - B-C-D - B-C-D - B-C-D - B-C-D - B - E.

Let's review before we move on. Anything we do with a `FOR` loop, we could achieve with a `WHILE` loop instead – and vice versa. So, when should we use `FOR` loops, and when should we use `WHILE` loops? Generally, use `FOR` loops when you know *exactly* how long a loop should run. Use `WHILE` loops when you have a condition that keeps the loop running (or that will cause the loop to stop), but you aren't sure exactly how many iterations that will require.

Chapter 0 – Foundation Concepts

Other Loop Tips

Some developers like to increment a variable's value by running `num += 1;` this is the same as typing `num = num + 1`. You may sometimes see `num++` or even `++num`; both are equivalent to +=.

```
var index = 2;
index = index + 1;
index++;
// index now holds a value of 4
```

By that same token, we can decrement the value of num by running simply `num--;` or `--num;`. This is exactly the same as running `num = num - 1;` or `num -= 1`. There are `*=` and `/=` operators as well, that multiply and divide a number as you might expect.

```
var counter = 5;
counter = counter - 1;   // counter now holds a value of 4
counter--;               // counter is now 3
counter *= 6;            // counter is 18
counter /= 2;            // counter == 9
```

Furthermore, not every loop must increment by one. Can you guess what the following would output?

```
for (var num = 10; num > 2; num = num - 1)
{
   console.log('num is currently', num);
}
```

Yes, that's right: this FOR loop counts backwards by ones, starting at 10, while num is greater than 2. So, it would count 10,9,8,7,6,5,4,3.

How would you print all *even* numbers from 1 to 1000000? How would you print all the *multiples of 7* (7, 14, ...) up to 100? Understanding how to use FOR loops is critical, so get really familiar with this.

Chapter 0 – Foundation Concepts

Loops and Code Flow

With more complex loops, you might need to break out of a loop early, or to skip the current pass but continue looping. In JavaScript, you can use special **BREAK** and **CONTINUE** keywords to do this. The **break** keyword *immediately exits the specific loop you are currently in* and continues immediately following the loop. Even the final end-loop statement (`num = num + 1` above) will not be executed. A **continue** *skips the rest of the current pass* through the loop, but any loop-end statement *is* executed and looping will continue. With both, once they run, <u>any subsequent code within the loop is skipped</u>.

Here's an example. The following code prints the first two lines, but then immediately exits the loop.

```
var num = 1;
while (num < 5)
{
   if (num == 3)
   {
      break;
      // if you have code here, it will never run!
   }
   console.log("I'm counting! The number is ", num);
   num = num + 1;   // if we break, these lines won't run
}
```
I'm counting! The number is 1
I'm counting! The number is 2

The below counts from 1 to 4, printing something about each number, but completely forgets about 3, because when num == 3, a **continue** skips the rest of the loop and proceeds (after adding 1 to *num*).

```
for (var num = 1; num < 5; num += 1)
{
   if (num == 3)
   {
      continue;
      // if you have additional code down here, it will never run!
   }
   console.log("I'm counting! The number is ", num);
}
```
I'm counting! The number is 1
I'm counting! The number is 2
I'm counting! The number is 4

Loops commonly use **break**. Get comfortable using it to loop for a number of iterations, then exit when you encounter a certain condition. With this, it isn't preposterous to see `while(true)`! My goodness.

Chapter 0 – Foundation Concepts

Parameters

Being able to call another function can be helpful for eliminating a lot of duplicate source code. That said, a function that always does exactly the same thing will be useful only in specific situations. It would be better if functions were more flexible and could be customized in some way. Fortunately, you can pass values into functions, so that the functions can behave differently depending on those values. The caller simply inserts these values (called *arguments*) between the parentheses, when it executes the function. When the function is executed, those values are copied in and are available like any other variable. Specifically, inside the function, these copied-in values are referred to as *parameters*.

For example, let's say that we have pulled our friendly greeting code above into a separate function, named `greetSomeone`. This function could include a parameter that is used by the code inside to customize the greeting, just as we did in our standalone code above. Depending on the argument that the caller sends in, our function would have different outcomes. Tying together the ideas of functions, parameters, conditionals and printing, this code could look like this:

```
function greetSomeone(person)
{
   if (person == "Martin") {
      console.log("Yo dawg, howz it goin?");
   }
   else
   {
      console.log("Greetings Earthling!");
   }
}
```

You might notice in the code above that there are curly braces that are not alone on their own lines, as they were in the previous code examples. The JavaScript language does not care whether you give these their own line or include them at the end of the previous line, as long as they are present. Really, braces are a way to indicate to the system some number of lines of code that it should treat as a single group. Without these, `IF..ELSE` and `WHILE` and `FOR` statements will only operate on a single line of code. Even if your loop *is* only a single line of code (and hence would work without braces), it is always safer to include these, in case you add more code to your loop later – and to reinforce good habits.

So, is it better to include these on their own lines, or to append them to the ends of the previous lines? This is really a matter of choice: *as long as you include them* (and you always should), JavaScript doesn't care about a few extra new-line characters or extra spaces. Over time you will develop your own **coding style**, writing source code in the way that is most understandable to you. Keep in mind though that when you join a software team, you will likely need to adopt the team's coding style (if they have one). If they don't, then even in that case you should generally match the style of existing code in the source files where you are working. So, as you develop your personal style, it is best to stay flexible.

Chapter 0 – Foundation Concepts

Foundations Review

Hopefully, this first chapter made you more comfortable with the essential building blocks of software. Below is a summary of the ideas we covered.

Computers can do amazing things but they need to be told what to do. We tell them what to do by running software. Software is generally built from *source code*, which is readable by humans, and is a sequence of basic steps that a computer will follow exactly. There are many different software languages (such as JavaScript), with different ways of expressing these basic steps, however most of the main concepts are universal. Our job is to break down problems into these steps, and then the computer will *run* that code when told. Generally, when source code is run, it executes from the first line linearly to the last line. However, we can change this flow by adding "fork-in-the-road" (conditional) or "do-that-part-a-few-times" (loop) structure to our source code.

A variable is a labeled, local space that can contain a value. We refer to a variable by its label if we want to read or change that value. Values can be a few different types, such as *numbers* or *strings* or *booleans*. A string is a sequence of characters, and a boolean is simply a true/false value. JavaScript (also known as JS) automatically changes values from one type to another as needed.

A single-equals (=) is used to set values in variables, and can be combined with normal mathematical operators (+ - * /). The == operator compares two values, allowing JS to convert data types if needed; the === operator does *not* allow the types to be converted. We print to the developer console using the `console.log` function, which accepts a string (or converts inputs to a string).

We can examine the values of variables, and divert the flow of source code execution depending on those values, using the **IF** statement. This can be combined with an **ELSE**, to cover the other side of a conditional as well; these **IF...ELSE** statements can be nested. One can create compound comparisons using logical operators that represent *and*, *or* and *not* (&&, ||, !).

To execute a specific piece of source code multiple times, there are two different types of *loops* available. A **FOR** loop is particularly useful when you know exactly how many times you need to loop; in other cases, a **WHILE** loop is simple and flexible. With both kinds of loops, you can use **BREAK** and **CONTINUE** statements to change the flow of code (to exit the loop or skip a certain iteration).

We can extract a piece of source code into a **FUNCTION** so that it can easily be called repeatedly. Functions (like variables) have labels, and to call a function, we list the function name with `()` following it. A function can require one or more values from outside, and we pass those values in by using parameters, which are included between the parentheses when calling the function, and similarly specified between the parentheses when defining the function.

The { and } characters are used to group code. How you choose to space (or compact) your source code will determine your personal *coding style*.

Chapter 1 – Fundamentals

OK Ninjas-in-training, use your new knowledge. Can you solve these?

☐ Setting and Swapping

Set `myNumber` to `42`. Set `myName` to your name. Now swap `myNumber` into `myName` & vice versa.

☐ Print -52 to 1066

Print integers from -52 to 1066 using a `FOR` loop.

☐ Don't Worry, Be Happy

Create `beCheerful()`. Within it, `console.log` string `"good morning!"` Call it 98 times.

☐ Multiples of Three – but Not All

Using `FOR`, print multiples of 3 from -300 to 0. *Skip* -3 and -6.

☐ Printing Integers with While

Print integers from 2000 to 5280, using a `WHILE`.

☐ You Say It's Your Birthday

If 2 given numbers represent your birth month and day *in either order*, log `"How did you know?"`, else log `"Just another day...."`

☐ Leap Year

Write a function that determines whether a given `year` is a leap year. If a year is divisible by four, it is a leap year, unless it is divisible by 100. However, if it is divisible by 400, then it *is*.

☐ Print and Count

Print all integer multiples of 5, from 512 to 4096. Afterward, also log how many there were.

☐ Multiples of Six

Print multiples of 6 up to 60,000, using a `WHILE`.

☐ Counting, the Dojo Way

Print integers 1 to 100. If divisible by 5, print `"Coding"` *instead*. If by 10, also print `" Dojo"`.

☐ What Do You Know?

Your function will be given an input parameter `incoming`. Please `console.log` this value.

☐ Whoa, That Sucker's Huge...

Add odd integers from -300,000 to 300,000, and `console.log` the final sum. Is there a shortcut?

☐ Countdown by Fours

Log positive numbers starting at 2016, counting down by fours (exclude 0), *without* a `FOR` loop.

☐ Flexible Countdown

Based on earlier "Countdown by Fours", given `lowNum`, `highNum`, `mult`, print multiples of `mult` from `highNum` down to `lowNum`, using a `FOR`. For `(2,9,3)`, print 9 6 3 (on successive lines).

☐ The Final Countdown

This is based on "Flexible Countdown". The parameter names are not as helpful, but the problem is essentially identical; don't be thrown off! Given <u>4</u> parameters `(param1,param2,param3,param4)`, print the multiples of `param1`, starting at `param2` and extending to `param3`. One exception: if a multiple is equal to `param4`, then skip (don't print) it. Do this using a `WHILE`. Given `(3,5,17,9)`, print `6,12,15` (which are all of the multiples of <u>3</u> between <u>5</u> and <u>17</u>, and excluding the value <u>9</u>).

Chapter 1 – Fundamentals

Return Values

Parameters give functions a lot more flexibility. However, sometimes you don't want a function to do *all* the work; maybe you just want it to give you information so that then your code can do something based on the answer it gives you. This is when you would use the *return value* for a function.

Functions have names (usually). They (often) have parameters. They have code that will run when the function is executed. They generally have a *return value* as well, which is simply a value that is returned to the caller when the function finishes executing. Not all functions have *return* values, and looking at source code you might think that not all functions have a return statement. However, they indeed *do*, because if there is nothing stated, an implicit `return` is added automatically at the end of the function.

In JavaScript, if a caller "listens" to a function that ends with `return`, the caller receives `undefined`. If we want to be more helpful, we can explicitly return a value (for example, a variable or a literal). In other words, our function could `return myNewName;` or could `return "Zaphod";`. In either case, once the `return` statement runs, any subsequent lines of code in our function will *not* be executed. When program execution encounters a `return`, it exits the current function immediately.

If functions can return values, to *tell us the answer*, then whoever calls those functions must *listen for that answer*. It is easy enough to execute a function (`greetSomeone(nameStr)`, below) that has no return. If a function *does* return a value, then to actually *receive* that value the caller should save the result into a `var`, or otherwise "listen" to what it says (`tellMeAGoodJoke()`, below after):

```
// Calling a function that           // This one DOES return a value
// does NOT return a value           var aJoke = tellMeAGoodJoke();
greetSomeone("Claire");              console.log(aJoke);
```

Above, `tellMeAGoodJoke()` returns a string which we copy into `aJoke` and display. See below for how to declare that function, but beware the function's sequel!

```
function tellMeAGoodJoke() {
   var jokeStr = "Have you heard about corduroy pillowcases?";
   jokeStr = jokeStr + " .... They're making headlines!";
   return jokeStr;
   jokeStr += "Thanks, I'm here all week...";   // this will never run!
}

// It may be a good joke, but it's a BAD FUNCTION. You only return once!
function tellMeAnotherOne() {
   var joke = "How many surrealists does it take to screw in a lightbulb?";
   return joke;
   return " .... A fish.";         // Wha? Oh I get it...but JavaScript won't.
}                                   // Remember: you can't return twice!
```

Chapter 1 – Fundamentals

Arrays

An array is like a cabinet with multiple drawers, where each drawer stores a number, string, or even another array. In JavaScript, arrays are created by code like this:

```
var arr = [2, 4, 6, 8];     // create array with four distinct values
```

In our example, we created an array called `arr`. This array `arr` is like a file cabinet with three drawers. To look into one of these file cabinets, we have to specify which one. Each drawer is numbered, starting at the number 0 (not 1). The first drawer, drawer 0, has a value of 2; the second drawer, labeled 1, has a value of 4; the next drawer, which we call drawer 2, has a value of 6. In our code, we reference the different locations in an array by specifying the 'drawer number', which is really the offset from the beginning of our array. Specifically, we read an array value by putting its offset between square-brackets, as follows:

```
console.log(arr[1]);        // "4" (Not 2 - this is at arr[0])
```

Arrays have three important built-in properties: `push`, `pop` and `length`. We add a value to the end of our array (which lengthens it by one) with `push`:

```
arr.push(777);              // arr was [2,4,6,8], is now [2,4,6,8,777]
```

This pushes a new value *onto the end of the array*, so `arr` has a new value and is slightly longer – it is now `[2,4,6,8,777]`.

Similarly, we *remove (and return) the value at the end of the array* (and we shorten our array by one) by using the `pop` function:

```
var last = arr.pop();       // arr was [2,4,6,8,777], is now [2,4,6,8]
console.log(last);          // "777" - this is what pop() returned
```

The examples we've used above have lengthened and shorted our array. We see this on the page by just looking at all the values, but how would we quickly do this in code? We would use a useful property on every array called `length`. This is attached to each array like pop and push are, but it is not a function, so you do not need parentheses when using it:

```
console.log(arr);           // "[2,4,6,8]"
console.log(arr.length);    // "4" - vals are stored at indices 0,1,2,3
```

Said another way, `arr.length` is always one greater than `arr`'s highest populated index.

Chapter 1 – Fundamentals

Writing Values into Arrays

In the previous example, our array `arr` had four (sometimes five) values. Each value in an array has its own space set aside for it, like the different drawers in a file cabinet.

```
var arr = [2, 4, 6, 8];   // create array with four distinct values
```

The beginning drawer (at index 0) has a value of 2; the second drawer (index 1) has a value of 4; the third drawer (index 2) has a value of 6. We change values within an array in the same way that we reference its values when reading from it: we enclose the index in square brackets, like this:

```
arr[1] = 10;              // arr was [2,4,6,8], is now [2,10,6,8].
```

This statement *sets* `arr[1]` *to be* 10. It puts value 10 into `arr[1]`: index (drawer) 1 within `arr`.

We often need to swap the values of two variables (this will be handy later, for algorithms such as "reverse an array"). We can treat the spaces in an array exactly the same. What if we tried swapping the value at index 1 with the value at index 3? We might try something like the below:

```
// arr is currently [2,10,6,8]. We want to change it to [2,8,6,10]
x[1] = x[3];
x[3] = x[1];
console.log(x);           // ...but this code won't work quite right.
                          // arr got messed up! It is now [2,8,6,8].
```

The code above wouldn't quite work. For example, let's talk through this code step by step.
- Before starting, `arr` is equal to `[2,10,6,8]`.
- In line 2, we set `arr[1]` to be the value in `arr[3]`, which is 8. Therefore, `arr` becomes `[2,8,6,8]`.
- When we run line 3, we set `arr[3]` to be the value in `arr[1]`, which is now 8. Thus, we overwrite an 8 with an 8, and `arr` remains `[2,8,6,8]`.

We can avoid this problem by creating a temporary variable to store the value of `arr[1]` before it is overwritten. To swap values (in an array or elsewhere), use a temporary variable. For example:

```
arr = [2, 10, 6, 8];
temp = arr[1];            // arr == [2,10,6,8], temp == 10
arr[1] = arr[3];          // arr == [2,8,6,8],  temp == 10
arr[3] = temp;            // arr == [2,8,6,10], temp == 10
console.log(arr);         // displays [2,8,6,10]
```

Success! Now, onward to algorithm challenges that use arrays.

Chapter 1 – Fundamentals

☐ Countdown

Create a function that accepts a number as an input. Return a new array that counts down by one, from the number (as array's 'zeroth' element) down to 0 (as the last element). How long is this array?

☐ Print and Return

Your function will receive an array with two numbers. Print the first value, and return the second.

☐ First Plus Length

Given an array, return the sum of the first value in the array, plus the array's length. What happens if the array's first value is *not* a number, but a string (like `"what?"`) or a boolean (like `false`).

☐ Values Greater than Second

For `[1,3,5,7,9,13]`, print values that are greater than its 2nd value. Return how many values this is.

☐ Values Greater than Second, Generalized

Write a function that accepts *any* array, and returns a new array with the array values that are greater than its 2nd value. Print how many values this is. What will you do if the array is only one element long?

☐ This Length, That Value

Given two numbers, return array of length `num1` with each value `num2`. Print `"Jinx!"` if they are same.

☐ Fit the First Value

Your function should accept an array. If value at `[0]` is greater than array's length, print `"Too big!"`; if value at `[0]` is less than array's length, print `"Too small!"`; otherwise print `"Just right!"`.

☐ Fahrenheit to Celsius

Kelvin wants to convert between temperature scales. Create `fahrenheitToCelsius(fDegrees)` that accepts a number of degrees in Fahrenheit, and returns the equivalent temperature as expressed in Celsius degrees. For review, `Fahrenheit = (9/5 * Celsius) + 32`.

☐ Celsius to Fahrenheit

Create `celsiusToFahrenheit(cDegrees)` that accepts number of degrees Celsius, and returns the equivalent temperature expressed in Fahrenheit degrees.

(optional) Do Fahrenheit and Celsius values *equate* at a certain number? Scientific calculation can be complex, so for this challenge just try a series of Celsius integer values starting at 200, going downward (descending), checking whether it is equal to the corresponding Fahrenheit value.

Chapter 1 – Fundamentals

Combining Arrays and FOR Loops

In programming, it's very common to loop through each array value. We can do this as follows:

```
var nums = [1,3,5,7];                            // set up our loop
for (var idx = 0;idx < nums.length;idx++)        // for each index in arr...
{
   console.log(nums[idx]);                       // ...print the value
}
```

This prints each value in the array, using a FOR loop that iterates once for each array value.

What if we wanted an array with multiples of 3 up to 99,999? We accomplish this with the code below:

```
var arr = [];                                    // create empty array
for (var val = 3;val <= 99999;val += 3)          // val will be 3,6,...99999
{
   arr.push(val);                                // add each val to arr
}
console.log(arr);                                // [3,6,9,12,..., 99999]
```

You will frequently write loops that, at each iteration's end, compare a variable (like `idx`) to the array's `.length`. Note: `push()` and `pop()` change an array's `.length`; if you need the original, save it off.

Here's an example of code that *does not* work as the programmer intended:

```
// BADCODE - intentionally buggy
function addEvenCount(arr) {
   // Count array even values & add that number to end of array
   for (var idx = 0; idx < arr.length; idx++) {
      if (idx == 0) {
         arr.push(0);                  // First time, add 0 to end.
      }
      if (arr[idx] % 2 == 0) {         // Then just add to it as we go.
         arr[arr.length - 1] += 1;
      }
   }
}                                      // Oops! We counted the "2" as well.
```

The problem, of course, is that if we push our zero to the end of the array, that increments `arr.length`, and now our `FOR` loop will run on the index we just added as well. Given `[0,3,6,5]`, we want to change the array to `[0,3,6,5,2]`, but would instead change it to `[0,3,6,5,3]`.

21

Chapter 1 – Fundamentals

☐ Biggie Size

Given an array, write a function that changes all positive numbers in the array to "big". Example: `makeItBig([-1,3,5,-5])` returns that same array, changed to `[-1,"big","big",-5]`.

☐ Print Low, Return High

Create a function that takes array of numbers. The function should print the lowest value in the array, and *return* the highest value in the array.

☐ Print One, Return Another

Build a function that takes array of numbers. The function should *print* second-to-last value in the array, and *return* **first odd** value in the array.

☐ Double Vision

Given array, create a function to return a *new* array where each value in the original has been doubled. Calling `double([1,2,3])` should return `[2,4,6]` without changing original.

☐ Count Positives

Given array of numbers, create function to replace last value with number of positive values. Example, `countPositives([-1,1,1,1])` changes array to `[-1,1,1,3]` and returns it.

☐ Evens and Odds

Create a function that accepts an array. Every time that array has three odd values in a row, print `"That's odd!"` Every time the array has three evens in a row, print `"Even more so!"`

☐ Increment the Seconds

Given `arr`, add 1 to odd elements (`[1]`, `[3]`, etc.), `console.log` all values and return `arr`.

☐ Previous Lengths

You are passed an array containing strings. Working within that same array, replace each string with a number – the length of the string at *previous* array index – and return the array.

☐ Add Seven to Most

Build function that accepts array. Return a new array with all values *except first*, adding 7 to each. Do not alter the original array.

☐ Reverse Array

Given array, write a function to reverse values, in-place. Example: `reverse([3,1,6,4,2])` returns same array, containing `[2,4,6,1,3]`.

☐ Outlook: Negative

Given an array, create and return a new one containing all the values of the provided array, made negative (*not simply multiplied by -1*). Given `[1,-3,5]`, return `[-1,-3,-5]`.

☐ Always Hungry

Create a function that accepts an array, and prints `"yummy"` each time one of the values is equal to `"food"`. If no array elements are `"food"`, then print `"I'm hungry"` once.

☐ Swap Toward the Center

Given array, swap first and last, third and third-to-last, etc. Input `[true,42,"Ada",2,"pizza"]` becomes `["pizza",42,"Ada",2,true]`. Change `[1,2,3,4,5,6]` to `[6,2,4,3,5,1]`.

☐ Scale the Array

Given array `arr` and number `num`, multiply each `arr` value by `num`, and return the changed `arr`.

Chapter 1 – Fundamentals

Using a T-Diagram

When trying to decipher complex code, particularly if someone else wrote it, T-diagrams can prove valuable. Eventually you may not need them, but while you are early in the journey to become a self-sufficient developer, you should use them frequently. Here's how they work:

T-diagrams record the state of local variables, including arrays and their indices. After each assignment in your code, update the diagram. Before a conditional (`IF/ELSE`, or each time through a `WHILE` or `FOR` loop) check variable values in a T-diagram to predict how code will behave. Let's try a short function.

Here's the code we will trace through. No sweat, right?

```
1. var arr = [1,3,5];
2. var idx = arr[1];
3. arr[idx] = arr[0];
4. idx--;
5. arr.push(arr[idx]);
6. idx = arr.length - arr[idx];
7. console.log(idx + arr[idx]);
```

T-Diagram A

arr	[1, 3, 5]
arr[1]	3
idx	3

T-Diagram B

arr	[1, 3, 5, 1]
arr[0]	1
idx	3

T-Diagram C

arr	[1, 3, 5, 1]
idx	2
arr[idx]	5

T-Diagram D

arr	[1, 3, 5, 1, 5]
idx	2
arr[idx]	5
arr.length	5

T-Diagram E

arr	[1, 3, 5, 1, 5]
idx	0
arr[idx]	1

Lines 1-2: following these lines, we have T-diagram A. We reflect that `idx` has been set to 3, so the following line refers to `arr[3]`.

Line 3: in this line, we set `arr[3]` to become 1, which is reflected in T-diagram B.

Line 4: after decrementing `idx`, we have T-diagram C, including the `arr[idx]` (which is `arr[2]`) needed by line 5.

Line 5: we push 5 to array's end. T-diagram D now represents our state (including the updated `arr.length`).

Line 6: this updates `idx`. T-diagram E reflects this value (5-5, or 0), and our updated `arr[idx]`.

Line 7: this line sums the two values (0 + 1), to determine what will be printed by `console.log`. T-diagram E makes it obvious: <u>1</u>.

We hope this quick walkthrough shows how T-diagrams can clarify even fairly complicated code.

Chapter 1 – Fundamentals

☐ Only Keep the Last Few

Stan learned something today: that directly decrementing an array's `.length` immediately shortens it by that amount. Given array `arr` and number `X`, remove all except the last `X` elements, and return `arr` (changed and shorter). Given `([2,4,6,8,10],3)`, change the given array to `[6,8,10]` and return it.

☐ Math Help

Cartman doesn't really like math; he needs help. You are given two numbers – coefficients `M` and `B` in the equation Y = MX + B. Build a function to return the X-intercept (his older cousin Fiaz wisely reminds him that X-intercept is the value of **X** where Y equals zero; Cartman just snorts in his general direction).

☐ Poor Kenny

Kenny tries to stay safe, but somehow *everyday* something happens. Out of the last 100 days, there were 10 days with volcanos, 15 others with tsunamis, 20 earthquakes, 25 blizzards and 30 meteors (for 100 days total). If these probabilities continue, write `whatHappensToday()` to print a day's outcome.

☐ What *Really* Happened?

Kyle (smarter than Kenny) notes that the chance of one disaster should be unrelated to the chance of another. Change `whatHappensToday()` function to create `whatReallyHappensToday()`. In this new function *test for each disaster independently*, instead of assuming exactly one disaster will happen. In other words, with this new function, *all five* might occur today – or *none*. Maybe Kenny will survive!

☐ Soaring IQ

Your time at the Dojo will definitely make you smarter! Let's say a new Dojo student, Bogdan, entered with a modest IQ of 101. Let's say that during a 14-week bootcamp, his IQ rose by .01 on the first day, then went up by an additional .02 on the second day, then up by .03 more on the third day, etc. all the way until increasing by .98 on his 98th day (the end of 14 full weeks). What is Bogdan's final IQ?

☐ Letter Grade

Mr. Cerise teaches high school math. Write a function that assigns and prints a letter grade, given an integer representing a score from 0 to 100? Those getting 90+ get an 'A', 80-89 earn 'B', 70-79 is a 'C', 60-69 should get a 'D', and lower than 60 receive 'F'. For example, given `88`, you should log `"Score: 88. Grade: B"`. Given the score 61, log the string `"Score: 61. Grade: D"`.

☐ More Accurate Grades

For an additional challenge, add '-' signs to scores in the bottom two percent of A, B, C and D scores, and "+" signs to the top two percent of B, C and D scores (sorry, Mr. Cerise never gives an A+). Given 88, console.log `"Score: 88. Grade: B+"`. Given 61, log `"Score: 61. Grade: D-"`.

Chapter 1 – Fundamentals

Comments

Source code containing good comments is a joy to work with. You don't spend as much time trying to figure it out, because the creator cared enough to spend just a few moments ahead of time to explain it. There are two ways to write comments in JavaScript source code.

One option is //. After a double-slash, the *rest of that line* is a comment. Your code might look like this:

```
// This is a very friendly function, if I do say so myself.
function greetSomeone(person) {
   if (person == "Martin")    // Check whether it is Martin...
   {
      console.log("Yo dawg, howz it goin?");
   }
   else                       // if not, probably some normal human.
   {
      console.log("Greetings Earthling!");
   }
}
```

Another option is /* ... */. These /* and */ bookends can span multiple lines, and *everything between them* is considered a non-source-code comment. This style would look like this:

```
/*
   Simple function that responds directly if the person is Martin,
   otherwise it provides a more generic salutation. No return value.
*/
function greetSomeone(person)
{
   if (person == "Martin") {
      console.log("Yo dawg, howz it goin?");
   } else {
      console.log("Greetings Earthling!");   /* no clue who this is... */
   }
}
```

Both are commonly used. Quick comments sprinkled throughout your code are usually //; larger comment blocks are often /* ... */. The main thing is simply to add a few comments. The next person to work with the code (perhaps a future YOU when you have forgotten details) will appreciate it.

Now that you have been introduced to the foundation concepts of source code execution, variables, conditionals, loops, arrays, functions, parameters, return values and comments, you are ready to continue onward to the rest of the algorithm materials. Enjoy!

Chapter 1 – Fundamentals

☐ Short Answer Questions: Fundamentals

What is source code?
What makes computers so "smart", anyway?
What is the purpose of a programming language?
What are 3 examples of programming languages? Why are there so many of these?
What is a variable? Why are variables useful?
What is the difference between a single-equals (=) and a double-equals (==)?
What is the difference between a double-equals (==) and a triple-equals (===)?
Why does the developer console exist?
When we talk about "conditional" statements, what does that mean? What is an example?
Why would we want `FOR` or `WHILE` loops in our source code?
When would you use a `WHILE` loop, instead of a `FOR` loop?
What is a function? Why would we use functions?
How many values can you receive back from a function? How many values can you send in?
What is an array? How many values does it hold?
What is a T-diagram and why should I know how to use one?
What are the two ways to comment JS code? When would you use one versus the other?

☐ Weekend Challenge: Fundamentals

This weekend, for a challenge, create a *fill-in-the-blank* quiz game. Ask the user's name, then refer to the user by name as you ask him/her a series of questions that you have stored in an array. Use the `prompt()` function to get each input from the user and compare it to the answer you expected. When the user enters "Q" (for quit), or perhaps when the user hits `[Cancel]`, exit the game and print the statistics of the game to the console: user name, number of questions answered and questions correct.

Fundamentals Review

This chapter covered a number of very important topics. Most importantly, we introduced you to the creation, reading, and changing of _arrays_, including using arrays in conjunction with FOR loops. We also showed how functions can not only accept input values (parameters), but also output a value back to the caller as well (_return values_). We gave our first example of how to use a _T-diagram_ (there will be more of these), to make sense of a piece of source code. Finally, we demonstrated two ways to add _comments_ to your source code, after talking about the importance of good commenting.

The "Basic 13"

These are Coding Dojo's foundation "Basic 13" algorithm challenges.
For each, write a JavaScript function - a suggested function name is included below.
Can you finish all of these challenges in less than two minutes each?

Print 1-255
`print1To255()`
Print all the integers from 1 to 255.

Print Odds 1-255
`printOdds1To255()`
Print all odd integers from 1 to 255.

Print Ints and Sum 0-255
`printIntsAndSum0To255()`
Print integers from 0 to 255, and with each integer print the sum so far.

Print Array Values
`printArrayVals(arr)`
Iterate through a given array, printing each value.

Print Max of Array
`printMaxOfArray(arr)`
Given an array, find and print its largest element.

Print Average of Array
`printAverageOfArray(arr)`
Analyze an array's values and print the average.

Return Odds Array 1-255
`returnOddsArray1To255()`
Create an array with all the odd integers between 1 and 255 (inclusive).

Square Array Values
`squareArrayVals(arr)`
Square each value in a given array, returning that same array with changed values.

Return Array Count Greater than Y
`returnArrayCountGreaterThanY(arr, y)`
Given an array and a value Y, count and print the number of array values greater than Y.

Zero Out Array Negative Numbers
`zeroOutArrayNegativeVals(arr)`
Return the given array, after setting any negative values to zero.

Print Max, Min, Average Array Values
`printMaxMinAverageArrayVals(arr)`
Given an array, print the max, min and average values for that array.

Shift Array Values Left
`shiftArrayValsLeft(arr)`
Given an array, move all values forward (to the left) by one index, dropping the first value and leaving a 0 (zero) value at the end of the array.

Swap String for Array Negative Values
`swapStringForArrayNegativeVals(arr)`
Given an array of numbers, replace any negative values with the string `'Dojo'`.

Chapter 2 – Fundamentals, Part II

This chapter, we will review basic blocks of programming: conditionals, logic operators, loops and a few techniques. All of the following concepts are used in this chapter:

Variables   *functions*   for *loops*   while *loops*   *conditional (if-else) statements*
   console.log   *parameters*   *return values*   *Math.random | Math.ceil | Math.floor | Math.trunc*

Review: define **variable**. Think of it as simply an empty container with a label. Once you put a value into the container, you can refer to this value by the label. We put a value into a variable using single-equals, which you read as "is set to a value of". In other words, `var name = "Zaphod"` can be read as *Variable labeled `"name"` <u>is set to a value of</u> `"Zaphod"`*. After this line of code, when you refer to `"name"`, you get a value of `"Zaphod"`. If you are still getting used to the idea of variables, *don't panic*.

☐ Sigma

Implement function `sigma(num)` that given a number, returns the sum of all positive integers up to number (inclusive). Ex.: `sigma(3)` = 6 (or 1 + 2 + 3); `sigma(5)` = 15 (or 1 + 2 + 3 + 4 + 5).

☐ Factorial

Just the Facts, ma'am. Factorials, that is. Write a function `factorial(num)` that, given a number, returns the product (multiplication) of all positive integers from 1 up to number (inclusive). For example, `factorial(3)` = 6 (or 1 * 2 * 3); `factorial(5)` = 120 (or 1 * 2 * 3 * 4 * 5).

☐ Star Art

Assume that you have a text field that is exactly 75 characters long. You want to fill it with spaces and asterisks (`'*'`), sometimes called *stars*. You should print the given number of asterisks consecutively. Depending on which function is called, those stars should be *left-justified* (first star would be very first char in the text field), or *right-justified* (last star would be very last char in the text field, with potentially some number of spaces at beginning of text field before the block of stars start), or *centered* in the 75-character text field (with same number of spaces on either side of the block of stars, plus/minus one).
- Write a function `drawLeftStars(num)` that accepts a number and prints that many asterisks.
- Write a function `drawRightStars(num)` that prints 75 characters total. Stars should build from right side. The last `num` characters should be asterisks; the other 75 should be spaces.
- Write function `drawCenteredStars(num)` that prints 75 characters total. The stars should be centered in the 75. The middle `num` characters should be asterisks; the rest of the 75 spaces.
- (optional) Create epic text-art Empire vs. Rebellion battle scenes, with ships like (=*=) and >o<.

☐ Character Art

From the above, derive the following that accept and draw the given characters, not just asterisks:
- `drawLeftChars(num,char)`   `// For all three of these, you`
- `drawRightChars(num,char)`   `// can safely assume that 'char'`
- `drawCenteredChars(num,char)`   `// is a string with length 1`

Chapter 2 – Fundamentals, Part II

It is imperative at this point in the bootcamp that you can rapidly complete the mandatory coding challenges from the **Algorithm Platform**. If you have not yet correctly answered *each* of them in under two minutes, then revisit the Algorithm Platform, "Reset All Challenges", and see how speedily you can complete them. Repeat until you can reliably finish each of them in less than two minutes.

Modulo Operator

So far you have learned about basic arithmetic operators to *add* (+), *subtract* (-), *multiply* (*) and *divide* (/). You may also have realized that JavaScript uses the + operator to *concatenate strings* as well! Now we want to introduce you to another operator, called *modulo* (%). Modulo is a companion operator to divide – think of it as "remainder". Given two numbers, modulo divides the second number into the first number an integer number of times, and returns the remainder. Examples: `(34 % 6)` is `4` because 34 integer-divides into 6 *five* times (30), leaving a remainder of 4. Modulo is great for determining if a number is even/odd: `(16 % 2)` is 0: it is even. Is 42 a multiple of ten? `(42 % 10)` is 2: no, it is not.

☐ Threes and Fives

Create `threesFives()` that adds values from 100 and 4000000 (inclusive) *if* that value is evenly divisible by 3 or 5 *but not both*. Display the final sum in the console.

Second: Create `betterThreesFives(start,end)` that allows you to enter arbitrary start and end values for your range. Think of `threesFives()` as `betterThreesFives(100,4000000)`.

☐ Generate Coin Change

Change is inevitable (especially when breaking a twenty). Make `generateCoinChange(cents)`. Accept a number of American cents, compute and print how to represent that amount with smallest number of coins. Common American coins are pennies (1 cent), nickels (5 cents), dimes (10 cents), and quarters (25 cents).

Second: can you simplify/shorten your code?

Example output, given `(94)`:

```
94 cents can be represented by:
    quarters:   3
    dimes:      1
    nickels:    1
    pennies:    4
```

Third: add half-dollar (50 cents) and dollar (100 cents) coins with 40 additional characters or less.

☐ Messy Math Mashup

Create a function `messyMath(num)` that will return the following sum: add all integers from 0 up to the given `num`, except for the following special cases of our `count` value:
   1. If current `count` (not `num`) is evenly divisible by 3, don't add to `sum`; skip to the next `count`;
   2. Otherwise, if current `count` is evenly divisible by 7, include it *twice* in `sum` instead of once;
   3. *Regardless* of the above, if current `count` is exactly 1/3 of `num`, return `-1` immediately.

For example, if given num is `4`, return `7`. If given num is `8`, return `34`. If given num is `15`, return `-1`.

Chapter 2 – Fundamentals, Part II

☐ Twelve-Bar Blues

Write a function that `console.log`s the number 1, then "`chick`", then "`boom`", then "`chick`", then 2, then "`chick`", "`boom`", "`chick`" – continuing the same cycle for each number up to (including) 12.

☐ Fibonacci

Create a function to generate *Fibonacci* numbers. In this famous mathematical sequence, each number is the sum of the previous two, starting with values 0 and 1. Your function should accept one argument, an index into the sequence (where 0 corresponds to the initial value, 4 corresponds to the value four later, etc). Examples: `fibonacci(0)` = 0 (given), `fibonacci(1)` = 1 (given), `fibonacci(2)` = 1 (`fib(0)+fib(1)`, or 0+1), `fibonacci(3)` = 2 (`fib(1)+fib(2)`, or 1+1), `fibonacci(4)` = 3 (1+2), `fibonacci(5)` = 5 (2+3), `fibonacci(6)` = 8 (3+5), `fibonacci(7)` = 13 (5+8), etc.

☐ Sum to One Digit

Kaitlin sees beauty in numbers, but also believes that less is more. Implement `sumToOne(num)` that sums a given integer's digits repeatedly until the sum is only one digit. Return that one-digit result. Example: `sumToOne(928)` returns 1, because 9+2+8 = 19, then 1+9 = 10, then 1+0 = 1.

☐ Clock Hand Angles

Regardless of how hard a Dojo student works (and they *should* work hard), they need time now and then to unwind – like hands on a clock. Traditional clocks are increasingly uncommon, but most can still read an analog clock's hands of hours, minutes and seconds. Create `clockHandAngles(seconds)` that, given a number of seconds since 12:00:00, prints angles (in degrees) of the hour, minute and second hands. As review, 360 degrees form a full rotation. For input of `3600` secs (equivalent to 1:00:00), print `"Hour hand: 30 degs. Minute hand: 0 degs. Second hand: 0 degs."` For an input parameter `seconds` of `119730` (which is equivalent to 9:15:30 plus 24 hours!), you should log `"Hour hand: 277.745 degs. Minute hand: 93 degs. Second hand: 180 degs."` Note: in the second example, the angle for the minute hand is not simply 90 degrees; it has advanced a bit further, because of the additional 30 seconds in that minute so far.

Second: also calculate and print degrees for an additional "week hand" that rotates once each week.

☐ Is Prime

Return whether a given integer is prime. Prime numbers are only evenly divisible by themselves and 1. Many highly optimized solutions exist, but for now just create one that is *easy to understand and debug*.

Chapter 2 – Fundamentals, Part II

Being able to write a T-diagram to keep track of your variables while you write out an algorithm by hand is extremely beneficial. You should use a T-diagram for algorithm challenges this chapter.

Math Library

A library is a related set of functions and values that have been grouped together under a common name. Traditionally this is done for less common functions, so they can be excluded from certain minimized versions of a language (e.g.: if we want a micro-JavaScript for some future Apple Ring™). Looking back now, it seems incredible that a language without math functions would be useful. Nonetheless JavaScript has grouped certain numerical functions and values into the Math library. When using these, put `Math.` before it (just like when using `log()` from `console` library!). Note that libraries are not limited to *just* functions. They can also include values such as `Math.PI`. Right now, however, we will focus on four functions in this library: `random()`, `floor()`, `ceil()` and `trunc()`.

The first, `Math.random`, returns a randomly generated decimal number between 0 and 1. It can theoretically return zero, but it cannot return one; for this reason, you can think of it as returning *some number between zero and 'almost-one'*. The other three functions are related: they accept a decimal number and return an *integer*. Given an integer, all three leave it *unchanged*. Otherwise, floor is a pessimist, ceil is an optimist, and trunc is a simplifier. `Math.floor` makes negative numbers more negative, and positives less positive. Conversely, `Math.ceil` makes positives more positive, and negatives less negative. `Math.trunc` drops any fraction, moving the number toward zero.

`Math.floor(2.718)` and `Math.trunc(2.718)` both return 2, but `Math.ceil(2.718)` returns 3. `Math.floor(-3.1416)` is -4; both `Math.trunc(-3.1416)` and `Math.ceil(-3.1416)` are -3.

Naturally, `Math.ceil(42) == Math.trunc(42) == Math.floor(42) == 42`.

One last idea. What if you want a random integer as low as 51 and as high as 100? <u>`Math.random()`</u> is "from 0 to almost-one". `Math.random()`<u>`*50`</u>, then, is "from 0 to almost-50". Let's turn those decimal ranges into integers: <u>`Math.trunc(Math.random()*50)`</u> is "50 possible integers from 0 to 49". Let's add an offset, so we start at 51: `Math.trunc(Math.random()*50)`<u>`+51`</u> is perfect. Whew!

☐ Rockin' the Dojo Sweatshirt

Ever since you arrived at the Dojo, you wanted one of those cool Coding Dojo sweatshirts – maybe even more than one. Let's say they cost $20 (including tax), but friendly Josh gives a 9% discount if you buy two, a nice 19% discount if you buy three, or a sweet 35% discount if you buy four or more. He only accepts cash and *says* he doesn't have coins, so you should round up to the nearest dollar. Build function `sweatshirtPricing(num)` that, given a number of sweatshirts, returns the cost.

☐ Clock Hand Angles, Revisited

Return to your previous `clockHandAngles` solution. Allow fractional values for input `seconds`, but change your implementation to print only *integer* values for angles (in degrees) of the various hands.

Chapter 2 – Fundamentals, Part II

Using Modulo to Extract a Digit

If variable `myBigNum` contained a big number, how would you get the value of the 'hundreds' digit? (To review, the *hundreds* digit of 32768 is '7', since it is thirty-two thousand, <u>seven hundred</u> sixty-eight.) First, you might `myBigNum = myBigNum / 100`, to shift the decimal point to exactly where you want (result: 327.68). Then, `Math.floor(myBigNum)` could remove any decimal leftovers (result: 327). Finally, you could use % to extract only the 'ones' digit. *What is % and how does it work?*

The % (modulo) operator often goes with / (divide). Basically, % *divides first number <u>evenly</u> by second, and returns remainder.* Example: `255 % 20` is 15, and `16 % 2` is 0. And ... `327 % 10` becomes the 7 we want. Putting it all together, we print the 'hundreds' digit like this:

```
console.log(Math.floor(myBigNum / 100) % 10);
```

Let's decode this. Formulas are computed inside out, so start with the division inside the parentheses. Once we've done that, our formula is simplified:

```
console.log(Math.floor(327.68) % 10);
```

Then comes the floor call. After evaluating that, our formula is:

```
console.log(327 % 10);
```

And finally comes the modulo operation, after which we have this!

```
console.log(7);
```

☐ Extract-o-matic

Create the `extractDigit(num,digitNum)` function that given a number and a digit number, returns the numeral value of that digit. 0 represents the ones digit, 1 represents the tens digit, etc. Given `(1824,2)`, return 8. Given `(1824,0)`, return 4. Given `(1824,7)`, return 0.

Second: handle negative `digitNum` values, where -1 represents tenths digit (0.x), -2 represents hundredths digit (0.0x), etc. Given `(123.45,-1)`, return 4.

Third: handle negative `num` values as well, doing what you think is appropriate.

☐ Most Significant Digit

If you already know who Ada Lovelace is, that's great! In a History of Science, she is *significant*. Given number of any size, return the most *significant* digit. If you already know what strings are, that's great! However, don't use them here ☺. Hint: use `WHILE` to bring the most significant digit into range where you can use the friendly modulus operator (%). The most significant digit is the *leftmost non-zero digit* of a number. Given `12345`, return 1. Given `67.89`, return 6. Given `0.00987`, return 9.

Second: handle negative `num` values as well, doing what you think is appropriate.

Chapter 2 – Fundamentals, Part II

Variables that Live Longer than a Single Function Call

If you declare a `var` within a function, it is created when entering, and destroyed when exiting that function. For a `var` to stay alive after you leave, you must declare it outside. That declaration will be called only once, when the file is loaded – including any initialization done on that variable. This can be useful if you want functions to "remember" values between successive calls to them. You should contain variables *within a function when possible*, but you *can* declare them outside if needed.

☐ Gaming Fun(damentals)

It's New Year's Eve, so let's play some dice games! It'll be fun. What could go wrong?

1) Create function `rollOne()` to return a randomly selected *integer* between 1 and 6 (inclusive).

2) Second, create a function `playFives(num)`, which should call `rollOne()` multiple times – '*num*' times, in fact, where 'num' is input parameter to `playFives(num)`. Each time, it should print the value `rollOne()` returns, and if that return value is 5, also print "That's good luck!"

3) Third, create a new function named `playStatistics()`, which should call `rollOne()` eight times (but not print anything after each call). After the last of these eight calls, it should print out the lowest and highest values that it received from `rollOne`, among those eight calls.

4) Fourth, make a copy of `playStatistics` and add code to make `playStatistics2()`, so that at the end (in addition to printing high/low rolls), it also prints the total sum of all eight rolls.

5) Fifth, copy `playStatistics2` and add code to it to make `playStatistics3(num)`, so that it will roll as many times as you want, instead of always doing this eight times.

6) Finally, make a copy of `playStatistics3` and change it to create `playStatistics4(num)`, so that at the end instead of the total sum, it prints the average roll.

☐ Statistics Until Doubles

Here's another game for our New Year's Eve party. Implement a '20-sided die' that randomly returns integers between 1 and 20 inclusive. Roll these, tracking statistics until you get a value twice in a row. Display *number of rolls*, *min*, *max*, and *average*.

☐ Claire is Where?

On New Year's Eve, have fun but don't forget your way home! For this challenge create four functions (`reset`, `moveBy`, `xLocation` and `yLocation`) to track the travels of Claire, a wanderer. Calling `reset()` moves Claire home to the origin `(0,0)`. The `moveBy(xOffset,yOffset)` function moves her by those amounts, in those directions. Finally, `xLocation()` and `yLocation()` return how far Claire is from home, in X and Y directions respectively. After the calls of `reset()`, `moveBy(1,-2)`, and `moveBy(3,1)`, subsequently calling `xLocation()` and `yLocation()` should return `4` and `-1`.

Second: create `distFromHome()`. Assuming she moves diagonally, return her distance from home.

Chapter 2 – Fundamentals, Part II

☐ Date, on a Deserted Island

After a particularly fabulous New Year's Eve party to end 2016, Eduardo wakes to find himself stranded on a deserted island. He misses his home in Burbank, but at least now he can spend plenty of time outdoors – and you can't beat the commute! To pass the time until he is rescued, he counts sunrises.

1) Help Eduardo track what day of the week it is. Create a `weekdayName(weekdayNum)` function that, given a number between 1 and 7, will `console.log` a string containing the day of the week for that number (given `1`, log `"Sunday"`). Use a `SWITCH` statement.
2) Expand `weekdayName()` to create `weekdayName2(dayNum)` accepting numbers up to 365. Return weekday as before, given number of days total. `"Sunday"` still corresponds to `1`.
3) Create a new function `someDays()` that calls `weekDayName2()` seventeen times, with randomly generated integers as high as 365. Log each result string. If it is a weekday, add the phrase `"Work hard!"`, and if it is a weekend day, add `"Enjoy your day off!"`
4) Build function `monthName(monthNum)` that, given a number from 1 to 12, returns a string containing month for that number (`"May"` corresponds to 5). Use an array, without loops.
5) Now expand `monthName()` to create `monthToDays(monthNum)`, returning the number of days in that month, in the year 2017. Hint: use a `SWITCH` statement for the days in each month.
6) Despite using his *ember* expertise to create a glowing SOS visible from space, the days go by and sadly Eduardo is still not rescued. Is it spring yet? It might as well be. Build on `monthName()` to create `dayToMonth(dayNum)`. If given a day number since the year began, return the current month (assume it is *not* a Leap Year). Given `75`, return `"March"`.
7) Eduardo builds a Dojo bootcamp on the island. Initially his students only find Ninja Gold in caves, but eventually even his tree sloths can write code quickly! Dojo classes meet Monday thru Friday, so let's reincorporate weekday to our calculations. Construct `fullDate(dayNum)` to accept number of days so far in 2017, and return a full date string. He hardly remembers that fateful New Year's Eve party, but he knows it was a Saturday. Given `142`, return `"Monday, May 22, 2017"`.
8) Times flies when you're at a Dojo – months in fact. Build `fullDate2(dayNum)` that will be given a 4-digit integer: the days that have passed since December 31, 2016. This number can stretch into future years! You can assume that any year number *divisible by four* is a leap year and has a 29-day February. Given `8475`, return `"Thursday, March 15, 2040"`.
9) Eduardo hacks the Google Maps API and adds this long-forgotten island back onto the map. Soon he is rescued! News of his Hemingway-like stoicism make him famous for centuries. Build `fullDate3(dayNum)` to handle days up to 140,000! Note: years 2100, 2200, and 2300 are *not* leap years (although 2400 *is*). Given `139947`, return `"Tuesday, February 29, 2400"`.

Having completed this epic saga, you are ready for additional concepts and chapters! Journey safely....

Chapter 2 – Fundamentals, Part II

☐ Short Answer Questions: Fundamentals, Part II

What is the JavaScript `Math` library? What does it contain?
Why aren't all those functions just included in JavaScript automatically?
If I call `Math.random()`, what will it return?
What do the following functions do: `Math.floor`, `Math.ceil`, `Math.trunc`, `Math.round`?
When do `Math.floor` and `Math.trunc` *not* return the same value?
What is the `%` operator? When is it useful?
How do I make variables declared outside (right next to) a function *visible* inside it?
Why should I comment my code? If I know what it does, isn't commenting just a waste of time?

☐ Weekend Challenge: Fundamentals, Part II

This weekend, complete the "Date, on a Deserted Island" problem series, if you have not yet done so.

Then, if time allows, incorporate the `Math` library into a new quiz game. See if users can memorize 10 digits of Pi. Do the same for the constant *e*, the square root of 2, as well as the square root of 1/2. These values are all available within the `Math` library. What other `Math` functions or properties can you incorporate? Continue to use prompt, and output the game statistics when the user quits.

Fundamentals Part II Review

The two chapters prior to this one rapidly introduced you to many important concepts that underlie all of computing. These include *source code*, *programming languages*, *code flow*, *variables* and *data types* (such as numbers, booleans and strings), *conditionals*, *operators* (such as =, ==, ===, &&, ||, !, +=, ++, -=, -- and %), *loops* (including `FOR`, `WHILE`, `BREAK`, `CONTINUE`), creating and executing your own *functions* (including input parameters and the return value), *arrays*, *T-diagrams* and *comments*.

This chapter added *numerical* tools to our palettes: including the `floor`, `ceil`, `round`, `trunc` and `random` functions from the `Math` library. We learned about the `%` operator, which is invaluable for determining remainders, or for extracting digits or fractional values from a compound number. We also were introduced to the concept of *scope*: a variable declared <u>within</u> a function is *not visible outside it*, but a variable declared <u>outside</u> a function *can be visible inside it*.

You are now fully equipped to solve a very broad number of basic computing challenges! There are still *many* more concepts for you to learn, so don't be discouraged if you go looking for interesting algorithm problems only to find that many of them are confusing or too difficult. Over time, with more repetition and practice, as these ideas sink in, and as we add more of these concepts, you will become better and better at breaking problems into understandable pieces that you can conquer with confidence. Onward!

Solving Whiteboard Problems (RIOT WALK)

When Donald Knuth solved his PhD thesis problem in less than two hours, he sent the *whiteboard* to his advisor's office as proof! Actually, I made up that whiteboard part – but it makes a good segue….

No company ships code on whiteboards, but most software interviewers still require candidates to write software on those pesky white surfaces. Regardless of tech skills needed once you are employed, you first must land the job in the first place. So, you should start practicing your whiteboarding skills *now*.

Here's the thing: technical interviewers don't just want correct code. They look for you to communicate, listen and respond. They expect you to break down problems logically. Got a consistent system? Ask and ye shall receive! OK maybe you didn't ask, but here it is. Use it, to pleasantly *stroll* through even the most turbulent and taxing of technology tests. It's called the **RIOT WALK**. Read on.

R – Recap
>First, just restate the problem back. Use your own wording, not the word-for-word description given. Demonstrate that you understand the problem (Pro tip: if an interviewer has a strong accent, this step is <u>critical</u>). Take the opportunity to ask clarifying questions – your interviewer will nod, contribute details, correct your description or otherwise reveal additional information.

IO – Inputs and Outputs
>State a few inputs with their outputs. "For the `IsOdd` function, if I pass in `3`, I expect `true`. For `6`, I expect `false`. Am I thinking about that right?" Listen for confirmation, then move on.

T – Test Cases
>Now you can channel your inner ETG[1]: in the whiteboard corner, list all the off-the-wall input parameters you can think of: negatives, non-integers, empty arrays, strings instead of arrays, really huge inputs, miraculously unlikely inputs, inputs that break the rules, missing parameters! For each of these, note the expected output (ask for clarification, if in doubt).

The space between **RIOT** and **WALK** is when you actually write the code. Yep, you still need to do this!

WALK – Walkthrough
>Finally, walk line-by-line through the code you just wrote, using your Test Cases from above. Make sure that all test cases return the required outputs before you say you are done.

With RIOT WALK you articulate problems and solutions clearly, identify ambiguity, dig for clarity, create tricky test cases and methodically walk through your code. Interviewers will be impressed!

---

[1] **Evil Test Genius** – the teammate that *always* knows how to break your code. Good software teams have at least one! You alternately fear, hate and admire this person, but always be glad s/he's on *your* team! When you manage a software team someday, find your ETG and keep him/her happy!

Chapter 3 – Arrays

This chapter explores the *array*: reading, changing, as well as adding and removing elements (which change the array's length). Before chapter's end, we touch on associative arrays as well. At this point we expect you to quickly complete the 13 mandatory algorithm challenges. Building array-inspection functions such as `min(arr)`, `max(arr)`, `sum(arr)` and `average(arr)` should be easy and rapid.

Let's review. Arrays store multiple values, which are accessed by specifying an *index* (offset from array front) in square brackets. This *random-access* makes arrays well-suited to be read in a different order than they were added. Arrays are less suitable (still common) in scenarios with many insertions and removals, if you need the array to stay in a particular sorted order. In that case, other values might need to be moved to create a space for inserting a new value (or, to fill a vacancy caused by removing a value). Arrays are not limited to one data type: one array can contain numbers, booleans, strings, etc.

Arrays are zero-based: *an array's first value is located at index 0*. Accordingly, array attribute `.length` literally means "one more than the last populated index." Like other interpreted languages, JavaScript arrays are not fixed-length; they automatically grow as values are set beyond the current length.

Tracking variables with T-diagrams can be very helpful when working with arrays. Use a T-diagram for this chapter's challenges. Below are constructs we'll use this chapter. Remember these building blocks!

Declaring a new array:
```
var myArr = [];
console.log(myArr.length);    // -> "0"
```

Setting and accessing array values:
```
myArr[0] = 42;                // myArr == [42], length==1
console.log(myArr[0]);        // -> "42"
```

Array.length is determined by largest index:
```
myArr[1] = "hi";              // myArr == [42,"hi"], length==2
myArr[2] = true;              // myArr == [42,"hi",true], length==3
```

Arrays can be sparsely populated:
```
myArr[myArr.length+1] = 2;    // myArr == [42,"hi",true,undefined,2]
console.log(myArr.length);    // -> "5"
```

Overwriting array values:
```
myArr[0] = 101;               // myArr == [101,"hi",true,undefined,2]
myArr[3] = "MG";              // myArr == [101,"hi",true,"MG",2]
```

Shorten arrays with pop(), lengthen with push():
```
myArr.pop();                  // myArr == [101,"hi",true,"MG"]
console.log(myArr.length);    // -> "4"
myArr.push("dat");            // myArr == [101,"hi",true,"MG","dat"]
console.log(myArr.length);    // -> "5"
```

Chapter 3 – Arrays

From your work with the Basic 13 challenges, we assume that you already know how to read from numerical arrays, and that you can easily create JavaScript functions to get the **minimum** or **maximum** value, the **sum** of all values in the array, or the **average** of all values in the array. If this is not the case, definitely review those implementations before continuing to today's challenges.

Here is a list of concepts to consider; some or all will be used in this chapter.

Array.pop() & Array.push()   arrays grow: Array.length == lastIdx-1   *if-else statements*
for /while loops   *arrays can contain different types*   *arrays are objects, passed by ref (ptr)*

☐ Array: Push Front

Given array and an additional value, *insert this value* at the beginning of the array. Do this without using any built-in array methods.

☐ Array: Pop Front

Given array, *remove and return the value* at the beginning of the array. Do this without using any built-in array methods except `pop()`.

☐ Array: Insert At

Given array, index, and additional value, *insert the value into array* at given index. Do this without using built-in array methods. You can think of `pushFront(arr,val)` as equivalent to `insertAt(arr,0,val)`.

☐ Array: Remove At

Given array and an index into array, *remove and return the array value* at that index. Do this without using built-in array methods except `pop()`. Think of `popFront(arr)` as equivalent to `removeAt(arr,0)`.

☐ Array: Swap Pairs

Swap positions of successive pairs of values of given array. If length is odd, do not change the final element. For `[1,2,3,4]`, return `[2,1,4,3]`. For example, change input `["Brendan",true,42]` to `[true,"Brendan",42]`. As with all array challenges, do this without using any built-in array methods.

☐ Array: Remove Duplicates

Sara is looking to hire an awesome web developer and has received applications from various sources. Her assistant alphabetized them but noticed some duplicates. Given a sorted array, remove duplicate values. Because array elements are already in order, all duplicate values will be grouped together. As with all these array challenges, do this without using any built-in array methods.

Second: solve this without using any nested loops.

Chapter 3 – Arrays

Array.length

Some programmers think of `Array.length` as the number of array elements. This is *usually* true, but certain things can cause it *not* to be the case. If you create and control an array (as opposed to working with an array received from some other code), then you can avoid these things, which will make your code less complex. Let's explore `.length`, so that we can keep life simple, for you and your arrays.

The array property `.length` is defined as *'one greater than the largest populated index'*:

```
var myArr == [42,"hi"];    // myArr.length == 2
myArr.push(true);          // myArr == [42,"hi",true] and length == 3
```

However, when directly setting values in arrays, we can add them at any (non-negative integer) index:

```
myArr[myArr.length+1] = 2; // myArr == [42,"hi",true,undefined,2]
console.log(myArr.length); // "5", although we set only 4 values
myArr.pop();               // myArr == [42,"hi",true,undefined]
console.log(myArr.length); // "4", although we never set myArr[3]
```

By setting an array value at an index beyond array's end, we created an empty space in our array – you could call it 'sparse' rather than having entirely contiguous values. Sparseness can be useful – in fact with *associative* arrays (objects), they will *always* be sparse – but generally with numerical arrays it vastly simplifies things to avoid this. How would you do this?

When adding a value to an array, use the `push()` function, or directly add the value to array's end (`arr[arr.length]`), or move another value there if you need the new value to be somewhere other than the array's end. In other words, if you don't use `push()`, make sure that `arr[arr.length]` is the next index in the array to be populated, rather than a larger index.

Likewise, when removing array values, use `pop()` or directly decrement the length (`arr.length--`). This means that if you need to remove a value from the middle of your array, you need to move the last value in the array into that middle index. Even though you are removing a middle value, you won't be removing that value's "chair". You'll actually be removing the last "chair" in the array, so the value currently there needs to be moved somewhere else!

Let's try these techniques on a few challenges. Remember, solve them without creating new arrays.

☐ Array: Min to Front

Given an array of comparable values, move the lowest element to array's front, shifting backward any elements previously ahead of it. Do not otherwise change the array's order. Given `[4,2,1,3,5]`, change it to `[1,4,2,3,5]` and return it. As always, do this without using built-in functions.

Chapter 3 – Arrays

Passing By Reference

Arrays are passed by *reference*. This means that when an array is sent as an argument, a pointer is sent. For this reason, even though parameters are always copies of the originals, with arrays (and all objects) a *pointer* is copied, resulting in caller and callee both having a copy of the same pointer. Hence both are looking at the same location in memory, and both will reference the same array. When we pass an array to another function, the array is passed "live" – changes the callee makes in that array are reflected when we return to the caller, regardless of whether the called function *returns* that array.

☐ Array: Reverse

Given a numerical array, reverse the order of values, in-place. The reversed array should have the same length, with existing elements moved to other indices so that order of elements is reversed. Working 'in-place' means that you *cannot use a second array* – move values within the array that you are given. As always, do not use built-in array functions such as `splice()`.

☐ Array: Rotate

Implement `rotateArr(arr, shiftBy)` that accepts array and offset. Shift `arr`'s values *to the right* by that amount. 'Wrap-around' any values that shift off array's end to the other side, so that no data is lost. Operate in-place: given `([1,2,3],1)`, change the array to `[3,1,2]`. Don't use built-in functions.
Second: allow negative `shiftBy` (shift L, not R).
Third: minimize memory usage. With no new array, handle arrays/`shiftBy`s in the millions.
Fourth: minimize the touches of each element.

☐ Array: Filter Range

Alan is good at breaking secret codes. One method is to eliminate values that lie within a specific *known* range. Given `arr` and values `min` and `max`, retain only the array values between `min` and `max`. Work in-place: return the array you are given, with values in original order. No built-in array functions.

☐ Array: Concat

Replicate JavaScript's `concat()`. Create a standalone function that accepts two arrays. Return a *new* array containing the first array's elements, followed by the second array's elements. Do not alter the original arrays. Ex.: `arrConcat( ['a','b'], [1,2] )` should return new array `['a','b',1,2]`.

☐ Skyline Heights

Lovely Burbank has a breathtaking view of the Los Angeles skyline. Let's say you are given an array with heights of consecutive buildings, starting closest to you and extending away. Array `[-1,7,3]` would represent three buildings: first is actually out of view below street level, behind it is second at 7 stories high, third is 3 stories high (hidden behind the 7-story). You are situated at street level. Return array containing heights of buildings you can see, in order. Given `[-1,1,1,7,3]` return `[1,7]`. Given `[0,4]` return `[4]`. As always with challenges, do not use built-in array functions such as `unshift()`.

Chapter 3 – Arrays

Another T-Diagram (Loops)

When working through a set of looping instructions with an array, a T-diagram can be especially useful. Let's do exactly that, with the following code and input array.

```
var arr = [42,68,7,21,243,512];
for (var x = arr.length-2; x > 1; x--) {
   arr[x - 1] = arr[x + 1];
}
console.log(arr);
console.log(x);// Does x exist out here?
```

As we enter the loop for the first time, here is our T-diagram:

arr	[42, 68, 7, 21, 243, 512]
arr.length	6
x	4

We enter the loop (because `x > 1`) then set `arr[x-1]` (or `arr[3]`, which is currently 21) to become `arr[x+1]` (`arr[5]`, or 512). Accordingly, within our diagram in the line for `arr`, we change the 21 to 512. Then x decrements, so we change that value in our diagram as well, from 4 to 3. Because we see that we will reference `arr[x+1]` repeatedly, we add that to our T-diagram as well, with a current value of 243. We need to remember to update this, each time we change x. Our updated T-diagram is as follows, as we return to loop's beginning, to evaluate whether to reenter:

arr	[42, 68, 7, <u>512</u>, 243, 512]
x	3
arr[x+1]	243 (x[4])

Because `x > 1`, we indeed reenter the loop. We now set `arr[x-1]` (`arr[2]`, currently 7) to become `arr[x+1]`, which is already in our diagram (243). Then x decrements to 2, so we must update our `arr[x+1]` reference: it is `arr[3]`, which is 512. We now return to the FOR loop's beginning. To the right is our updated T-diagram, as we check whether to reenter the loop:

arr	[42,68,<u>243</u>,512,243,512]
x	2
arr[x+1]	512 (x[3])

You can probably complete the exercise on your own at this point, but we'll continue onward for completeness. Again `x > 1`, so we do in fact reenter. Again, we set `arr[x-1]` (`arr[1]`, currently 68) to become `arr[x+1]` (512 in our diagram). We decrement x to 1 and update our `arr[x+1]` reference to 243 (although ultimately we won't need this). Returning to our FOR loop's beginning, here is our updated T-diagram at this point:

arr	[42,<u>512</u>,243,512,243,512]
x	1
arr[x+1]	243 (x[2])

Looking now at x, we see we will *not* reenter the FOR. We will `console.log` both `arr` and `x`. The final value of `arr` is [42,512,243,512,243,512]. Yes, x has meaning outside the FOR: a value of 1.

We hope this second walkthrough shows the clarity that T-diagrams can bring when iterating arrays.

Chapter 3 – Arrays

Here are the concepts/methods we've discussed; some or all will be used in this chapter's challenges. As always, don't use built-in array methods.

for / while loops   *Array.pop() & push()*   *avoid sparseness*
       arrays grow: arr.length == lastIdx-1   *if / else statements*
can contain different data types in JS   *arrays are objects, passed by reference (ptr)*

☐ Array: Remove Negatives

Implement `removeNegatives()` that accepts an array, removes negative values, and returns the same array (not a copy), preserving non-negatives' order. As always, do not use built-in array functions.

Second: don't use nested loops.

☐ Array: Second-to-Last

Return the second-to-last element of an array. Given `[42,true,4,"Kate",7]`, return `"Kate"`. If array is too short, return `null`.

☐ Array: Nth-to-Last

Return the element that is N-from-array's-end. Given `([5,2,3,6,4,9,7],3)`, return `4`. If the array is too short, return `null`.

☐ Array: Second-Largest

Return the second-largest element of an array. Given `[42,1,4,Math.PI,7]`, return `7`. If the array is too short, return `null`.

☐ Array: Nth-Largest

Liam has `"N"` number of Green Belt stickers for excellent Python projects. Given `arr` and `N`, return the Nth-largest element, where `(N-1)` elements are larger. Return `null` if needed.

☐ Credit Card Validation

The Luhn formula is sometimes used to validate credit card numbers. Create the function `isCreditCardValid(digitArr)` that accepts an array of digits on the card (13-19 depending on the card), and returns a boolean whether the card digits satisfy the Luhn formula, as follows:

1) Set aside the last digit; do not include it in these calculations (until step 5);
2) Starting from the back, multiply the digits in odd positions (last, third-to-last, etc.) by 2;
3) If any results are larger than 9, subtract 9 from them;
4) Add all numbers (not just our odds) together;
5) Now add the last digit back in – the sum should be a multiple of 10.

For example, when given digit array `[5,2,2,8,2]`, after step 1) it becomes `[5,2,2,8]`, then after step 2) it is `[5,4,2,16]`. Post-3) we have `[5,4,2,7]`, then following 4) it becomes `18`. After step 5) our value is `20`, so ultimately we return `true`. If the final digit were any non-multiple-of-10, we would instead return `false`.

Chapter 3 – Arrays

"Truthy" and "Falsey"

JavaScript is well known for its 'loose' treatment of data types. In actuality, JavaScript considers almost everything *an object*, since almost every possible value has a set of methods attached (`valueOf`, `toString`, etc). That said, `typeof` returns six possible values, suggesting that there are six top-level data types: `boolean`, `number`, `string`, `object`, `function`, and `undefined`. (A seventh, introduced in ES6, is left as an exercise for the reader.) JavaScript converts values between data types, as needed. For example, `if()` converts any value to a boolean, to decide which way to branch.

Most values are considered *something* and if converted to a boolean, equate to `true`. Only six values are considered *nothing*: `false`, `0`, `NaN`, `""`, `null`, `undefined`; these six are "falsey", because when converted to a boolean, they equate to `false`. All other values are "truthy", including all functions, objects, non-0 numbers (e.g.: `-Infinity`) and non-empty strings (e.g.: `"0"` or `"false"`).

☐ Array: Shuffle

In JavaScript, the `Array` object has numerous useful methods. It does not, however, contain a method that will randomize the order of an array's elements. Let's create `shuffle(arr)`, to efficiently shuffle a given array's values. Work in-place, naturally. Do you need to return anything from your function?

☐ Array: Remove Range

Given array, and indices `start` and `end`, remove vals in that index range, working in-place (hence shortening the array). Given `([20,30,40,50,60,70],2,4)`, change to `[20,30,70]` and return it.

☐ Intermediate Sums

You will be given an array of numbers. After every tenth element, add an additional element containing the sum of those ten values. If the array does not end aligned evenly with ten elements, add one last sum that includes those last elements not yet been included in one of the earlier sums. Given the array `[1,2,1,2,1,2,1,2,1,2,1,2,1,2]`, change it to `[1,2,1,2,1,2,1,2,1,2,15,1,2,1,2,6]`.

☐ Double Trouble

Create a function that changes a given array to list each original element twice, retaining original order. Convert `[4,"Ulysses",42,false]` to `[4,4,"Ulysses","Ulysses",42,42,false,false]`.

☐ Zip It

Create a standalone function that accepts two arrays and combines their values sequentially into a new array, at *alternating indices* starting with first array. Extra values from either array should be included afterward. Given `[1,2]` and `[10,20,30,40]`, return new array containing `[1,10,2,20,30,40]`.

Second: combine the two arrays' values *into the first array*, instead of into a new array. Much more fun!

Chapter 3 – Arrays

☐ Short Answer Questions: Arrays

What is an array?
What types of values can be held in an array?
What happens if you try to contain values of different data types in an array?
What is the index of the first element in an array?
What is the index of the last element in an array?
If you control an array, what is the easiest way to determine the number of values?
When would the above method *not* work well, and what must you do in that case?
What are two ways to make an array one element longer?
What are two ways to make an array two elements shorter?
What is the upper limit on the number of values an array can hold?
When working with arrays, does working "in-place" really matter? If so, when and why?
Which values are "falsey" in JavaScript, and what does "falsey" mean anyway?
What does "passing by reference" mean?

☐ Weekend Challenge: Arrays

For this weekend challenge, consider the game Tic-Tac-Toe. How would you represent a 3x3 game board: specifically, whether each square is unoccupied or claimed by a player? Could you represent this with an array? What would the array contain? Is there a benefit from having an array of *arrays*?

Once you have a good design in mind, create a function that, given one of these gameboards, automatically determines and returns the overall state of the game. A game is always in one of five different states – one state might be "Player 1's turn"; another might be "Game over: player 2 has won."

Once you have mastered that, can you extend this function to handle gameboards of arbitrary size?

Arrays Review

This chapter covered JavaScript arrays in more depth. We showed how to *declare and initialize* arrays, how to *read* from specific indices, and how to *write* values into arrays – both overwriting existing values, as well as writing into new index locations that likely extend an array's length. We made significant use of the property `.length` that is present in every array, and we discussed how this property is usually (but *not always*) equal to the *number of elements* present in the array. Specifically, we mentioned that arrays can be *sparse*, which means we can configure an array so that certain index locations have not yet been written with any value (and hence contain `undefined`). We rehearsed numerous times the iteration of an array, using a `FOR` loop. We touched on the subject of function parameters that are *passed by reference*, and how that changes a function from purely returning advisory information to making permanent changes in the array (or another parameter). We did an exhaustive walkthrough of *debugging FOR loops with arrays*. Finally, we built on our new understanding of JavaScript data types, and discussed the values that (across type conversion) all equate to `false` – the six *"falsey"* values.

"Basic 13" Review

Solutions for the "Basic 13" algorithm challenges.

Print 1-255
Print all the integers from 1 to 255.

```
function print1to255()
{
   var num = 1;
   while (num <= 255) {
      console.log(num);
      num = num + 1;
   }
}
```

Print Ints and Sum 0-255
Print integers from 0 to 255, and the sum so far.

```
function printIntsAndSum0to255()
{
   var sum = 0;
   for (var num = 0; num <= 255; num++) {
      sum += num;
      console.log("New number:" + num + "Sum:" + sum);
   }
}
```

Print Max of Array
Print the largest element in a given array, by iterating through it and comparing values.

```
function printMaxOfArray(arr)
{
   if (arr.length == 0) {
      console.log("Empty array, no max value.");
      return;
   }

   var max = arr[0];
   for (var idx = 1; idx < arr.length; idx++) {
      if (arr[idx] > max) {
         max = arr[idx];
      }
   }
   console.log("Max value is:" + max);
}
```

"Basic 13" Review

Solutions for the "Basic 13" algorithm challenges.

Print Odds 1-255
Print all odd integers from 1 to 255.

```
function printOdds1to255() {
   var num = 1;
   while (num <= 255) {
      console.log(num);
      num = num + 2;
   }
}
```

Return Odds Array 1-255
Create an array with odd integers from 1-255.

```
function returnOddsArray1to255() {
   var oddArray = [];
   for (var num = 1;num <= 255;num += 2)
   {
      oddArray.push(num);
   }
   return oddArray;
}
```

Print Array Values
Print all values in a given array by iterating through it.

```
function printArrayValues(arr) {
   for (var index = 0; index < arr.length; index++) {
      console.log("array[" + index + "] is equal to" + arr[index]);
   }
}
```

Print Average of Array
Analyze an array's values and print the average.

```
function printAverageOfArray(arr) {
   if (arr.length == 0) {
      console.log("Empty arr, no average val");
      return;
   }

   var sum = arr[0];
   for (var idx = 1; idx < arr.length; idx++) {
      sum += arr[idx];
   }
   console.log("Average value is:" + sum / arr.length);
}
```

"Basic 13" Review

Solutions for the "Basic 13" algorithm challenges.

Greater than Y

Count and print the number of array values less than a given Y.

```
function numGreaterThanY(arr, y) {
   var numGreater = 0;
   for (var idx = 0; idx < arr.length; idx++) {
      if (arr[idx] > y) { numGreater++; }
   }
   console.log("%d values are greater than %d", numGreater, y);
}
```

Print Max, Min, Average Array Values

Given an array, print max, min and average values.

```
function printMaxMinAverageArrayVals(arr) {
   if (arr.length == 0) {
      console.log("Null arr, no min/max/avg");
      return;
   }
   var min = arr[0];
   var max = arr[0];
   var sum = arr[0];
   for (var idx = 1; idx < arr.length; idx++) {
      if (arr[idx] < min) { min = arr[idx]; }
      if (arr[idx] > max) { max = arr[idx]; }
      sum += arr[idx];
   }
   console.log("Max:" + max + " Min:" + min);
   console.log("Avg value:" + sum / arr.length);
}
```

Square Array Values

Given an array, square each value in the array.

```
function squareArrVals(arr) {
   for (var idx = 0; idx < arr.length; idx++) {
      arr[idx] = arr[idx] * arr[idx];
   }
   return arr;
}
```

"Basic 13" Review

Solutions for the "Basic 13" algorithm challenges.

Zero Out Array Negative Values

Set negative array values to zero.

```
function zeroOutArrayNegativeVals(arr)
{
   for (var idx = 0; idx < arr.length; idx++)
   {
      if (arr[idx] < 0)
      {
         arr[idx] = 0;
      }
   }
   return arr;
}
```

Shift Array Values Left

Shift array values: drop the first and leave '0' at end.

```
function shiftArrValsLeft(arr)
{
   for (var idx = 1; idx < arr.length; idx++)
   {
      arr[idx - 1] = arr[idx];
   }
   arr[arr.length - 1] = 0;
   return arr;
}
```

Swap String for Array Negative Values

Replace any negative array values with 'Dojo'.

```
function swapStringForArrayNegativeVals(arr)
{
   for (var idx = 0; idx < arr.length; idx++)
   {
      if (arr[idx] < 0)
      {
         arr[idx] = "Dojo";
      }
   }
   return arr;
}
```

Chapter 4 – Strings and Associative Arrays

More About Strings

Of our basic JavaScript data types, strings are our third focus (after *Number* and *Boolean*).

Strings are arrays of characters (more accurately, you can *read* individual characters the same way you read specific values in a numerical array, and these individual values are *strings of length 1*). However, you cannot write individual characters in a string in this same way. Once a string is defined, individual characters can be *referenced* by [ ] but *not changed*. Strings are *immutable*: they can be completely replaced in their entirety, but not changed piecewise. To manipulate string characters, you must split the string into an *array*, make individual changes within that array, then join the array to reform a string.

Below are examples of declaring strings, referencing individual elements, using `String.length`, converting string to array with `String.split`, and converting array back to string with `Array.join`.

```
var funStr = "Emma shreds on her electric cello";
console.log(typeof funStr);          // "string"
var oneChar = funStr[26];            // "c"
console.log(typeof oneChar);         // "string"
```

`String.length` method

```
console.log(funStr.length);          // 33
console.log("".length);              // 0
```

`String.split` (converts string to array, splitting on the provided parameter)

```
wordArray = funStr.split(" ");       // Note: " " never appears in result:
                                     // [ "Emma", "shreds", "on", "her",
                                     // "electric", "cello" ]
console.log(wordArray[5].split(""));  // Split on every letter:
                                     // [ "c", "e", "l", "l", "o" ]
```

`Array.join` (converts array to string, using provided parameter as separator)

```
console.log(wordArray.join());       // Note: "," is used by default:
                                     // "Emma,shreds,on,her,electric,cello"
console.log(wordArray.join("-"));    // Param "-" inserted between words:
                                     // "Emma-shreds-on-her-electric-cello"
console.log(wordArray.join(""));     // "Emmashredsonherelectriccello"
```

Challenge: what is displayed by the following? Why?

```
console.log(1 + 2 + "3" + "4" + 5 + 6);
```

49

Chapter 4 – Strings and Associative Arrays

This chapter explores strings – a special case of the basic array – then associative arrays. By now you should be able to easily complete the "Basic 13" algorithm challenges in less than 2 minutes each.

☐ Remove Blanks

Create a function that, given a string, returns all of that string's contents, but without blanks. If given the string `"  Pl   ayTha  tF   u  nkyM  usi    c  "`, return `"PlayThatFunkyMusic"`.

☐ String: Get Digits

Create a JavaScript function that given a string, returns the integer made from the string's digits. Given `"0s1a3y5w7h9a2t4?6!8?0"`, the function should return the number `1357924680`.

☐ Acronyms

Create a function that, given a string, returns the string's acronym (first letters only, capitalized). Given `"  there's no free lunch   -  gotta pay yer way.  "`, return `"TNFL-GPYW"`. Given `"Live from New York, it's Saturday Night!"`, return `"LFNYISN"`.

☐ Count Non-Spaces

Accept a string and return the number of non-space characters found in the string. For example, given `"Honey pie, you are driving me crazy"`, return `29` (not `35`).

☐ Remove Shorter Strings

Given a string array and value (length), remove any strings shorter than *length* from the array.

Chapter 4 – Strings and Associative Arrays

Switch/case statements

Think of `SWITCH` statements as a series of `IF` statements, based on a single `value` (a number or string). From the `switch`, execution jumps forward to the `case` that matches (or `default` if no match is found). Execution continues until it hits a `break`, exiting the switch statement. If you omit a `break`, execution continues even into a subsequent `case:`! Here are examples:

```
switch (favoriteLanguageString) {
   case 'JavaScript':  console.log("Ah so, we thrive on chaos!"); break;
   case 'Python':      console.log("Parenthesis-haters, unite!"); break;
   case 'PL/I':        console.log("Wha? Who let you in here?");
   default:            console.log("Why don't you choose a different one.");
}
```

Note that if `favoriteLanguageString` is equal to `'PL/I'`, we log two messages. After the `"Wha?"` `console.log`, we continue onward to the next console.log at the end of the `SWITCH`, since we hit no `break`. Switch statements are not always the right choice, but may prove valuable below.

☐ String: Reverse

Implement `reverseString(str)` that, given string, returns that string with characters reversed. Given `"creature"`, return `"erutaerc"`. Tempting as it seems, do not use the built-in `reverse()`!

☐ Remove Even-Length Strings

Build a standalone function to remove strings of *even lengths* from a given array. For array containing `["Nope!","Its","Kris","starting","with","K!","(instead","of","Chris","with","C)","."]`, change that same array to `["Nope!","Its","Chris","."]`.

☐ Integer to Roman Numerals

Given a positive integer that is less than 4000, return a string containing that value in Roman numeral representation. In this representation, `I` is 1, `V` is 5, `X` is 10, `L` = 50, `C` = 100, `D` = 500, and `M` = 1000. Remember that 4 is IV, 349 is CCCIL and 444 is CDXLIV.

☐ Roman Numerals to Integer

Sept 16, 2014 headline: *"Ancient Computer Found in Roman Shipwreck"*. Comprising 30 bronze gears, its wooden frame features 2000 characters. Given a string containing a Roman numeral representation of a positive integer, return the integer. Remember that `III` is 3, `DCIX` is 609 and `MXDII` is 1492.

Challenge answered: `console.log(1 + 2 + "3" + "4" + 5 + 6)` will output `"33456"`. Num+num is a num, but num+str or str+num is a str: `1+2==3`. `3+"3"=="33"`. `"334"+5=="3345"`.

Chapter 4 – Strings and Associative Arrays

Getting the hang of strings? Good! As far as we know, this data structure is important in *every* programming language.

☐ Parens Valid

Create a function that, given an input string `str`, returns a boolean whether parentheses in `str` are valid. Valid sets of parentheses always open before they close, for example. For `"Y(3(p)p(3)r)s"`, return `true`. Given `"N(0(p)3"`, return `false`: not every parenthesis is closed. Given `"N(0)t )0(k"`, return `false`, because the underlined `")"` is premature: there is nothing open for it to close.

☐ Braces Valid

Given a sequence of parentheses, braces and brackets, determine whether it is valid. Example: `"W(a{t}s[o(n{ c}o)m]e )h[e{r}e]!"` => `true`. `"D(i{a}l[ t]o)n{e"` => `false`. `"A(1)s[O (n]0{t) 0}k"` => `false`.

Strings like `"Able was I, ere I saw Elba"` or `"Madam, I'm Adam"` could be considered *palindromes*, because (if we ignore spaces, punctuation and capitalization) the letters are the same when reading from the back to the front.

☐ String: Is Palindrome

Create a function that returns a boolean whether the string is a *strict* palindrome. For `"a x a"` or `"racecar"`, return `true`. Do **not** ignore spaces, punctuation and capitalization: if given `"Dud"` or `"oho!"`, return `false`.

Second: now *do* ignore white space (spaces, tabs, returns), capitalization and punctuation.

☐ Longest Palindrome

For this challenge, we will look not only at the entire string provided, but also at the substrings within it. Return the longest palindromic substring. Given `"what up, daddy-o?"`, return `"dad"`. Given `"uh... not much"`, return `"u"`. *Include spaces* as well (i.e. be strict, as in previous challenge): given `"Yikes! my favorite racecar erupted!"`, return `"e racecar e"`. Strings *longer or shorter* than complete words are OK.

Second: re-solve the above problem, but ignore spaces, tabs, returns, capitalization and punctuation. Given `"Hot puree eruption!"`, return `"tpureeerupt"`.

Chapter 4 – Strings and Associative Arrays

Fast-Finish / Fast-Fail

The idea of *quickly exiting a function if a special case is detected* likely does not seem all that revolutionary. However, this not only simplifies the code, but make its average running time faster as well. Whether to apply them to failure (fast-fail) or success (fast-finish) cases will depend on the specifics of the challenge, but in any case they can quickly narrow a problem to the mainline case that remains.

This chapter's challenges focused on *strings*, then *maps / hashes*. These concepts might be useful:

.length *.split* *.join* *.concat* *for...in loops* *switch/case*

☐ Is Word Alphabetical

Nikki, a queen of gentle sarcasm, loves the word *facetiously*. Lance helpfully points out that it is the only known English word that contains *all five vowels* in alphabetical order, and it even has a 'y' on the end! Nikki takes a break from debugging to turn and give him an acid stare – indeed a look that was delivered *arseniously*. Given a string, return whether all contained letters are in *alphabetical order*.

☐ D Gets Jiggy

Write a function that accepts as a parameter a string containing someone's name. Return a string containing the following oh-so-cool greeting: strip off the first letter of the name, capitalize this new word, and add " `to the` [first letter]`!`" Given `"Dylan"`, return `"Ylan to the D!"`

☐ Common Suffix

Lance is writing his opus: Epitome, an epic tome of beat poetry. Always ready for a good rhyme, he constantly seeks words that end with the same letters. Write a function that, when given a word array, returns the largest suffix (word-end) common to *all words* in the array. For inputs `["deforestation", "citation", "conviction", "incarceration"]`, return `"tion"` (not all that creative a rhyming point). If it is `["nice", "ice", "baby"]`, return `""`, because that's just ... *not*.

☐ Book Index

Martin is writing his opus: a book of algorithm challenges, set as lyrics to a suite of *a cappella* fugues. Some of 'those fugueing challenges' are less popular than others, so he needs an index. Given a sorted array of pages where a term appears, produce an index string. Consecutive pages should form ranges separated by a hyphen. For `[1,13,14,15,37,38,70]`, return string `"1, 13-15, 37-38, 70"`. Take care to get all the commas and spaces correct: Martin is palpably particular (practically persnickety!) about patchy punctuation.

☐ Drop the Mike

Create a standalone function that accepts an input string, removes leading and trailing white space (at beginning and end only), capitalizes the first letter of every word, and returns that string. If original string contains the word `"Mike"` *anywhere*, immediately return `"stunned silence"` instead.

Chapter 4 – Strings and Associative Arrays

Before we dive into a new area, let's remind ourselves of some of the best practices mentioned previously. Make sure to understand the problem thoroughly – ask clarifying questions before rushing to write code. Challenge yourself to think of any special cases your solution might need to handle: can you trust the input data you are given? Note any interesting "corner cases" for later, when you test your code. Restate the problem back to the interviewer, and (again, before you start coding) note a few important test cases along with what output they should produce. *Then* start coding. Once you finish, verify your code using the test cases you identified earlier, perhaps using T-diagrams. OK, onward.

Associative Arrays (Objects)

"Regular" (numerically indexed) arrays are handy. They can contain many values, any of which can be instantly accessed simply by providing the index. Arrays have *order* – indices are numerically arranged. However, sometimes we want more than just a number to describe what is stored in an array cell. If we held `["John", "Watson", "221B Baker Street"]`, we *might* remember that `[0]` meant first name, `[2]` stored the address, etc., but numerical indices are often not descriptive enough.

What if, for each specific cell in our array, instead of associating it with an *index number*, we associated it with a *string* – <u>any</u> string we wanted? This is essentially the *associative array*. Just as we place a numerical index within square brackets to reference a cell in a numerical array, similarly with an associative array we place a string (whether literal or in a variable) within the same square brackets. As a structure that organizes and stores data, most programming languages have this concept, referring to it as an associative array, a dictionary, a map, a hashtable, or (in JavaScript) simply an *object*.

This data structure consists of key-value pairs: *keys* (strings) that are associated with *values* (the contents of the array cell). Just as (regular) arrays are initialized by `[]`, JavaScript objects are initialized by `{}`. The syntax for assigning values to keys *during object initialization* is this:

```
var myAssocArr = { fName: "Kaitemma", "lName": "Claiben"};
// notice that keys can be strings (quoted) or symbols (without quotes)
```

Once created, we access an object's keys as *array indices* (with `[]`) or *object properties*:

```
myAssocArr["fun"] = "shreds on electric cello";
console.log(myAssocArr);     // { fName: "Kaitlemma", lName: "Claiben",
                             //   fun: "shreds on her electric cello"  }
myAssocArr.IQ = 144;
console.log(myAssoc["IQ"];   // 144
console.log(myAssoc.fun);    // "shreds on her electric cello"
```

☐ Coin Change with Object

As before, given a number of U.S. cents, return the optimal configuration of coins, in an object.

☐ Max/Min/Average with Object

Given an array, return an object containing the array's max, min and average values.

Chapter 4 – Strings and Associative Arrays

FOR ... IN Loops

When working with arrays (whether they are associative or numerical), one of the most common tasks is to iterate through all keys or values in the array. With this type of array, the keys are not numerical: there isn't a predictable first index, like `[0]`. Furthermore, there is no obvious last index such as `[arr.length-1]`. Without something new that we have not yet learned, we don't know how many keys an object contains.

Fortunately **for in**siders like us, we needn't import anything **foreign** from outside JavaScript: it has just what we need: the `FOR...IN` loop. Objects do not have a `.length` property, but with `FOR...IN` we can still iterate through each of the object's keys. There is no real guarantee on the *order* in which we will be handed these keys, but we will be handed each key exactly once. Many students, when encountering `FOR...IN` or `FOREACH` for the first time, are confused about whether the loop iterator represents a *key* or a *value*. For the JavaScript `FOR...IN`, *always think of it as* `FOR (key IN obj)`. The loop iterator represents *keys*, not *values*. If you need to iterate values within an object, then within a `FOR (key IN obj)` loop, reference `obj[key]`.

Using your new knowledge and skills with JavaScript objects (the equivalent in other programming languages to an associative array, dictionary or hashtable), try your hand at the following challenges:

☐ Zip Arrays into Map

Associative arrays are sometimes called *maps* because a key (string) maps to a value. Given two arrays, create an associative array (map) containing keys of the first, and values of the second. For `arr1 = ["abc", 3, "yo"]` and `arr2 = [42, "wassup", true]`, return `{"abc": 42, 3: "wassup", "yo": true}`.

☐ Invert Hash

Associative arrays are also called *hashes* (we'll learn why later). Build `invertHash(assocArr)` to convert hash keys to values, and values to keys. Example: given `{"name": "Zaphod", "charm": "high", "morals": "dicey"}`, return object `{"Zaphod": "name", "high": "charm", "dicey": "morals"}`.

☐ Associative Array: Number of Values (without .Length)

Without using the `.length` property that is present on all arrays, determine and return the number of values in the given array. If we were to do this on a numerical array, we might check to see whether the element at a certain numerical index was `undefined`. Unfortunately, we can't do that here because the keys don't have any sort of predictable order or first value.

So, for object `{ band: "Travis Shredd & the Good Ol' Homeboys", style: "Country/Metal/Rap", album: "668: The Neighbor of the Beast" }`, you should return the value 3, because there are three keys in this object: `band`, `style` and `album`.

Chapter 4 – Strings and Associative Arrays

Why Don't We Allow Built-In Functions?

Knowing available services for a language or framework is essential for unlocking its value. That said, there is power in knowing how to recreate those services – if they don't work as expected, or when you must extend them for new scenarios. Furthermore, having a sense for how services work 'under the hood' deepens your understanding about how/when to use them. Knowing for example that `push()` and `pop()` are *significantly* faster than `splice()` might make a difference in which you choose.

For extra algorithm practice, recreate these built-in functions from JavaScript's string library.

☐ String.concat

`String.concat(str2,str3,...,strX)` - add string(s) to end of existing one. Return new string.

☐ String.slice

`String.slice(start,end)` - extract part of a string and return in a new one. *Start* and *end* are indices into the string, with the first character at index 0. *End* param is optional and if present, refers to one beyond the last character to include.

Bonus: include support for negative indices, representing offsets from string-end. Example: `String.slice(-1)` returns the string's last character.

☐ String.trim

`String.trim()` - remove whitespace (spaces, tabs, newlines) from both sides, and return a new string. Example: `" \n  hello goodbye \t  ".trim()` should return `"hello goodbye"`.

☐ String.split

`String.split(separator,limit)` - split string into an array of substrings, returning array. `Separator` specifies where to divide substrings and is not included in any substring. If `""` is specified, split the string on every character. `Limit` is optional and indicates number of splits; additional post-limit items should be discarded. Note: existing string is unaffected.

☐ String.search

`String.search(val)` - search `string` for the given `val` (another string). Return the index position of the first match found (or `-1` if not found).

Chapter 4 – Strings and Associative Arrays

☐ Short Answer Questions: Strings and Associative Arrays

What is a string? How is it different than an array?
What is a data type? Is this what `typeof` tells us? What JavaScript data types have we learned?
What does `typeof` return, if given a string? What does `typeof` return, if given an array?
How do you quickly determine the number of characters in a string?
Are spaces counted toward the length of a string?
What are a few of the built-in (method) functions available on every string?
Is there a built-in function to easily convert a string to an array? Show me how to do this.
Is there a built-in function to easily convert an array to a string? Show me how to do this.
Is there a built-in function to easily convert a string to a boolean? Show me how to do this.
Is there a built-in function to easily convert a number to a string? Show me how to do this.
What is a `switch` statement, and when would you best use one?
What is a fast-finish check? Does it actually make your code faster?
What is an associative array? How does one differ from a traditional 'array classic'?
What is a JavaScript object? Featurewise, how does it differ from an associative array?
Is an object the closest thing – in JavaScript – to an associative array? What is its data type?
What does 'immutable' mean? Is a string immutable? Is an array immutable? Is an object?
To manually iterate through the keys and values in an object, what type of loop do I need?
Does this type of loop give you the keys, or the values?
Why does the Dojo frown on the use of built-in functions, during most algorithm challenges?

☐ Weekend Challenge: Strings and Associative Arrays

This weekend, go online and find a long text file (such as http://www.classicreader.com/book/206/1, for example – although any multi-page text would suffice). We want to do some analysis on this text! Find a way to get the text into your JavaScript code, and then determine the following:

- How many letters (including spaces) are in the text? How many words?
- How many *unique* letters are in the text? Ignoring punctuation, how many *unique* words?
- What are the unique-letter and unique-word results if you ignore capitalization?
- List all the unique words in alphabetical order. Put them into an array in this order.
- What are the ten *most common* words in this text? How frequently do each of them occur?
- Create an array of unique words and number of appearances, *in ascending count order*. What is your best choice of data structure here?

Strings and Associative Arrays Review

In this chapter, we learned about the **string** data type: how to access specific characters, determine the length, and use built-in string functions. We learned about the `switch` statement, as well as the concepts of **fast-finish** and **fast-fail**. We introduced the concept of associative arrays (and objects, which are the closest concept in JavaScript to an associative array). We also discovered the `FOR..IN` loop and used it to iterate through the *keys* (not *values*) of an object.

Debugging Your JavaScript Code

There are various ways to test and debug JavaScript code using artificial environments such as JSBin or plugins for your code editor. However, we prefer the real-world JS environment that *truly* matters: *browsers*. This way you test your code in a way that doesn't *emulate* the real-world: it *is* the real-world environment. Here are steps for one workflow that uses both editor and browser when creating/testing:

1) Go to Sublime/Atom, create a new file with the HTML file extension, and save it.

2) Within that file, type `html` and hit [tab]. Sublime will create the basic html tags for you.

3) Within the `<head>` section, type `script` and again hit [tab], to create `<script>` tags. You can delete the other attributes inside the `<script>` tag, as well as the `<style>` and even `<body>` tags; you don't *need* those if all you are doing is writing/testing JavaScript.

4) As the very first line after the <script> tag, always include `"use strict";` .

5) Now write JS code as you wish. Remember to save as you go, of course.

6) When you are ready to test your code (which should be early and often), right-click on the Sublime file and select "Open in Browser".

7) Your default browser will open a window. We prefer Chrome for testing JS, but any browser is fine. Within that window, open the Developer Console (the MacOS key sequence is *cmd-opt-J*).

8) Type JS into the console such as `returnGreaterThanSecond([1,3,5,7,9,11,15])` or `var arr=[];returnGreaterThanSecond(arr)` or `printOdds()` to exercise your code.

9) To change or add to your code, cmd-tab back to Sublime/Atom, make your change, then Save.

10) Switch back to browser and Refresh, returning to step 8. You will soon memorize the quick-key sequence for saving in Sublime, returning to browser, and refreshing (cmd-s, cmd-tab, cmd-r).

Ultimately, your JavaScript code will run in the browser JS runtime environment, rather than an artificial environment such as JSBin. They produce slightly different results sometimes, so why bother....

Chapter 5 – Linked Lists

This chapter explores linked lists, a data structure used widely in backends, frameworks, runtimes and operating systems. You will become familiar with concepts such as the *reference*: not a local copy of a value, but a pointer to the value in shared memory.

How does your operating system keeps track of the files in a directory? Modern systems do not do this with an array. They use a data structure called a *linked list*. Linked lists are easily reordered and well-suited for large data collections because (unlike arrays) they store data in small pieces of memory that "fit in the holes" between variables, rather than requiring a large chunk of contiguous memory. Linked lists are the first data structure we discuss as an *object*; they use *references*.

Objects and Classes

A **class definition** is like a blueprint of a complex machine, from which many copies can be made. Actually, constructing a machine is a separate step. Likewise, *declaring* a class merely informs us of that blueprint; actual objects must be individually constructed. In JavaScript, class declarations take the form of functions called *object constructors* – when called, they create an **object** for the caller. An object is an instance of the class, brought to life, just like a physical copy of the ideas in the blueprint.

Not all machines are complex; not all objects complicated. However, code can add or remove attributes of objects on the fly, so this makes them different than a boolean or number which always occupies the same amount of memory space. Why does this matter? If you have debugged JavaScript code in the browser, you may understand the *call stack* idea. This series of function calls led the computer to where it is right now. Whenever the currently running function returns, the JavaScript runtime looks to the call stack to help it "remember" which function it came from, as well as the state of all local variables when it called into another function. The runtime stores variables in the stack while changing execution to another function. Setting aside call stack space for booleans and numbers is easy – regardless of value, numbers occupy a 64-bit memory chunk. However, objects are tricky: JavaScript cannot determine *a priori* how much space to set aside for objects. How can it quickly construct a call stack?

The answer is that objects are created using a common chunk of memory set aside for variable-sized allocations. This memory is called the *heap*, and it is used for any unpredictable memory needs. When the system looks at your 'blueprint' and constructs a 'machine' corresponding to those plans, it goes to the heap and sets aside space for all that object's attributes and functions. If the object needs more space, it expands into adjacent heap memory. During normal operation, the heap is wide-open for large and small allocations. The call stack is apartment space in a high-rise tower; the heap is Montana.

When you create an object and store it in a local `var`, the system doesn't put the object in that memory slot the way it does for a number or a boolean. It puts a *reference* to that heap location into your local `var`. References (called pointers) are fixed-size, so this enables the runtime do its stack magic. A pointer represents an object's location in memory, but you can think of it as an object's contact info: its email address. True to its name, a pointer *points* to where the object is found. If you have information to retrieve from (or store to) an object, you "go there" by dereferencing that pointer, followed by the attribute you want within the object. This could look like `myProject.name` or `myQuizzes[3]` or even `getAverage(myArr)`. Yes, arrays, strings and even functions are objects – dereferenced by . or [or (.

59

Chapter 5 – Linked Lists

Linked Lists

Consider a row of gymnasts, all facing left so that all they can see is the gymnast immediately ahead in line. Now imagine that each of the gymnasts raises a right arm to put a right hand on the shoulder of the next gymnast in line. This mental picture is akin to a *linked list*. Many languages and systems use linked lists heavily, and they are frequently used in interview questions. Why are they so popular?

Linked lists provide a way to store a large amount of information without (as arrays do) forcing the runtime to find a large contiguous chunk of memory (as arrays do). Indeed, a linked list of 1000 pieces of information could use 1000 small spaces in memory. Like an array, they keep information in a certain *order*. However, unlike arrays, you need not relocate everything in order to add a value to the middle! Linked lists introduce the *reference* concept – essentially, storing the location of the variable, instead of its value. This reference is 'just another' attribute in the `node` object that can be compared, set, etc.

Over the chapter's course, we'll coalesce a considerable collection of concepts to contemplate. Some or all of these will be used in this chapter's challenges.

classes and *objects* *object constructors* *local vars vs. heap allocations* *pointers*
reference vs. *value* *private* vs. *public* === vs. == *push( ) & pop( )*

Here is a definition of a **node** object. A node simply holds a value and a *pointer* linking it to the next node in sequence, if there is one. A sequence of node objects is called a *linked list*.

```
function ListNode(value)
{
    this.val = value;
    this.next = null;
}
```

☐ List: Add Front

Rudy isn't nice: he cuts in line in front of everyone else. Given a pointer to the first `ListNode` and a value, create a new node, assign it to the list head, and return a pointer to the new head node.

☐ List: Contains

Sam thinks Tad might be somewhere in a very long line waiting to attend the Superman movie. Given a `ListNode` pointer and a val, return whether val is found in any node in the list.

☐ List: Remove Front

Ha! Rudy is getting what he deserves – kicked out of line. Given a pointer to the first node in a list, remove the head node and return the new list head node. If list is empty, return `null`.

☐ List: Front

Finally, Tad and Sam reach the front of the line to get movie tickets. Oh no – only one seat remains! Who was earlier in line: Tad or Sam? Return the *value* (not the node) at the *head* of the list. If list is empty, return `null`.

Chapter 5 – Linked Lists

This chapter we will familiarize ourselves with basic manipulation of the *singly linked list* data structure. Why is it referred to as a *singly* linked list? Well, there are other ways to arrange node objects; some feature more than one linkage between nodes. For example, *doubly linked list* nodes each connect to *two* others: the next as and previous. *Singly* linked list nodes contain only a *next* pointer.

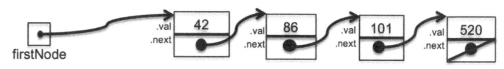

The list above is comprised of four nodes. Each node (*object*) has two properties: `.val`, and `.next`. The `.val` property stores anything the user chooses to put there. The `.next` property has one job: 'point' to the next node in the list (not unlike the gymnast's right hand on the shoulder of the next gymnast). The subsequent node does not know who is pointing to it; all it knows about is its own `.next` pointer. That might be pointing to yet another node, or might be `null` if that node is the last in the line.

So how do we work with linked lists? A common pattern is to declare a local variable called `runner`, set it to reference the first node, use it to access that node, then update it to point to the second node, use it to access that node, and so on until runner reaches the end of the list. To update `runner` to point to the next node, we would execute `runner=runner.next;`. This sets runner to be equal to the node's `.next` attribute. Setting a variable to a pointer makes it *point to* what the other *points to*. Example: per drawing above, `firstNode` points to the first node. We could change the `'101'` value to `'100'` with the code `firstNode.next.next.val=100;`. To have `firstNode` point instead to the subsequent node (the one with 86), we would simply execute `firstNode = firstNode.next;`. This sets the `firstNode` variable to be equal to the node's `.next` pointer. In other words, `firstNode` will point to what that node's `.next` points to, which is the subsequent node.

For these challenges, use this `ListNode` definition as a starting point. Note: some refer to *singly linked lists* as **SLists** (not **SLLists**).

```
function ListNode(value) {
    this.val = value;
    this.next = null;
}
```

☐ SList: Length

July 20, 2013: about 5000 people wait in line for a chance to audition for American Idol. Create a function that accepts a pointer to the first list node, and returns *number of nodes* in that SList.

☐ SList: Display

Create `display(node)` for debugging that returns a string containing all list values. Build what you wish `console.log(myList)` did!

☐ SList: Max

American Idol seems to air singers that are the *best*, and a few that seem like the *worst*! Create function `max(node)` to return list's largest val.

☐ SList: Min

Create `min(node)` to return list's smallest val.

☐ SList: Average

Create `average(node)` to return average val.

Chapter 5 – Linked Lists

Over the chapter's course, we coalesce a considerable collection of concepts to contemplate. Some or all of these will be used in this chapter's challenges.

classes and *objects*   *object constructors*   *local vars* vs. *heap allocations*   *pointers*
reference vs. *value*   *private* vs. *public*   === vs. ==   *push( )* & *pop( )*

As always, here's our node object:

```
function ListNode(value) {
   this.val = value;
   this.next = null;
}
```

☐ SList: Back

Create a function that accepts a `ListNode` pointer and returns the last value in the list.

☐ SList: Remove Back

Create a standalone function that removes the last `ListNode` in the list and returns the new list.

☐ SList: Add Back

Create a function that creates a `ListNode` with given value and inserts it at end of a linked list.

☐ SList: Move Min to Front

Create a standalone function that locates the minimum value in a linked list, and moves that node to the front of the list. Return the new list, with all nodes still present, and all (except for the new head node) in their original order.

☐ SList: Move Max to Back

Create a standalone function that locates the maximum value in a linked list, and moves that node to the back of the list. Return the new list, with all nodes still present, and all in their original order except for the node you moved to the end of the singly linked list.

Chapter 5 – Linked Lists

Prompts

For fifty pages now, you have used `console.log` every time you needed to display something. By now you know (more than) your fair share of HTML, so why do we continue to insist that you do this? Because in algorithm challenges, we want you focused on core algorithmic ideas, not presentation.

Having said that, you may sometimes want to request text from the user (when testing your code, for example). In these times, the `prompt()` function is what you need. `Prompt` accepts a string and raises an input dialog. The dialog displays your string and accepts an input from the user. An optional second parameter is set as the default value of the input field (IE and Edge require this parameter). If the user clicks `[OK]`, the input field's contents are returned. If the user clicks the `[Cancel]` button, `prompt()` returns `null` (exception: Safari returns `""`). Although not the most professional way to interact with your user, `prompt()` is sometimes appropriate, such as getting a quick value for a new `ListNode`.

Here is the humble-but-mighty `ListNode` class:

```
function ListNode(value) {
    this.val = value;
    this.next = null;
}
```

☐ SList: Prepend Val

Create `prependVal(ListNode,val,before)` to insert a new `ListNode` with `val` immediately before the node containing `before` (or at end, if no node contains `before`). Return the new list.

☐ SList: Append Val

Create `appendVal(list,val,after)` that inserts a new `ListNode` containing given `val` immediately after the node containing `after` (or at end, if `after` not found). Return the new list.

☐ Create SList (prompt)

Create an `SList` with values entered. Use the `prompt` function to gather values one at a time from the user, putting each into a `ListNode` that you add to the end of the list. When the user hits `[Cancel]`, return the list you have created.

☐ SList: Remove Val

Create `removeVal(ListNode,val)`. Given a pointer to the head `ListNode`, remove the node with the given `val`. Return the new list. What will you do if `val` is not found?

Chapter 5 – Linked Lists

Alerts

If you know about `prompt()`, you should also know about `alert()`. Neither are appropriate choices when writing professional web applications, but they may occasionally be useful in our *algorithmic challenge* context, such as when surfacing a particularly unusual error.

Put simply, `alert()` accepts a string and raises a dialog displaying that string. The user must click `[OK]` for the dialog box to be dismissed. The `alert()` function has no return value.

Here's our `ListNode` class:

```
function ListNode(value) {
    this.val = value;
    this.next = null;
    this.front = function() { ... }
    // more functions here
}
```

☐ SList: Split on Value

Create `splitOnVal(list,num)` that, given **number**, splits a list in two. The latter half of the list should be returned, starting with node containing **num**. E.g.: `splitOnVal(5)` for the list (1=>3=>5=>2=>4) will change list to (1=>3), and the return value will be (5=>2=>4).

☐ SList: Remove Negatives

Given a pointer to the head node of a singly linked list, remove any nodes containing negative values and return (a pointer to) the new list.

☐ SList: Concat

Given two pointers to separate linked lists, concatenate the second list to the end of the first one, and return the new list.

☐ SList: Partition

Create `partition(ListNode,value)` that locates the first node with that value, and moves all nodes with values *less than* that value to be earlier, and all nodes with values *greater than* that value to be later. Otherwise, original order need not be perfectly preserved. Return the new head `ListNode`.

Chapter 5 – Linked Lists

This chapter you familiarized yourself with basic manipulation of the *singly linked list* data structure. Here are concepts used in this chapter's challenges.

classes and *objects*   *object constructors*   *local variables* vs. *heap allocations*
         push() and *pop()*   *pointers*   *private* vs. *public*
=== vs. *==*   *reference* vs. *value*   *time* vs. *space tradeoff*

Here is what we have so far for `ListNode`:

```
function ListNode(value) {
    this.val = value;
    this.next = null;
    this.front = function() { ... }
    // more functions here
}
```

☐ SList: Second to Last Value

Create a standalone function that, given a pointer to the first node in a singly linked list, will return the second-to-last value in that list. What will you return if the list is not long enough?

☐ SList: Copy

Given a pointer to a singly linked list, return a copy of that list. Do not return the same list, but instead make a copy of each node in the list and connect them in the same order as the original.

☐ SList: Delete Given Node

Create `ListNode` *method* `removeSelf()` to disconnect (remove) itself from linked lists that include it. Note: the node might be the first in a list (it won't be the *last*), and you do NOT have a pointer to the previous node. Also, don't lose any subsequent nodes pointed to by `.next`.

☐ SList: Filter

Given a `headNode`, a `lowVal` and a `highVal`, remove from the list any nodes that have values less than `lowVal` or higher than `highVal`. Return the new list.

Chapter 5 – Linked Lists

This chapter you familiarized yourself with basic manipulation of the *singly linked list* data structure. Here are concepts used in this chapter's challenges.

classes and *objects* *object constructors* *local variables* vs. *heap allocations*
push() and *pop()* *pointers* *private* vs. *public*
=== vs. == *reference* vs. *value* *time* vs. *space tradeoff*

Here, as usual, is the definition of our node class. Note that going forward we will refer to this as `SLNode` instead of `ListNode`, to avoid ambiguity about what *kind* of list will contain this node.

```
function SLNode(value) {
    this.val = value;
    this.next = null;
    this.front = function() { ... }
    // more functions here
}
```

☐ SList: Second Largest Value

Given a pointer to the first node in a singly linked list, return the second-largest value contained in the list.

☐ Zip SLists

Provided two pointers to independent linked lists, 'zip' the two lists together by alternating nodes. Start with the first list, and return the new combined list.

☐ Dedupe SList

Remove nodes with duplicate values. Following this call, all remaining nodes should have unique values. Retain only first instance of each value.

☐ Dedupe SList Without Buffer

Can you accomplish deduplication without using a secondary buffer? What are the performance ramifications? How long would you expect the function to take to finish, if it was sent an `SList` of length 5 million?

Chapter 5 – Linked Lists

Write Understandable Code!

What is a software engineer paid to deliver? Generally, they are paid to *solve a business problem*, specifically through software that they write. How do we know if it's *good* software? This is an excellent question, and one we will explore more fully, later. Generally, software is *good* if it solves the business problem inexpensively. We're talking at a very high level, so let's continue drilling in on this.

What does *inexpensive* mean, when applied to software? It could mean the literal cost, such as the expenses to purchase developer tools or servers. An expense that is just as important though, is the time required to write it. The costs associated with time include salary expense, as well as the cost of lost opportunities if a problem is not solved soon enough. As the saying goes: *time is money*.

We constantly face a tradeoff between cost *now* versus cost *later*. Taking a shortcut right now might seem smart, but sometimes it is not. Writing software as rapidly as possible might seem like the lowest-cost approach, but this is not always true. I think we can agree that if, in order to make a small change to a project, you had to completely rewrite it from the ground up, this Situation A is more expensive than a different Situation B in which you keep most of the previous work when a small change is needed. Unfortunately, shortcuts taken by the original engineer might lead to the Situation A we described.

Great software engineers can write source code that is easily understood, and for this reason their work is more useful in the future. It is inexpensive to make changes to code that is easy to understand – you spend less time trying to figure out what it does, and you can be targeted (spend less time) in verifying that your change didn't break something else.

What are things you can do to make your code more understandable? Organize your code into related sections. Name functions and variables clearly. If you label a function `func4()`, you require the reader (which might be *you*, in the future) to read the entire function in order to understand what it does and how it fits with everything else. Something like `findTreeSize()` is much clearer. Don't use single-letter variable names; there is no real speed difference gained by using '`i`' instead of '`index`' or '`idx`'. In brief, code that is *self-describing* is more valuable because it is less expensive to maintain. You should also add useful (not obvious) comments to your code, particularly block comments at the beginnings of source files and functions. That said, self-describing code will require fewer comments, because the names of functions and variables convey your basic intentions.

Remember: friends don't let friends use one-letter variable names!

Chapter 5 – Linked Lists

☐ Short Answer Questions: Objects, Classes and Linked Lists

What is an object?
How is an object different than an *associative* array?
Are local variables allocated in the memory heap or the call stack?
What is this so-called *call stack*, anyway?
And what is this *memory heap*. When do we use it?
What is the difference between a *class* and an *object*?
What is an object constructor?
What code is needed to create new object instances?
What is a pointer? Is this the same thing as the index of an array?
What is `null`? What would `typeof` tell us, if given `null`?

What is a Singly Linked List (`SList`)?
Generally, what are the attributes within a singly linked list?
Why is it called a *Singly* Linked List?
Under what circumstances is an `SList` a better choice than an array?
What would `typeof` tell us, if given an `SList`?
What is a Singly Linked List Node (`SLNode`)?
What are attributes of a singly linked list node? Do `SLNode`s always have only two attributes?
How would you determine whether an `SList` is empty?
What would `typeof` tell us, if given an `SLNode`?
Are `SList` and `SLNode` objects built into JavaScript?
What are the differences between a `DList` and an `SList`?
What are the differences between an `SLNode` and a `DLNode`?
Why might we use a `DList` instead of an `SList`?

In JavaScript, what is the difference between `alert()` and `prompt()` and `console.log()`?
Personally, what do you do to make your code more understandable? Why do you do this?

☐ Weekend Challenge: Linked Lists

This weekend, create an `SList` with nodes containing `.id`, `.firstName` and `.lastName` in addition to the obligatory `.next`. After creating `SList` and `SLNode` constructors, write code to do the following:
- Create a list and at least five unique nodes, and add the nodes to the list.
- Build a function that reorders list nodes to be alphabetized by `.lastName`.
- Refactor this code to accept a boolean, representing whether to sort *ascending* or *descending*.
- Now, augment the code to sort by any of these attributes, as well as ascending or descending.
- Refactor the function to sort by more than one attribute. For example, we may want to "Sort the list by last name (ascending), using ID (descending) as a tiebreaker if last names are equal."
- Is any of this challenge easier if our nodes contain a `.prev` in addition to a `.next`?

Chapter 5 – Linked Lists

Linked Lists Review

Objects are a collection of attributes and functions. Because they are variable in size, they are allocated in the **memory heap**. Object constructors return **pointers**, which are fixed in size and hence can be held in local variables. Conceptually, a pointer is just some particular memory location (not unlike "P.O. Box 5588"), referring to a location in the heap where some object has been allocated. Although calling `console.log()` on some variable containing a pointer will display the contents of the allocated object, this is only because the browser is trying to be helpful – the actual contents of that variable (the pointer itself) is merely a number representing some memory location (not what is *stored* at that location). *Dereferencing* a pointer means traveling across it, to the attributes and functions within the object on the other side. To dereference an object pointer, append `.` plus an attribute name.

A **linked list** is a sequence of connected **node** objects. Nodes contain `.next` pointers, plus other attributes as needed. In our examples, node objects often contain only `.val` and `.next`, but in real-world scenarios you find much larger objects with dozens of attributes, *including* a `.next` so that these object records can be sequenced, grouped and sorted.

Linked lists are preferable to arrays if frequently adding/removing values mid-sequence. Unlike arrays, singly linked lists directly access only the first node – to reach later ones, we **traverse** from one node to the next one by following the sequence of `.next` pointers. Singly linked lists have the ability to traverse only forward through the list, because they contain only a single link between nodes. A doubly linked list is comprised of nodes containing both `.next` and `.prev` pointers, and for this reason they are useful when we need to traverse back and forth in our sequence; that said, doubly linked lists are slightly more complicated to build and maintain (as we will see in a future chapter).

`alert()` and `prompt()` are useful in debugging and quick prototypes, but not customer-facing views.

Creating **clear, understandable code** is well worth the effort needed, because this code is more easily and quickly understood, and can be extended with more confidence. Taking the time to do this is the professional way to approach any code, and it is doing any future engineer in your code a favor. Do it!

The "Buggy 13" (#1)

Below are submissions for the "Basic 13" challenges. Unfortunately, some of these contain errors. Which solutions have bugs, what are they, and how would you fix them?

Print1To255()
Print all the integers from 1 to 255.

```
function print1to255()
{
   var num = 1;
   while (num < 255) {
      console.log(num);
      num = num + 1;
   }
}
```

PrintIntsAndSum0To255()
Print integers from 0 to 255, and the sum so far.

```
function printIntsAndSum0to255()
{
   var sum = 0;
   for(var num = 0;num <= 255;num++)
   { sum += num; }
   return sum;
}
```

PrintMaxOfArray(arr)
Print the largest element in a given array.

```
function printMaxOfArray(arr) {
   if (arr.length == 0) {
      console.log("[], no max val.");
      return;
   }
   var max = 0;
   for (var idx = 0;
        idx < arr.length; idx++) {
      if (arr[idx] > max)
      { max = arr[idx]; }
   }
   console.log("Max val is:", max);
}
```

PrintOdds1To255()
Print all odd integers from 1 to 255.

```
function printOdds1to255()
{
   var num = 1;
   while (num <= 255)
   {
      console.log(num + 2);
   }
}
```

PrintArrayVals(arr)
Print all values in a given array.

```
function printArrayVals(arr) {
   for var idx = 0;idx < arr.length;
                  arr++) {
      console.log("array[", idx,
                  "] =",arr[idx]);
   }
}
```

PrintAverageOfArray(arr)
Analyze an array's values and print the average.

```
arr = [1,4,7,2,5,8];
if (arr.length == 0) {
   console.log("[ ], no avg val.");
   return;
}
var sum = arr[0];
for (var idx=1;idx<arr.length;idx++)
{
   sum += arr[idx];
}
console.log("Avg val:",
sum/arr.length);
```

The "Bug-Ridden 13" (#1) – continued

(continued)

ReturnOddsArray1To255()
Create & return array with odd integers 1-255.

```
function returnOddsArray1to255() {
  var oddArray = [];
  for (var num=1; num<=255; num+=2)
  { oddArray.push(num); }
}
```

ReturnArrayCountGreaterThanY(arr, y)
Given an array, return count greater than Y.

```
function countGreaterThanY(arr, y) {
  var numGreater = 0;
  for(var idx = 0;
      idx < arr.length; idx++) {
    if (arr[idx] > y)
    { numGreater++; }
  }
  return arr[y];
}
```

PrintMaxMinAverageArrayVals(arr)
Print the max, min and average array values.

```
function printMaxMinAverage(arr) {
  if (arr.length == 0) { return; }
  var min = arr[0];
  var max = arr[0];
  var sum = arr[0];
  for (var idx = 1;
       idx <= arr.length; idx++) {
    if (arr[idx] < min)
    { min = arr[idx]; }
    if (arr[idx] > max)
    { max = arr[idx]; }
    sum += arr[idx];
  }
  return min;
  return max;
  return avg;
}
```

SquareArrayVals(arr)
Given an array, square each value in the array.

```
function squareArrVals(arr) {
  for ( var idx = 0;
        idx < arr.length; idx++){
    arr[idx] = arr[idx] + arr[idx];
  }
}
```

ZeroOutArrayNegativeVals(arr)
Given an array, set negative values to zero.

```
zeroOutArrayNegativeVals(arr) {
  for ( var idx=0; idx<arr.length;
        idx++){
    if (arr[idx]<0) { arr[idx]=0; }
  }
}
```

ShiftArrayValsLeft(arr)
Shift array values forward, leaving '0' at end.

```
function shiftArrayValsLeft(arr) {
  for(var ix=1;ix<arr.length;ix++){
    arr[ix - 1] = arr[ix];
  }
  arr.length--;
  return arr;
}
```

SwapStringForArrayNegativeVals(arr)
Replace negative array values with 'Dojo'.

```
function swapStringForArrNegs(arr){
  for (var idx = 0; idx<arr.length;
       idx++){
    if(idx < 0) { arr[idx]="Dojo" }
  }
  return arr;
}
```

Chapter 6 – Queues and Stacks

Hey! Hold this book for me. Also, could you take this note-to-self I wrote on a slip of paper? Oh, and I almost forgot – someone important called for you. Here's the phone number – ready?

It's crazy how much we are asked to commit to, and recall from, memory on a daily basis. That's why we have machines save this information for us! Devices are better than humans at storing data *primarily* they are <u>faster</u> (and not forgetful!) and have an expandable amount of storage space.

When we create software systems, we make choices about how to store and organize information, and these choices significantly impact the performance of our systems. It is always wise to borrow great ideas from the past, and over time well-known patterns have emerged for storing, managing and retrieving information. These patterns are reflected in reusable code called *data structures*.

Put simply (and obviously), data structures handle *data* – they store, organize, and retrieve information. There are many different data structures; each exists because it is optimized for a certain set of usage scenarios. Said another way, each data structure has its own priorities about what aspects are important. As a result, each data structure has strengths and weaknesses that make it a good choice for certain situations and a poor choice for others. Everything is a tradeoff after all – if you optimize for everything, then you are really optimizing for nothing.

In general, these choices are design tradeoffs that data structure creators make: how the data structure consumes memory, which of its functions it expects to be most frequently called, etc. Understanding these tradeoffs enables you to make intentional decisions about which data structure to use in your particular situation. If you know, for example, that you will constantly search your data structure for random values, but will rarely add or remove values from it, then instead of a linked list you might choose an array (or perhaps a tree, as we'll see in a few weeks) for your data structure.

You have already worked closely with a few data structures– these include arrays, strings (closely related to arrays) and singly linked lists. This chapter we will learn about a number of new data structures, including the Stack and various flavors of Queues. We will also dive into how existing data structures change when we alter how they deal with duplicate values.

As we study data structures, it is important to keep in mind that these data structures could be implemented in a number of ways, using different building blocks underneath. For this reason, data structures such as Queues are considered *Abstract Data Types*. They are considered *abstract* because the outward behavior of the data structure is well understood, but there is no requirement on how the data structure is constructed internally. We could choose to reimplement an existing Abstract Data Type in an entirely different manner, and as long as we maintain the same Abstract interface, this should cause no problems for all other software that uses that Abstract Data Type.

Chapter 6 – Queues and Stacks

Queues

We're told: *wait our turn*. Queues enforce this, as *Sequential* data structures. Values emerge in order we add them. Like waiting in line at a store, first value to enter is the first to exit (first customer to wait in line is the first to get a tasty treat!). For this reason, Queues contain only a few methods:

`enqueue(val)`: add `val` to Queue
`dequeue()`: remove & return front value
`front()`: return (not remove) first val
`contains(val)`: Queue contains `val`?
`isEmpty()`: Queue contains *no* values?
`size()`: return num of vals in Queue

We can implement Queues in many ways; we will create a Queue using *singly linked list*, starting with:

```
function SLNode(value) {
   this.val = value;
   this.next = null;
}
```

```
function SLQueue() {
   var head = null; // these point
   var tail = null; // ->Node objs
}
```

☐ SLQueue: Enqueue

Create `SLQueue` method `enqueue(val)` to add the given value to end of our queue. Remember, `SLQueue` uses a singly linked list (not an array).

☐ SLQueue: Dequeue

Create `SLQueue` method `dequeue()` to remove and return value at front of queue. Remember, `SLQueue` uses singly linked list (not array).

☐ SLQueue: Front

Create `SLQueue` method `front()` to return the value at front of our queue, without removing it.

☐ SLQueue: Contains

Create method `contains(val)` to return whether given value is found within our queue.

☐ SLQueue: Is Empty

Create `SLQueue` method `isEmpty()` that returns whether our queue contains no values.

☐ SLQueue: Size

Create `SLQueue` method `size()` that returns the number of values in our queue.

☐ SLQueue: Compare Queues

Given two `SLQueue` objects, create a standalone function that returns whether they are equal. Queues are equal only if they have equal elements in identical order. Allocate no other object, and return the queues in their original condition upon exit.

☐ SLQueue: Remove Minimums

Create a standalone function to remove an `SLQueue`'s lowest value, otherwise leaving values in the same sequence. Use only local variables; allocate no other objects. Remove all duplicates of this value.

Bonus: Remove only the *last* minimum value. Convert `[7,2,5,2,4]` to `[7,2,5,4]`.

☐ SLQueue: Interleave Queue

Reorder `SLQueue` values to alternate first half values with second half values, in order. For example: `(1,2,3,4,5)` becomes `(1,4,2,5,3)`. You may create one additional `SLQueue`, if needed.

Chapter 6 – Queues and Stacks

Stacks

Stacks and Queues are companion data structures. Both are *sequential*, meaning they manage data according to the order in which they were added. A Queue data structure operates by a principle of "First-In becomes First-Out" (FIFO); a Stack is quite the opposite (Last-In, First-Out or LIFO).

Consider a pile of papers. With this stack of papers, we can only get a good look at the top of the pile. When we add another paper, *that* page becomes the only one visible. We can only add and remove papers from the *top*. We cannot add a page mid-stack (just as one should not cut into the middle of a *queue* at the ice cream store). In this way, Stacks and Queues mirror one another. Their methods correspond: substitute **push / pop / top** for **enqueue / dequeue / front**, and they become identical.

Stack Implementation Based on Array

Build essential methods `push`, `pop`, `top`, `contains`, `isEmpty`, `size` for `ArrStack` using an *array*. Make sure you designate the underlying array as *private* (declared `var`), not *public* (attached to `this`).

☐ **ArrStack: Push**

Create `push(val)` that adds val to our stack.

☐ **ArrStack: Pop**

Create `pop()` to remove and return the top val.

☐ **ArrStack: Top**

Return (not remove) the stack's top value.

☐ **ArrStack: Contains**

Return whether given val is within the stack.

☐ **ArrStack: Is Empty**

Return whether the stack is empty.

☐ **ArrStack: Size**

Return the number of stacked values.

Now that you're warmed up, create a list-based class `SLStack`, with a *singly linked list*:

☐ **SLStack: Push**

Create `push(val)` that adds val to our stack.

☐ **SLStack: Pop**

Create `pop()` to remove and return the top val.

☐ **SLStack: Top**

Return (not remove) the stack's top value.

☐ **SLStack: Contains**

Return whether given val is within the stack.

☐ **SLStack: Is Empty**

Return whether the stack is empty.

☐ **SLStack: Size**

Return the number of stacked values.

☐ **Compare Stacks**

Given two Stack objects, create a standalone function to return whether they are equal. Stacks are equal only if they have equal elements in identical order. You can use an additional third Stack for storage; you will need it because you must return the given Stacks to their original condition upon exit.

Chapter 6 – Queues and Stacks

In the code you've written the past few days, you may have seen the significant similarity between Queues and Stacks. Today, along with other challenges, we will use that similarity to our advantage, reducing our code *footprint*.

☐ Stack: Copy

Given a Stack, create a new second Stack and copy values from first Stack into second Stack, so they pop in same order. Use only one Queue for additional storage, and only *public* Stack/Queue interfaces.

☐ Create Queue Using Two Stacks

Using only two Stack objects for the underlying data storage, recreate a Queue class.

☐ Queue: Is Palindrome

Given a `Queue`, return `true` if its values are a palindrome (if they are same in reverse order), else return `false`. Restore `Queue` to original state before exiting. For storage, use one additional `Stack`.

☐ Stack / Queue Code-Sharing

As a design exercise, think through how you would combine the `SLQueue` you wrote previously with the `SLStack` class you just created. Would you use object-oriented design? If so, which class inherits from which? Is there a parent class that is neither?

Once you've done the thought work, now it is time to code it: rework what you wrote for `SLQueue` and `SLStack` (or start from scratch, calling these `SLQueue2` and `SLStack2`) with code sharing in mind. When you are done, someone should be able to create new queue and stack objects and use all the methods for those classes. Your combined codebase should be only about 15% larger than `SLQueue`!

☐ Deque: Implementation

Having combined the *designs* of Stack and Queue, why not combine *features* as well. Let's create a class Deque (pronounced 'deck') representing a *double-ended queue*. On top of the basic six methods, enable it to push and pop from opposite ends. Specifically, build class `Deque` with `pushFront(val)`, `pushBack(val)`, `popFront()`, `popBack()`, `front()`, `back()`, `contains(val)`, `isEmpty()`, and `size()`.

☐ Stack: Remove Stack Min

Remove a Stack's minimum value, otherwise leaving values in order. If duplicate min values are found, *remove them all* (see below). Use only one additional Queue (plus primitive local vars) for storage.

Bonus: Create `removeNewestMin()` and `removeOldestMin()` that remove only *one* min value.

Chapter 6 – Queues and Stacks

We created an `SLQueue` and an `SLStack`. We created an `ArrStack`, but no `ArrQueue`. Why not? Singly linked lists have a beginning, a direction and an end; using a list to implement a Queue feels natural. What if we wanted to use an underlying *array*? Why would we do this? In high-performance scenarios, when working with our queue we may not be able to allocate memory for new node objects. Although we could allocate a large number of empty node objects *ahead of time* and keep them in a resource pool, what if instead we built a Queue class *using an array* as the underlying data structure?

Arrays are a natural choice for a *Stack data structure*, since Stacks add and remove from the same end, just like Stacks do. They even both have push() and pop() methods. To use an array underneath a *Queue*, however, there is a wrinkle – at least after a while. With both Queue and Stack, as we add elements our array gets longer, since elements are placed at the end of the array. With a Stack, as we remove elements our array grows and shrinks back like an accordion, since they are removed from the end (the [0] side of the array never changes). This isn't the case with a Queue: we add elements to the end, but we remove them from the beginning. We will need to track the head index and the tail index. Unfortunately (and here is the wrinkle), over time as elements are added and removed, our array will get very large, as our head and tail indices grow higher and higher. This eats up memory even worse than allocating (and freeing!) `ListNode` objects. What to do? Start by capping our array's size!

Circular Queues

When queue's tail or head approaches `size`, wrap around to `[0]` and continue. `tail` and `head` shouldn't meet – one can't "lap" the other. Instead, `enqueue(val)` *fails*: a *full* queue. Ditto `dequeue()`, if *empty*. Constructor requires a `size` argument. Starting there, implement a circular queue!

```
function CirQueue(cap) {
    var head = 0;
    var tail = 0;
    var capacity = cap;
    var arr = [];
}
```

☐ CirQueue: Front

Return (not remove) the queue's front value.

☐ CirQueue: Is Empty

Return whether queue is empty.

☐ CirQueue: Is Full

Return whether queue is full.

☐ CirQueue: Size

Return number of queued vals (not capacity).

☐ CirQueue: Enqueue

Create `enqueue(val)` that adds val to our `CirQueue`, or returns `false`. Wrap if needed!

☐ CirQueue: Dequeue

Create `CirQueue` method `dequeue()` that removes/returns front value, or `null` on fail.

☐ CirQueue: Contains

Return whether given val is within the queue.

☐ CirQueue: Grow

(advanced) Create method `grow(newSize)` that expands a `CirQueue` to a new given size.

Chapter 6 – Queues and Stacks

We know you can't get enough and would *wait in line* to receive a *stack* of additional challenges, so here are a few more! Solve them using the data structures as directed.

☐ Reorder Absolute Queue

Rob sees the world in clear black-and-white terms. Scott, however, is more likely to say "it depends" and see shades of grey. Create a standalone function that accepts a Queue of numbers, sequenced in *absolute-value* order, such as `(10,-20,30,-40,50)`. Using only an additional Stack for storage, reorder the Queue values so that they are in increasing order, such as `(-40,-20,10,30,50)`.

☐ Stack: Partition

Numerous values are stored in a Stack. Divide the values into a group of positive numbers and a group of zero-or-negative numbers. Rearrange the Stack's values so that when popping, all non-positive values come before all positive numbers. The original order can otherwise be disregarded. Use only one Queue for additional storage.

☐ Stack: Switch Pairs

Given Stack containing integers, switch successive pairs of values starting at bottom of stack. If there is an odd number of values, the top value is unaffected. For example, assuming we list top values first, Stack `(1,2,3,4,5,6,7)` should become `(1,3,2,5,4,7,6)`. Use only one additional Queue for storage.

☐ Stack: Is Sorted

Given a Stack containing numerical values, write a standalone function that returns a boolean to represent whether the stack's values are sorted from smallest (at Stack top) to largest (at bottom). Use only one another Stack or a Queue (not both) for storage.

☐ Stack: Mirror

Anna has a curiosity with numbers and strings that are the same forwards and backwards. Mirror a Stack's existing values onto itself, in reverse. Sending Stack `(1,3,5,7)` to your function should change it to `(1,3,5,7,7,5,3,1)`. Use one other Stack or Queue (not both) for storage.

Is your mental queue *overly full* of queue/stack problems? Here's something different:

☐ Weak Finger

Let's count on our fingers! Write a function to return how far you can count on one hand, continually from finger 1 to 5 then back again. *However*, one finger is *weak* and limits the number of times you can use it. You are sent the *number of the weak finger*, and *how many times* you can use it. After that, you can neither count on it nor skip it. If you count the sequence 1,2,3,4,5,4,3,2,1,2,3, you would return 11 as number of counts. Given `(5,0)` return 4, as you would count fingers 1,2,3,4 (stopping before first 5). Given `(2,1)` return 7: you'd count 1,2,3,4,5,4,3 (stopping before second 2).

Chapter 6 – Queues and Stacks

With short answer questions, you can demonstrate *technical depth* as well as *clarity of communication*. How would you answer the following, if asked in an interview?

☐ Short Answer Questions: Queues and Stacks

What is a Queue? When would I use one?
What's the best way to implement a Queue?
Can you implement this a different way? How would you do this, and why?
Is there such thing as 'unbalanced' Queue?

For a list-based Queue that contains the following methods – *push, pop, top, min, max, size, contains, prevVal/nextVal* – which of these are considered *relatively fast*?
Conversely, which of these methods would be considered *relatively slow*? <u>How</u> slow?
Would you change this implementation if your list-based Queue required rapid sequential access in both the forward *and reverse* directions (`removeFirst`, `removeLast`)? How?
When would a list-based Queue be considered 'full'?

For an array-based Queue that contains the following methods – *push, pop, top, min, max, size, contains, prevVal/nextVal* – which of these are considered *relatively fast*?
Conversely, which of these methods would be considered *relatively slow*? <u>How</u> slow?
Would you change this implementation if your array-based Queue required rapid sequential access in both the forward *and reverse* directions (`removeFirst`, `removeLast`)? How?
When would an array-based Queue be considered 'full'?

What is a Stack? When would I use one?
What is the most common underlying implementation for a Stack?
When and why would you choose to implement this differently?
For a Stack built with common implementation, containing the following methods – *push, pop, top, min, max, size, contains, prevVal/nextVal* – which methods are considered *relatively fast*?
Likewise, which of these methods are considered *relatively slow*? <u>How</u> slow?
Is there such thing as 'unbalanced' Stack?
When would this type of Stack be considered 'full'?

Is there such thing as a hybrid Queue/Stack? Does it have a name?
How are these most commonly implemented? Is there more than one common implementation?

Chapter 6 – Queues and Stacks

☐ Weekend Challenge: Stacks and Queues

This weekend, build a card game named **Fives!** that makes use of `Stack` and `Queue` objects. Integrate the classes that you have created, and use queues and stacks where these make sense (and *don't* use any Array objects). Your game should do the following:
- The game uses a single deck of 52 cards: four sets of 13 cards. Each set contains a card with value 1, a card with value 2, up thru value 13 (game doesn't need suits such as "clubs", etc).
- Allow any number of players from two to six.
- Get the number of players, plus each player's name, via `prompt()`.
- Each player starts with five cards. For each turn, a player must do the following three things:
    1. Either draw one new card from the remaining undrawn cards (if any remain), or pick up one or more consecutive cards from the pile of discards;
    2. Optionally, lay down a set of cards that add up to a multiple of 5 (that player would then increment his/her score by one);
    3. Discard from his/her hand one remaining card.
- Gameplay begins with Player 1, then the others in order, until all cards have been discarded.
- The player with the most points – the most laid-down card sets – wins.

Queues and Stacks Review

Data structures hold and manage data. Each data structure is optimized for some specific use and as a result is less optimized for other uses. In this chapter, we studied data structures that are good *abstract data types*. An **abstract data type** satisfies a specific external interface (such as `push`, `pop`, `top`, `isEmpty`, `size` and `contains`) but can be internally implemented in different ways (e.g. with an `Array` or with an `SList`).

Queues and **stacks** are abstract data types that manage data *sequentially*, based on the order in which this data was added. Queues manage data in a **FIFO** (first-in, first-out) manner, and stacks manage data in a **LIFO** (last-in, first-out) manner. Queues are considered *inherently fair* data structures and commonly used when managing a running list of tasks or objects. Stacks are invaluable when you pause what you are doing to handle something new, before returning to the task at hand.

Working with queue and stack objects ('reverse this queue, using only one other queue') has long been a staple of entry-level software interviews, as they force you to think abstractly but also work with basic objects to build more complex behaviors. Queue/stack questions are not as common as they once were (generally interview questions are more advanced nowadays). Don't fret though – we are only a fraction of the way through our algorithm journey as well.

Keep working hard, and you'll be fluent in abstract data types (and other data structures) in no time!

Chapter 7 – Arrays, Part II

Working with arrays grows our dexterity with foundation concepts such as loops and conditionals. Now we can use newer concepts such as recursion. Knowing how to *test your code* is another critical skill.

Test-Driven Development

Stated simply, test-driven development (TDD) is a technique where you first build a test that fails before creating any new code. Your sole objective is then to write "just enough" clean code to pass this test. If *any* test (including a preexisting one) is failing, consider your status *red*; your only goal is to *get green* again. With TDD, software development becomes: **create a new test, write code to get green, refactor as necessary, repeat**. This practice is very common in industry, particularly when the cost of a bug is unusually high, or when code is long-lived or likely to become complicated. Conversely, when writing quick prototypes that are very likely to be rewritten (or even in a final product, if the costs of defects are manageably low), a significant investment in TDD may be unwarranted.

Even in that situation, though, you should constantly think about different inputs that might break your code. For every challenge, think about (and ideally write down or state aloud) the pertinent test cases. Over time you will know the common "corner cases" to include (empty array, extremely long list, etc). Listing these on the whiteboard before coding is something that interviewers will appreciate. Once your code is done, then revisit your tests by hand or with test code. Always ask yourself "where's the bug?"

☐ Array: Average (Warmup)

(Warm-up) Always run through some quick algorithm problems before any coding interview, to get yourself warmed up. How about this one: *return the average value of an array of unsorted numbers*.

☐ Balance Point

Write a function that returns whether the given array has a balance point between indices, where one side's sum is equal to the other's. Example: `[1,2,3,4,10]` → `true` (*between indices 3 & 4*), but `[1,2,4,2,1]` → `false`.

☐ Balance Index

Here, a balance point is *on* an index, not *between* indices. Return the *balance index* where sums are equal on either side (exclude its own value). Return -1 if none exist. Ex.: `[-2,5,7,0,3]` → `2`, but `[9,9]` → `-1`.

☐ Taco Truck

Joe drives a taco truck in the booming town of Squaresburg. He uses an array of `[x,y]` coordinates corresponding to locations of his customers. They walk to his truck, but he is fair-minded so he wants to *minimize total distance* from truck to customers. City blocks are perfect squares, and every street is two-way, at perfect right angles. He only parks by street corners (coordinates like `[37,-16]`). Customers only travel on streets: coordinate `[2,-2]` is distance 4 from `[0,0]`. Joe checks the array before deciding where to park. Given a customer coordinate array, return an optimal taco truck location. Example: given `[ [10,0], [-1,-10], [2,4] ]`, return `[2,0]`, as total distance is `25` (8+13+4).

Chapter 7 – Arrays, Part II

Divide and Conquer

If you looked for a word ("stentorian", for example) in an actual book dictionary, would you turn to the first page, then the second page, then the third, examining all pages until you found the word? Of course not! You'd open to the center, finding the word *"lightweight"*. Undaunted by such name-calling, and based on your alphabetical prowess, you'd look halfway further towards book's end, where you might find *"ridicule"*. Again, you would throw off this insult, looking even further toward the end of the book. The word you'd find might be *"terrible"*, but like all Dojo students you wouldn't give up. Eventually you would find your word "stentorian", nestled amidst stenographers and stepbrothers.

This is an example of a technique known as *"divide and conquer"*. When you haven't yet opened the dictionary, you don't know much about which of the 3350 pages contains *your* word. After looking at page 1, all you really know is that the word is somewhere in the 2-3350 range – you haven't narrowed it down much! If, instead of reading the first page, you glanced at a page in the middle (p.1675, let's say), then with a single look you have cut the problem space in half. With a second glance at page 2513, you narrowed it even further and by looking at page 2900, you narrow the possibilities from 3350 pages down to "only" 400 pages: an 8x drop by checking only 3 pages. You can "divide and conquer" the problem space in this way, because words are listed *in-order*.

☐ Array: Binary Search

Given a sorted array and a value, return whether the array contains that value. Do not sequentially iterate the array. Instead, 'divide and conquer', taking advantage of the fact that the array is *sorted*. As always, only use built-in functions that you are prepared to recreate (write yourself) on demand!

☐ Min of Sorted-Rotated

You will be given a numerical array that has first been sorted, then rotated by an unknown amount. Find and return the minimum value in that array. Don't use built-in functions (surprise!). Given the input array `["Gigli","Jay is cool","Mavis","Phoebe","Thurber","Anna","Celeste","Elon"]`, you should return `"Anna"`. Remember, do not linearly iterate the array!

☐ String: Binary Search

You will be given a very long string and a single character. Return whether that character is present in the string. Note: the characters in the string have been arranged so that the `charCodeAt()` values for each character are monotonically ascending from the beginning of the string to the back. Use the fact that the string is effectively *sorted*. Don't use built-in functions. Note: characters may not be exactly as you might have considered 'alphabetized', but `char.charCodeAt()` works well. Example: if your function is given the inputs `(" &-0379DEFXZ[abcz|", "6")`, it should return `false`. If instead it is sent `(" &-0379DEFXZ[abcz|", "c")`, return `true`. Remember, don't iterate the string linearly!

Chapter 7 – Arrays, Part II

Don't panic   Think out loud   Ask clarifying questions   Draw diagrams
Error and corner cases   List example inputs and what they should return
Admit when it is suboptimal (but keep going)   Ask "what are we optimizing for?"

☐ Array: Flatten

Flatten a given array, eliminating nested & empty arrays. Do not alter it; return a new one retaining order. For `[1,[2,3],4,[]]` return `[1,2,3,4]`.

Second: work *'in-place'* in the given array (do not create another). Alter order if needed. Ex.: `[1,[2,3],4,[]]` could become `[1,3,4,2]`.

Third: make your algorithm both *in-place* and *stable*. Do you need a return value?

☐ Array: Mode

Back in the Basic 13, you wrote code to compute an array's minimum and maximum values. You also wrote code to determine average value (the "mean"). What about the "mode" – the most common value in that data set. Create a function that, given an array, returns the most frequent value in the array.

Second: memory constraints prevent your using a new array. How does this affect your solution?

☐ Array: Remove Duplicates

Remove array duplicates. Do not alter original. Return new array with results 'stable' (original order). For `[1,2,1,3,4,2]` return `[1,2,3,4]`.

Second: work *'in-place'* in given array. Alter order if needed (*stability* is not required). Ex.: `[1,2,1,3,4,2]` could become `[1,2,4,3]`.

Third: make it *in-place* and stable.

Fourth: eliminate any second (inner) loop.

☐ Array: Buffer Copy

Create `arrBufferCopy(sourceArr,destArr,sourceStartIdx,destStartIdx,numVals)` to copy `numVals` values starting at `sourceArr[sourceStartIdx]` to `destArr[destStartIdx]` etc. Do not lengthen `destArr`, nor read off the end of `sourceArr`.

Second: if you reach either array's end, *wraparound* to continue writing/reading at beginning of array.

Third: if `numVals > destArr.length`, only copy the minimum needed amount.

Fourth: `sourceArr` can now be the same array as `destArr`! Only handle the non-wrap case. That is, you can assume that you won't need to read beyond `arr.length`. You can extend the array on writes.

Fifth: if you made it this far, good job! Now for a real challenge: handle *all possible cases* where `sourceArr` and `destArr` are the same array, including wraparound, not overwriting original array data prematurely, nor extending it, but copying all data *in-place*. If `arr.length` is 100, how would you handle significant wraparound and overwriting, such as `arrBufferCopy(arr,arr,30,80,95)`?

Chapter 7 – Arrays, Part II

Time-Space Tradeoff

Good engineering is all about tradeoffs: knowing what tradeoffs are available, and knowing when to use them. In software engineering, one important tradeoff is *time vs. space*. If you know you will be asked to solve a certain formula repeatedly, you can keep track your previous answer and simply provide that answer rather than recomputing it. For certain problems, whether in algorithms class or in the workplace, *caching* (saving) the results will not make the function any faster when it is first called, but it can make subsequent calls *much* faster. Use this concept in today's algorithm challenges!

☐ Smarter Sum

Use time-space tradeoff to accelerate average running time for `iSigma(num)` that returns sum of integers from 1 to num. Recall `iSigma(1)=1`, `iSigma(2)=3`, `iSigma(3)=6`, `iSigma(4)=10`.

☐ Faster Factorial

Remember `Factorial(num)`? It returned the product of positive integers from 1 to num. Examples: `Factorial(1) = 1`, `Factorial(2) = 2`, `Factorial(3) = 6`. For these purposes, `Factorial(0) = 1`. Recreate this function, but use a time-space tradeoff to accelerate the average running time.

☐ Fancy Fibonacci

Use time-space tradeoff to accelerate running time of `iFib(num)` that returns `num`th number in the Fibonacci sequence. Recall `iFib(0)=0`, `iFib(1)=1`, `iFib(2)=1`, `iFib(3)=2`.

☐ Tricky Tribonacci

Why stop with fibonacci? Create a function to retrieve a "Tribonacci" number, which we will define as the sum of the previous 3 values. Tribonaccis start with { 0, 0, 1, 1, 2, 4, 7, 13, 24, 44, 81, ... }. Again, use a time-space tradeoff to make it fast.

Chapter 7 – Arrays, Part II

This chapter we dive deeply into arrays. Put yourself into the mindset of a technical interview during this chapter's algorithm challenges, using the following concepts:

*Don't panic   Think out loud   Clarifying questions   Error and corner cases   Example inputs
       Diagrams   Admit when it is suboptimal (but keep going)   "What are we optimizing for?"*

☐ Median of Sorted Arrays

Given two arrays that are sorted but not necessarily the same length, find the median value. Given (`[1,5,9]`, `[1,2,3,4,5,6]`), return `4`. If the number of values is even, return the average of the two middle values. Given (`[1,5,9]`, `[1,2,3,4,5]`), return `3.5`.

Second: accept three arrays instead of two.

Third: handle an arbitrary number of arrays.

☐ Time to English

You are given an integer representing the number of minutes that have elapsed since midnight. You should return a string representing the current time, in traditional spoken convention. Use numerals, except specifically the following words – *midnight, noon, past, til, half, quarter*. Examples: if given `30`, return `"half past midnight"`. If given `75`, return `"quarter past 1 am"`. If given `710`, return `"10 til noon"`. If given `1000`, return `"20 til 5 pm"`.

☐ Missing Value

You are given an array of length `N` that contains, in no particular order, integers from `0` to `N`. One integer value is missing. Quickly determine and return the missing value. Given (`[3,0,1]`), return `2`.

Second: now the lowest value can now be *any* integer (including negatives), instead of always being 0. Given (`[2,-4,0,-3,-2,1]`) return `-1`. Given (`[5,2,7,8,4,9,3]`), return `6`.

☐ Rain Terraces

The Seattle Coding Dojo wants to send excess water to the Burbank Coding Dojo, so it landscapes its rooftop with a set of unusual elevated terraces. The terraces are all the same width, but have varying heights. When it rains, water gathers in the low terraces that are surrounded by taller ones. For example, if we have terraces with heights `[3,1,1,4,2]`, then as much as 4 units of water could be gathered, because water would pool 2-deep on two different terraces (both of the 1-high terraces: between the 3-high and 4-high terraces). Water on the other terraces just runs off the sides. Given an array of terrace heights, return the maximum amount of water that is trapped when rains come.

Chapter 7 – Arrays, Part II

Data Sufficiency

One important problem solving concept is the idea of *data sufficiency*. In algorithm challenges and real-world problems, having a piece of data doesn't necessarily make it important. Often code will run faster if we discard unneeded data. In fact, sometimes your code *cannot* run *until* you let go of it!

☐ Last Digit of A to the B

Modern computers can handle very large numbers, but they do have their limits. A number that is repeatedly multiplied by itself will eventually exceeds a computer's ability to accurately represent it. (Note: the number of times it is multiplied by itself is called an *exponent*.) For an optional end-of-chapter challenge, determine the smallest (least significant) digit of a number that is potentially very, very large. You may find that you must do this without computing the actual (unimaginably large) number.

Implement a function `lastDigitAtoB(a,b)` that accepts two non-negative integers. It should return the last digit of a number found by raising the first number (`a`) to an exponent of the second number (`b`). Examples: given `(3,4)`, you should return 1 (3 * 3 * 3 * 3 is 81, whose last digit is 1). Given `(12,5)`, return 2 (which is the least significant digit of 248832: 12 * 12 * 12 * 12 * 12). How high can you scale your solution? For example, what is the return value for `(237,124)`?

☐ Matrix Search

Mike digs image recognition and wants to create a JavaScript Imaging Library, just like PIL for Python. He is given 2 different two-dimensional arrays, containing integers between 0 and 65535. Each two-dimensional array represents a gray-scale image, where each integer value is a pixel. The second image *might* be found somewhere within the larger one. Return whether it is.

Given array: `[ [12,34,45,56],`   and array: `[ [67,78],`   return `true`.
              `[98,87,76,65],`   `[43,32]]`
              `[56,67,78,89],`
              `[54,43,32,21]]`

Second: Return location of first match found (`[-1,-1]` if no match). In example above, return `[2,1]`.

☐ Max of Subarray Sums

How efficient can you be on this following final challenge? The input may hold many million values.

Given a numerical array that is potentially very long, return the maximum sum of values from a subarray. Any *consecutive sequence* of indices in the array is considered a subarray. Create a function that returns the highest sum possible from these subarrays. Given `[1,2,-4,3,-2,3,-1]`, you should return **4** (for subarray `[3,-2,3]`), and given `[-1,-2,-4,-3,-2,-3]`, return **0** (for `[]`). This problem has many possible implementations. Which do you prefer & why?

The "Bugful 13" (#2)

Below are submissions for the "Basic 13". What errors can you find?

Print1To255()
Print all the integers from 1 to 255.

```
function print1to255()
{
   for(var num = 1;num <= 255;num--)
   {
      console.log(num);
   }
}
```

PrintIntsAndSum0To255()
Print integers from 0 to 255, and the sum so far.

```
function printIntsAndSum0to255()
{
   var sum = 0;
   for (var num=0; num<=255; num++){
      console.log(num," Sum:",sum);
      sum += num;
   }
}
```

PrintMaxOfArray(arr)
Print the largest element in a given array.

```
function printMaxOfArray(arr)
{
   if (arr.length == 0) {
      console.log("[], no max val.");
      return;
   }
   var max = arr[0];
   for ( var idx = 1;
         idx < arr.length; idx++){
      if (arr[idx] > max) {
         max = arr[idx];
      }
      console.log("Max val:", max);
   }
}
```

PrintOdds1To255()
Print all odd integers from 1 to 255.

```
function printOdds1to255() {
   var num = 1;
   while (num <= 255) {
      console.log(num);
      num ++= 2;
   }
}
```

PrintArrayVals(arr)
Print all values in a given array.

```
function printArrayVals(arr)
{
   for( var idx=0; idx<arr.length;
         idx++) {
      console.log("array[", idx,
                  "] =", idx);
   }
}
```

PrintAverageOfArray(arr)
Analyze an array's values and print the average.

```
function printAverageOfArray(arr)
{
   if (arr.length == 0) {
      console.log("[], no avg val.");
      return;
   }
   var sum = arr[0];
   for ( var idx = 0;
         idx < arr.length; idx++ )
   {sum += arr[idx];}
   console.log(sum/arr.length);
}
```

The "Bugger's Banquet 13" (#2) – continued

ReturnOddsArray1To255()
Create & return an array with odd integers from 1-255.

```
function returnOddsArray1to255() {
   // create empty array
   // setup for loop, with max iterations
   // { add # to array }
   // return array
}
```

ReturnArrayCountGreaterThanY(arr, y)
Given an array, return the count that is greater than Y.

```
function returnArrayCountGreaterThanY(arr, y) {
   var numGreater = 0;
   for (var idx = 0;idx < arr.length;idx++){
      if (arr[idx] > y) { y++; }
   }
   console.log("%d values greater than %d", numGreater, y);
}
```

PrintMaxMinAverageArrayVals(arr)
Given an array, print max, min and average values.

```
function printMaxMinAverageArrayVals(arr)
{
   if (arr.length == 0) {
      console.log("[] arr, no min/max/avg");
      return;
   }
   var min = arr[0];
   var max = arr[0];
   var sum = arr[0];
   for (var idx=1; idx <= arr.length;idx++){
      if (arr[idx] < min) { min = arr[idx]; }
      if (arr[idx] > max) { max = arr[idx]; }
      sum += arr[idx];
   }
   console.log("Max val:", max);
   console.log("Min val:", min);
   console.log("Avg val:", sum/arr.length);
   return [max, min, avg];
}
```

"Exterminator's Delight" (#2) – continued

SquareArrayVals(arr)
Given an array, square each value in the array.

```
function squareArrVals(arr) {
   for (idx = 0; idx < arr.length; idx++) {
      arr[idx] = arr[idx * idx];
   }
}
```

ZeroOutArrayNegativeVals(arr)
Given an array, set negative values to zero.

```
function zeroOutArrayNegativeVals(arr) {
   for (var idx = 1;idx < arr.length;idx++){
      if (arr[idx] < 0) {
         arr[idx] = 0;
      }
   }
}
```

ShiftArrayValsLeft(arr)
Given an array, shift values leftward by one. Drop first values and leave extra `'0'` value(s) at end.

```
function shiftArrValsLeft(arr) {
   for (var idx = 1;idx < arr.length;idx++) {
      arr[idx + 1] = arr[idx];
   }
   arr[arr.length - 1] = 0;
   return arr;
}
```

SwapStringForArrayNegativeVals(arr)
Given an array, replace negative values with `'Dojo'`.

```
function swapStringForArrayNegativeVals(arr) {
   for (var idx = 0;idx < arr.length;idx++) {
      if (arr[idx] <= 0) {
         arr[idx] = "Dojo";
      }
   }
   return arr;
}
```

Chapter 8 – Linked Lists, Part II

This week involves *linked list* and *object pointer manipulation*. Later we'll see a list where nodes connect to *two* others, but in this linked list, each node links only to the *next*. It is accurately called a <u>*singly linked list*</u>, where iterating forward is easy; backward is tricky. Start from this SList object:

```
function SLNode(value) {
   this.val = value;
   this.next = null;
}
function SList() {
   this.head = null;
   this.back = function() {
      if (!this.head) { return null;}
      var runner = this.head;
      while (runner.next)
      { runner = runner.next; }
      return runner.val;
   }
   this.pushBack = function(value) {
      var newNode =new SLNode(value);
      if (!this.head)
      { this.head = newNode; }
      else {
         var runner = this.head;
         while (runner.next)
         { runner = runner.next; }
         runner.next = newNode;
      }
   }
   this.popBack = function() {
      if (!this.head) {return null; }
      var returnVal;
      if (!this.head.next) {
         returnVal = this.head.val;
         this.head = null;
         return returnVal;
      }
      var runner = this.head;
      while (runner.next.next)
      { runner = runner.next; }
      returnVal = runner.next.val;
      runner.next = null;
      return returnVal;
   }
   this.pushFront = function(value){
      var oldHead = this.head;
      this.head = new SLNode(value);
      this.head.next = oldHead;
   }
   this.popFront = function() {
      var returnVal = null;
      if (this.head) {
         returnVal = this.head.val;
         this.head = this.head.next;
      }
      return returnVal;
   }
   this.contains = function(value) {
      var runner = this.head;
      while (runner) {
         if (runner.val === value)
         { return true; }
         runner = runner.next;
      }
      return false;
   }
   this.removeVal = function(value){
      if (!this.head){ return false;}
      if (this.head.val === value) {
         this.head = this.head.next;
         return true;
      }
      var runner = this.head;
      while (runner.next) {
         if(runner.next.val===value){
            runner.next =
                  runner.next.next;
            return true;
         }
         runner = runner.next;
      }
      return false;
   }
}
```

Chapter 8 – Linked Lists, Part II

Runners and Linked List Iterators

By now you know well how to iterate through the values of an array. You set up your `FOR` loop, with an `idx` variable that starts at 0 and advances by 1 until `idx` equals `Array.length`. We want to easily iterate through the values of a linked list as well, and this is easy enough. Instead of an `idx` that starts at the beginning of the array, we start with a pointer to the first node (or `SList.head`, if we are working with an `SList` object). This pointer will ultimately run through all the nodes in our list, so we use a convention of calling this variable `runner`. Just as `idx` advances by 1 until it equals `Array.length`, likewise our `runner` will follow each node's `.next` pointer to the subsequent node, until it is `null`.

How would we compare runners to other iterators? One important aspect is that in singly linked lists (`SLists` for shorthand), `.next` pointers flow in only one direction. To check whether an *array* is a palindrome, we can directly compare `arr[idx]` to `arr[arr.length-idx-1]`; runners can't do that. We *can*, however, have more than one! In addition to our normal `runner`, we could have 1) a second runner that trails by some number of nodes, or 2) a second runner that is actually a 'walker' – the two runners could advance at different speeds. This is sometimes called a 'tortoise and hare' pattern, and is useful in a number of situations.

This chapter's challenges have an <u>optional additional twist</u>, *if you so choose*. If the challenge asks for a method in the `SList` class, then to accept this optional challenge, solve it three ways: as a standalone function that accepts an `SList` object, as an `SLNode` method, and as an `SList` method.

☐ SList: Reverse

Reverse the node sequence. Given an `SList` object, the `.head` property should point to the previously-last node, and the rest of the nodes should follow similarly from back to front.

☐ SList: Kth-Last Node

Given k, return the value that is 'k' nodes from the list's end. If given `(list,1)`, return the list's last value. If given `(list,4)`, return the value at the node that has exactly 3 nodes following it.

☐ SList: Shift Right

Given a list, shift nodes to the right, by a given number *shiftBy*. These shifts are circular: when shifting a node off list's end, it reappears at list's start. For list a=>b=>c, `shift(1)` should return c=>a=>b.

Second: also handle negative *shiftBy* (to left).

☐ SList: Is Palindrome

Return whether a list is a palindrome. *String* palindromes read the same front-to-back and back-to-front. Here, compare *node values*. N.B.: to be accurate in JavaScript, use `===` instead of `==`, since `1 == true == [1] == "1"`.

Second: you may not have plentiful memory. Can you solve this without an additional array?

Chapter 8 – Linked Lists, Part II

Over the chapter's course, we'll coalesce a considerable collection of cool concepts for contemplation:

Classes and *objects*   *Private* vs. *public*   *Prototype*   === vs. ==   *Reference* vs. *value*

Today's challenges should all be implemented as *standalone functions*.

☐ SList: Sum Numerals

You are given two lists, each representing a number. Every node value is a 0-9 digit, with *first* node representing *least significant digit*. Return a *new* list representing the sum. Given 2=>0=>1 & 8=>4, return 0=>5=1 because 102 + 48 = 150.

Second: what if first node is **most** significant?

☐ SList: Flatten Children

Why limit nodes to contain only one pointer? In this challenge, each node has `.next`, but also `.child` that is either `null` or points to another head. In turn each *child* node could point to another list. Don't alter `.child`; arrange `.next` pointers to 'flatten' the hierarchy into one linear list, from head through all others via `.next`.

☐ SList: Setup Loop

In preparation for tomorrow, create a sequence of `slNodes` that form a closed loop. Your function's first argument should signify how many nodes total, and the second should be which node number is pointed to by the last node. Give nodes sequential numbers as values, for clarity. Calling setupLoop(5, 3) should return a circular list of 1=>2=>3=>4=>5=>3=>4=>5=>3....

☐ SList: Unflatten Children

Take the output from your "flatten child lists" function (a linear linked list containing nodes with `.child` pointers), and restore it to its original state. Do you need to change your *flatten* function to enable this?

Second: for `flatten` & `unflatten`, in the case of really complex inputs, how many nested `FOR` (or `WHILE`) loops might you have? Can you solve without nested loops, even for complex inputs?

Chapter 8 – Linked Lists, Part II

Be mindful of these ideas as you work through the chapter's challenges:

Classes and *objects*   *Private* vs. *public*   *Prototype*   === vs. ==   *Reference* vs. *value*

Build standalone functions <u>and</u> `SList` & `SLNode` methods. Your `setupListLoop()` may be useful.

☐ SList: Has Loop

Ben sends linked lists to Emma, but she doesn't quite trust him. Is he trying to make her code spin infinitely? Given a linked list, determine whether it has a loop, and return a boolean accordingly.

☐ SList: Loop Start

For Emma to expose Ben's nefarious intentions, she needs to locate the loops. Given a linked list, return a pointer to the node where a loop begins (where the last node points), or `null` if no loop.

☐ SList: Break Loop

Even better than finding where the loops start would be to just fix them. You will be given a *potentially loopy list*; determine whether there is a loop, and if so, break it. Retain all nodes, in original order.

☐ SList: Number of Nodes

Given a linked list *with or without* a loop, return total number of nodes. Given circular list `k=>e=>l=>v=>i=>n=>l=>v=>`..., return `6`.

☐ SList: Swap Pairs

Given a singly linked list, rearrange the nodes so that successive pairs of nodes are swapped in sequence. If list has an odd number of nodes, the final node (not part of a pair) should be unchanged. For `mySList` a=>b=>c, `mySList.swapPairs()` should change the `mySList` object to b=>a=>c. For `mySList` a=>b=>c=>d, `mySList.swapPairs()` should change it to b=>a=>d=>c.

Chapter 8 – Linked Lists, Part II

☐ Where's the Bug? (SList version)

Without peeking at previous code, how many bugs can you find in the below `SList`/`SLNode` methods?

```
function SLNode(val) { this.val = value; this.next = null;}

function SList() {
   this.head = null;
   this.back = function() {
      if (!this.head) return null;
      var runner = this.head;
      while (runner)
      { runner = runner.next; }
      return runner.val;
   }
   this.pushBack = function(value) {
      var newNode = SLNode(value);
      if (!this.head)
      { this.head = newNode; }
      else {
         var runner = this.head;
         while (runner.next)
         { runner = runner.next; }
         runner.next = newNode;
      }
   }
   this.popBack = function() {
      if (!this.head) { return null; }
      var returnVal;
      if (!this.head.next) {
         returnVal = this.head.val;
         this.head.val = null;
         return returnVal;
      }
      var runner = this.head;
      while (runner.next)
      { runner = runner.next; }
      returnVal = runner.val;
      runner.next = null;
      return returnVal;
   }
   this.pushFront = function(value) {
      var oldHead = this.head;
      this.head.next = oldHead;
      this.head = new SLNode(value);
   }
   this.popFront = function() {
      var returnVal = this.head.val;
      this.head = this.head.next;
      return returnVal;
   }
   this.contains = function(value) {
      var runner = this.head;
      while (runner) {
         if (runner.val == value)
         { return true; }
         runner = runner.next;
      }
      return false;
   }
   this.removeVal = function(value) {
      if (!this.head) { return false;}
      if (this.head.val === value)
         this.head = this.head.next;
         return true;

      var runner = this.head;
      while (runner.next) {
         if (runner.next.val!==value) {
            runner.next=runner.next.next;
            return true;
         }
         runner = runner.next;
      }
      return false;
   }
```

Chapter 8 – Linked Lists, Part II

Doubly Linked List

There is certainly no reason why a linked list node must refer to only one other node. For the best flexibility when traversing a list, we might want to be connected in both directions: forward and backward. Whereas singly linked lists feature nodes that only know about their forward neighbor (unable to look backward), *doubly linked lists* are more like lines of preschoolers holding hands as they walk down the street together, on a field trip to the fire station. This expands our ability to easily iterate back and forth through the `DList`, forming a much better parallel with our `idx` array iterator.

For the Doubly Linked List, all the concepts and techniques of Singly Linked Lists apply (see below). This extra flexibility comes with a cost, however. Maintaining both sets of pointers can be tedious.

Classes and *objects*   *Private* vs. *public*   *Prototype*   === vs. ==   *Reference* vs. *value*

```
function DLNode(value)                  function DList()
{                                       {
   this.val = value;                       this.head = null;
   this.prev = null;                       this.tail = null;
   this.next = null;                    }
}
```

☐ DList Class

Given the above reference implementations for doubly linked node and doubly linked list, can you construct the rest of a basic `DList` class? This would include `DList` methods `push()`, `pop()`, `front()`, `back()`, `contains()`, and `size()`.

Second: implement these so that they are available as *standalone functions* as well as methods on both `DLNode` *and* `DList` classes.

Chapter 8 – Linked Lists, Part II

Take on as many `DList` challenges as possible, before next chapter starts!

☐ DList: Prepend Value

Given `DList`, new `val`, and existing `val`, insert new `val` into `DList` *before* existing `val`.

☐ DList: Append Value

Given `DList`, new `val`, and existing `val`, insert new `val` into `DList` *after* existing `val`.

☐ DList: Kth-to-Last Value

Given `k`, return the value 'k' from a `DList`'s end.

☐ DList: Delete Middle Node

Given `node` in the middle of a `DList`, remove it.

☐ DList: Is Valid

Determine whether given `DList` is valid: whether next and prev pointers match, no loops, etc.

☐ DList: Partition

Given `DList` and partition `val`, perform a simple partition (no need to return the pivot index).

☐ DList: Palindrome

Determine whether a `DList` is a palindrome

☐ DList: Reverse

Create function to reverse nodes in a `DList`.

☐ DList: Loop Start

Given `DList` that may contain a loop, return node where loop begins (or `null` if no loop).

☐ DList: Break Loop

Given `DList` that may contain a loop, break the loop while retaining original node order.

☐ DList: Repair

Combine previous work with a function that fixes errors found by `isValid` and breaks loops.

With short answer questions, you can demonstrate *technical depth* as well as *clarity of communication*. How would you answer the following, if asked in an interview?

☐ Short Answer Questions: DLists

**When are linked lists useful, compared to arrays? Conversely, when are arrays a better choice?
What is the difference between SList & DList? When would I use one versus the other?
How are DLists implemented?
Which linked list methods are significantly different, between SLists and DLists? (these include front, back, pushFront/popFront, pushBack/popBack, min/max, contains, nextVal/prevVal, size)
Is there such thing as an 'unbalanced' DList? Is there such thing as a 'full' DList?
How would one check whether a DList is valid?**

Chapter 9 – Recursion

This chapter covers *recursion* and *dynamic programming*. Recursion occurs when a *function calls itself*. Dynamic programming is more general: breaking large problems into smaller, more solvable ones.

Let's consider an example: "I'm thinking of an integer between 1 and 120. Guess it." If you were to guess '61', and I said "nope, that's too high," *then* how would you respond? You would treat this exactly as if we had just started and I had said "I'm thinking of an integer between 1 and 60." In doing this, you reframed the problem as a less complex one, a technique called *dynamic programming*.

Let us continue: if next you guessed '30', and I said "nope, too low," then you could again reframe the problem as "I'm thinking of a number from 31 to 60." Let's say you then guessed '42', to which I said "Yes, you guessed it! How did you know *that* was the answer?!" With this 'divide- and-conquer' approach, you could guess the correct number in a 1-120 range, in just 6 guesses on average.

Why is dynamic programming useful? This is used when a function can make progress toward solving a problem, but is not able to solve the entire problem immediately. In these cases, if we always make at least a little *forward progress*, continually revisiting the problem to try again, then ultimately we will complete the task (this is a great metaphor for the power of focus and persistence in daily life as well!). Dynamic programming is an effective way to decompose a problem so that it takes advantage of multiple machines. For our purposes, however, we will use it to better understand *recursion*.

Three requirements for effective recursion

a) **Base cases:**
When a function *can* determine (and return) an answer immediately, this is a *'base case'*. If you successfully guess my number, I know right away that the game is over. Conversely, if you search for *'spizzwink'* in an alphabetized word list and find nothing between *'spitz'* and *'splash'*, you need not continue: *'spizzwink'* was not found. There are *positive* and *negative* base cases.

b) **Forward progress:**
When a function *cannot* solve a problem but can narrow the range of possibilities, this is *'forward progress'*. Learning that '61' is *too high*, you have made forward progress because you now know the solution is outside the '61-120' range. For recursion to be effective, you must make at least a little forward progress in every possible case. If there is a case in which you can neither solve the problem nor break it down further, then your solution is not complete.

c) **Calling back into itself as if it were the original problem:**
If my initial challenge were "I'm thinking of an integer between 1 and 60", you would proceed just as you did in originally after your first guess. If "taking a guess" is a function call, this function wouldn't know the difference between initial and subsequent calls. A recursive function calls *itself* to narrow things down, but like most functions it generally does not need to know anything about its caller – the fact that *the caller might be itself* is not an important distinction.

When creating (and debugging) recursive code, remember: each function call creates a new stack frame (essentially, a new T-diagram). Call stack space is limited, so *recurse with care*.

Chapter 9 – Recursion

Writing great code to solve a well-understood problem is only part of a software engineer's job. You should also consider how your code responds when given unexpected inputs. Thinking of possible "corner cases" ahead of time allows you to create much more resilient code that stands the test of time.

This chapter you will familiarize yourself with recursion. Some or all of the following important concepts will be used in this chapter's challenges.

    Base cases   Forward Progress   Call Stack   Dynamic Programming

☐ Recursive Sigma

Write a recursive function that given a number returns sum of integers from 1 to that number. Example: `rSigma(5)` = 15 (1+2+3+4+5); `rSigma(2.5)` = 3 (1+2); `rSigma(-1)` = 0.

☐ Recursive Factorial

Given `num`, return the product of ints from 1 up to `num`. If less than zero, treat as zero. If not integer, truncate. Experts tell us `0!` is `1`. `rFact(3)` = 6 (1*2*3). Also, `rFact(6.5)` = 720 (1*2*3*4*5*6).

☐ Flood Fill

Most graphical "paint" applications, have a 'paintcan fill' function that floods part of an image with a certain color. We change the image as if we painted a canvas: a two-dimensional array of integers, where each integer represents a color for that pixel. The canvas `Array.length` is the Y dimension of our canvas; each spot in the canvas array is a row in our image, with a length equal to our canvas' X dimension. You are given a canvas (2-dimensional array of integers), starting coordinate (2-element array), and the color to flood (integer value). Build `floodFill(canvas2D,startXY,newColor)`! Replace a pixel's color value only if it is the *same* color as the origin coordinate and is directly adjacent via X or Y to another pixel you will change. Note: *diagonally related pixels are not considered adjacent.*

Given `canvas2D` of   [[3,2,3,4,3],
                         [2,3,3,4,0],
                         [7,3,3,5,3],   …plus `startXY` of [2,2] and `newColor` of 1 …
                         [6,5,3,4,1],
                         [1,2,3,3,3]]

… we examine the cells that are directly (not diagonally) adjacent to `startXY`, which is `[2,2]`. If any have a value of 3 (the original value at `startXY`), we change its value to 1 (`newColor`) and repeat the process with *its* directly-adjacent neighbor cells. We repeat this until the entire zone of similarly-colored cells is changed.

Our `canvas2D` becomes: [[3,2,1,4,3],
                                [2,1,1,4,0],
                                [7,1,1,5,3],
                                [6,5,1,4,1],
                                [1,2,1,1,1]]

Chapter 9 – Recursion

T-Diagrams and Recursion

Recursion is a powerful technique but may be difficult to understand initially. Tracing recursive functions can be confusing unless we remember that <u>each successive recursive call is a different context</u>, with a completely new T-Diagram.

Let's trace `rSigma()` when given 2.718:

```
function rSigma(num) {
    var returnVal = 0;
    if (num >= 1) {
        var intNum = Math.trunc(num);
        var prevVal = rSigma(intNum-1);
        returnVal = prevVal + intNum;
    }
    return returnVal;
}
```

Upon entering, we set `returnVal`, enter an IF, set `intNum` and call `rSigma`. At this point, the eventual value of `prevVal` is unknown. All we know is that it will be set to the return value from `rSigma(1)`, which has not yet returned. Once it does, we can continue onward in this diagram. Let's now work through `rSigma(1)`. This new function call will have a new T-diagram.

rSigma(2.718)	
num	2.718
returnVal	0
intNum	2
prevVal	rSigma(1)

As above, upon entering `rSigma(1)` we set `returnVal`, test `num`, enter IF, set `intNum` and call `rSigma(0)`. Note the T-diagrams:

rSigma(1)	
num	1
returnVal	0
intNum	1
prevVal	rSigma(0)

rSigma(2.718)	
num	2.718
returnVal	0
intNum	2
prevVal	rSigma(1)

We are now two levels deep into `rSigma`, but this should not cause concern. The only effect those calls `rSigma` call is the input: 0. Unlike previous calls, this one (as `num` is 0) does not enter the IF; instead returning 0, here:

rSigma(0)	
num	0
returnVal	0

rSigma(1)	
num	1
returnVal	0
intNum	1
prevVal	rSigma(0)

rSigma(2.718)	
num	2.718
returnVal	0
intNum	2
prevVal	rSigma(1)

On exiting `rSigma(0)`, that T-diagram is destroyed; we return to previous `rSigma(1)` context. We update `prevVal` to 0 (return value from `rSigma(0)`) and continue immediately after the previous recursive call, setting `returnVal` to `prevVal+intNum`, which in our diagram is 0+1. Immediately before we return from `rSigma(1)`, here are our diagrams:

rSigma(2.718)	
num	2.718
returnVal	0
intNum	2
prevVal	rSigma(1)

rSigma(1)	
num	1
returnVal	1
intNum	1
prevVal	0

rSigma(2.718)	
num	2.718
returnVal	3
intNum	2
prevVal	1

Back at last in our original context, we now know the value of `prevVal`: 1. Substituting this into our diagram and continuing from immediately after the recursive call, we set `returnVal` to 1+2, and return final value <u>3</u>, shown here:

Hopefully this sheds some light on how recursive code works!

Chapter 9 – Recursion

☐ Recursive Fibonacci

Write `rFib(num)`. Recursively compute and return numth Fibonacci value. As earlier, treat first two (num = 0, num = 1) Fibonacci vals as 0 and 1. Examples: `rFib(2)` = 1 (0+1); `rFib(3)` = 2 (1+1); `rFib(4)` = 3 (1+2); `rFib(5)` = 5 (2+3). `rFib(3.65)` = `rFib(3)` = 2, `rFib(-2)` = `rFib(0)` = 0.

☐ Recursive "Tribonacci"

Write function `rTrib(num)` to mimic Fibonacci, adding previous *three* values instead of *two*. First three Tribonacci numbers are 0, 0, 1, so `rTrib(3)` = 1 (0+0+1); `rTrib(4)` = 2 (0+1+1); `rTrib(5)` = 4 (1+1+2); `rTrib(6)` = 7 (1+2+4). Handle negatives and non-integers appropriately and inexpensively.

☐ Paging Dr. Ackermann

The Ackermann function is among the earliest examples of a computable but not primitive-recursive function. It grows rapidly, and hence can overflow the JavaScript stack frame even at very low values. This function accepts two non-negative integer values, `num1` and `num2`, and follows these rules:
1) `ackermann(0,num2)` == `num2+1`;
2) `ackermann(num1,0)` == `ackermann(num1-1,1)` if num1 > 0 (otherwise see #1);
3) `ackermann(num1,num2)` == `ackermann(num1-1,ackermann(num1,num2-1))`.

Don't be dismayed if a `num1` value as low as 4 "blows your stack". That's the nature of this function!

☐ Zibonacci

This function borrows ideas from the Fibonacci series, but the calculated results appear to zig and zag, hence the name. A so-called 'Zibonacci' series would be defined by the following rules:

1) `Zib(0)` == 1;
2) `Zib(1)` == 1;
3) `Zib(2)` == 2;
4) `Zib(2n+1)` == `Zib(n)+Zib(n-1)+1`, if n > 0 (i.e. odd values 3 and higher);
5) `Zib(2n)` == `Zib(n)+Zib(n+1)+1`, if n > 1 (i.e. even values 4 and higher).

Create the `Zibonacci(num)` function. What is `Zibonacci(10)`? `Zibonacci(100)`?

Second: For a given number that *might* be a Zibonacci result, find the largest index that maps to that result. `bestZibNum(3186)` == `2467`, `bestZibNum(3183)` == `null`.

Chapter 9 – Recursion

Dynamic Programming and Memoization

(No, it's not a typo – it really is 'memoization', not 'memorization'.)

Recursion is a powerful technique that allows us to explore multiple pathways. In general, we break a problem into smaller problems; often we simply feed those smaller problems in to the same function to eventually get a solution. Sometimes, it isn't that clean – sometimes we need to save some partial progress to build upon in subsequent recursive calls. This is when a '*memo*' is valuable.

A memo is any of 'note to self' that you send along with a recursive call, so that it can take advantage of previous progress you have made. You might be able to incorporate this into a single-function recursive solution, by adding an additional parameter that is `undefined` when your function is called externally. In subsequent recursive calls you make to yourself, you could include a *memo* here that might be a fragment of a solution that you are trying to complete, or an array to which you are pushing all possible solutions – or perhaps both, using two parameters that are not in the original function call. Other times, your original function is an entry point, calling a recursive function using additional parameters, like this:

```
///// Simple function to kick off the recursive version, with default
// values for the number of opens pending (0), the substring fragment
// we've built so far (""), and the array of complete solutions ([]).
function allValidNParens(numParens) {
   var solutions = [];
   rValidNParens(numParens, 0, "", solutions);
   return solutions;
}

///// Recursive All-Valid-Combinations-Of-N-Pairs-Parentheses func.
// Parameters: number of parens remaining, number of opens pending,
// unfinished substring fragment we're building, array of solutions
function rValidNParens(parens, opens, subStr, solutions) {
   // If no parens/opens remain, this fragment is a valid solution.
   if (!parens && !opens) {
      solutions.push(subStr);
   }
   // If opens remain, one option is to close one.
   if (opens) {
      rValidNParens(parens, opens-1, subStr + ")", solutions);
   }
   // If unused parens remain, one option is to open a new one.
   if (parens) {
      rValidNParens(parens-1, opens+1, subStr + "(", solutions);
   }
   // solutions array is a 'live' obj; we don't need to return it.
}
```

Chapter 9 – Recursion

This chapter you will familiarize yourself with recursion. Some or all of the following important concepts will be used in this chapter's challenges.

Base Cases   Forward Progress   Call Stack   Memoization   Dynamic Programming

☐ Recursive Binary Search

Given a sorted array and a value, recursively determine whether value is found within array. `rBinarySearch([1,3,5,6],4)` = `false`; `rBinarySearch([4,5,6,8,12],5)` = `true`.

☐ Greatest Common Factor

Given two integers, create `rGCF(num1,num2)` to recursively determine Greatest Common Factor (the largest integer dividing evenly into both). Greek mathematician Euclid demonstrated these facts:

1) `gcf(a,b) == a`, if a == b;
2) `gcf(a,b) == gcf(a-b,b)`, if a>b;
3) `gcf(a,b) == gcf(a,b-a)`, if b>a.

Second: rework facts #2 and #3 to reduce stack consumption and expand `rGCF`'s reach. You should be able to compute `rGCF(123456,987654)`.

☐ Tarai

The `tarai` (Japanese: "to pass around") function was created to profile recursive performance in various systems and languages. Unlike other functions, numbers don't get particularly large, but the amount of recursion is significant. The tarai function accepts three parameters, and is defined as:
1) `tarai(x,y,z) == y`, if x <= y (otherwise see rule #2);
2) `tarai(x,y,z) == tarai(tarai(x-1,y,z),tarai(y-1,z,x),tarai(z-1,x,y))`.

Calling `tarai(10,2,9)` should return 9 (after recursing 4145 times!).

☐ String: In-Order Subsets

Create `strSubsets(str)`. Return an array with every possible *in-order character subset* of str. The resultant array itself need not be in any specific order – it is the subset of letters in each string that must be in the same order as they were in the original string. Given `"abc"`, return an array that includes `[""`, `"c"`, `"b"`, `"bc"`, `"a"`, `"ac"`, `"ab"`, `"abc"]` (in any order).

Chapter 9 – Recursion

This chapter you will familiarize yourself with recursion. Some or all of the following important concepts will be used in this chapter's challenges.

Base Cases   Forward Progress   Call Stack   Memoization   Dynamic Programming

☐ Recursive List Length

Given first node of a singly linked list, create a recursive function that returns number of nodes in that list. Assume list contains no loops and is short enough that you will not 'blow your stack'.

☐ Got Any Grapes?!?

Martin loves grapes. He sees a number of baggies containing grapes, all in a row. Stephen tells him that he can take as many of the baggies as he wants, as long as he doesn't take two that are next to each other. Martin wants to maximize his number of grapes. Grapes are pretty healthy, so let's help him out. Create a function to accept an array of non-negative integers representing number of grapes in each adjacent baggy. Your function should return the maximum number of grapes he can obtain.

☐ Collatz-apalooza

Define a function that, given positive integer `num`, returns `num/2` if `num` is even or `3*num + 1` if `num` is odd. Continuously feeding result back into function results in numerical series such as `5,16,8,4,2,1`. According to Dr. Lothar Collatz, the series always reaches 1 (and then repeats `4,2,1,4,2,1,`…). What starting number requires the most iterations before reaching 1 the first time?

☐ Telephone Words

Nikki has a new phone number (304-5083) and wants to create a clever way for everyone to remember it. On older telephones, the keypad associates letters with each numeral. Given a seven-digit telephone number, return an array of all possible strings that equate to that phone number. For reference, here is the mapping: `[2:ABC; 3:DEF; 4:GHI; 5:JKL; 6:MNO; 7:PQRS; 8:TUV; 9:WXYZ]` – for completeness, map 1 to `I` and zero to `O`. For example, given a phone number 818-2612, return an array of 243 different strings, including "vitamic" and "titania".

Chapter 9 – Recursion

☐ Rising Squares

Ever since her dad discovered universal truths about triangles, Sophia Pythagoras has loved square numbers. Given positive integer, successively print squares of integers up to that integer, first ascending odds, then descending evens. Solve recursively with no loops. Ex.: `risingSquare(5)` returns `"1, 9, 25, 16, 4"`, `risingSquare(8)` returns `"1, 9, 25, 49, 64, 36, 16, 4"`.

☐ Binary String Expansion

You are given a string containing chars '0', '1', and '?'. For every '?', either '0' or '1' can be substituted. Write a recursive function to return array of *all* valid strings with '?' chars expanded to '0' or '1'. `binStrExpand("1?0?")` => `["1000","1001","1100","1101"]`. If you use string functions such as `slice()`, use them sparingly, as they are expensive.

☐ String Anagrams

Given a string, return array where each element is a string representing a different anagram (a different sequence of the letters in that string). Example: if given `"lim"`, return `["ilm", "iml", "lim", "lmi", "mil", "mli"]`. For this challenge, you can use built-in string functions such as `split()`.

☐ Climbing Stairs

Speros walks the stairs at the Dojo multiple times every day. Often he takes 2 stairs at a time, to work his quadriceps; he's just that way. Other days he mixes it up: with every footstep, he randomly chooses to take 1 stair or 2. You are given an integer representing the total number of stairs. Determine all ways to walk the stairs. Given 4, return `[[1,1,1,1], [1,1,2], [1,2,1], [2,1,1], [2,2]]`. Solve recursively with no loops. And don't forget to get *yourself* some exercise during the bootcamp, as well.

Second: assuming you always start with a left foot, return only those ways that *end with a right step*. So, given 4, you should return `[[1,1,1,1], [2,2]]`.

Third: instead of only returning those that end with a right step, only return those where the total number of steps climbed with left foot equal those climbed with right. So, given 4, you should return `[[1,1,1,1], [1,2,1], [2,2]]`.

Chapter 9 – Recursion

This chapter you will familiarize yourself with recursion. Some or all of the following important concepts will be used in this chapter's challenges.

Base Cases   Forward Progress   Call Stack   Memoization   Dynamic Programming

☐ Sum of Squares

Mike enjoys teaching the "lego concept" to beginning HTML/CSS students: breaking a web page into different rectangles. There is something about squares that appeals to his sense of balance. Given an integer, calculate and print all combinations of *square integers* that sum to that integer. No duplicates are allowed among smaller integers. `sumOfSquares(10)` => "1 + 9". `sumOfSquares(30)` => "1 + 4 + 25, 1 + 4 + 9 + 16". Solve recursively with no loops.

☐ All Valid N Pairs of Parens

Given the number of pairs of parentheses, return an array of strings, where each string represents a different valid way to order those parentheses. Example: given 2, return `["()()", "(())"]`.

☐ Towers of Hanoi

Create an algorithm to solve the Towers of Hanoi game. In the Towers of Hanoi, there are three poles and a stack of disks that fit onto the poles. The disks range from largest (on bottom) to smallest (on top), currently all on pole A. Moving only one disk at a time, move the stack to pole C. You can use any of the three poles you wish. A larger disk can never be placed on top of a smaller disk. How many moves does it take to relocate six disks from pole A to pole C? What is the first move?

☐ IP Addresses

Given string containing digits, add three decimal points to convert into a valid IP address, and return that string. Each of the four *quads* in a `"###.###.###.###"` IP address is a number between 0 and 255. Given `"255255255"`, you could return `"2.55.255.255"`, or `"25.5.255.255"`, or others. **Second:** return an array of *all possible* valid IP address combinations, for the given string.

☐ Uneven Digits

Cami doesn't know why, but she's just in an odd mood today. Let's make all numerals odd for her. Given an integer, recursively return the integer formed by stripping out all even digits in original. Solve without loops. `uneven(-1845)` = -15; `uneven(79)` = 79; `uneven(20)` = 0; `uneven(-92)` = -9.

☐ Generate All Possible Coin Change

Create `generateAllCoinChange(cents)`. Given a number of American cents, compute and return an array enumerating all possible ways to represent it, with pennies (1 cent), nickels (5 cents), dimes (10 cents), quarters (25 cents). For 5, return `[{dimes:0,nickels:1,pennies:0,quarters:0}, {dimes:0,nickels:0,pennies:5,quarters:0}{}]`. Do not return duplicate results.

Chapter 9 – Recursion

Some of these end-of-chapter challenges all assume that you have some familiarity with the game *chess*. If you don't, here is all you need to know. Chessboards are square, with 8 rows of 8 squares each. Queens are one type of chess piece, and in a single move they can travel any number of squares in either of the horizontal directions (along a *row*), or either of the vertical directions (along a *file* or *column*), or either of the diagonal directions. A piece is considered under threat from a queen if it is situated in a square where that queen can directly move.

☐ Is Chess Move Safe

`isChessMoveSafe(intendedMove,queen)` returns `true` if square is threatened, else `false`. It takes a location object for both the square to check, and current location of opposing queen.

Second: accept an *array of queens*.

☐ All Safe Chess Squares

Build on your solution to the previous challenge, to create `allSafeChessSquares(queen)` that returns all chessboard squares not threatened by a given queen.

Second: accept an *array of queens*.

☐ Eight Queens

Build `eightQueens()` using previous solutions. Return all arrangements of eight queens on an 8x8 chessboard, so no queen threatens any other. How would you best return these results?

Second: write a helper function that displays the queens-located-on-the-board results returned, in awesomely-retro character graphics, using `console.log()`.

☐ N Queens

Create `nQueens(n,xSize,ySize)` using previous work, returning all arrangements of N unthreatened queens on X by Y rectangular board. `eightQueens() == nQueens(8,8,8)`.

Second: optimize your solution so that you can extend `n`, `xSize` and `ySize` as far as possible before you exhaust the available memory. Can you get as high as 15 queens on a 15x15 board?

Chapter 9 – Recursion

☐ **Where's the Bug? (recursion version)**

Without peeking at previous code, how many bugs can you find in the recursive code below?

```
function rFib(num)
{
   if (num <= 1) { return 1; }

   return rFib(num) + rFib(num - 1);
}



function rListLength(node) {
   if (!node) {
      return 0;
   }
   else {
      return rListLength(node.next);
   }
   return rListLength(node) + 1;
}



function rSigma(num)
   if (num == 0) { return 0; }
   return num + rSigma(num - 1);
}



function rFactorial(num) {
   if (num === 0) {return 0; }
   return rFactorial(num + 1) * num;
}
```

Chapter 10 – Strings, Part II

This chapter we revisit strings, having mastered the fine art of *recursion*. Remember: recursion is not an answer to every problem; everything that can be solved with recursion can also be solved without.

Recall that strings are *immutable*. Individual elements (characters) within the set cannot be altered, but an entire string can be replaced by a new one. For this reason, one can (even though it feels like cheating) execute a statement like `myString = myString + ", dude!"`. The entire `myString` object is replaced by a new one that just so happens to be based on the old one.

When string questions are asked in interviews, it is *always* worth asking whether you are allowed to use built-in string library functions. It might be the case that the interviewer just wants to know whether you are aware of the built-ins, and will readily allow you to avail yourself of them. In many other cases, though, the intention is for you to work in low-level primitives, often duplicating one or more built-in string library functions. These questions can be tedious, but they are still exceedingly common.

In challenges this chapter, *do not use built-in string methods* unless they are explicitly mentioned. This means you must work with strings simply as immutable arrays of characters. One exception: when capitalization is mentioned, you are allowed to use `.toLowerCase()` and `.toUpperCase()`.

☐ String to Word Array

Given a string of words (with spaces, tabs and linefeeds), returns an array of words. Given `"Life is not a drill!"` return `["Life", "is" "not", "a", "drill!"]`.

Bonus: handle punctuation.

☐ Reverse Word Order

Create a function that, given a string of words (with spaces), returns new string with words in reverse sequence. Given `"This is a test"`, return `"test a is This"`.

Bonus: handle punctuation and capitalization. Example: given `"Life is not a drill, go for it!"` you should return `"It for go, drill a not is life!"`

☐ Longest Word

Create a function that, given a string of words, returns the longest word. Example: given `"Snap crackle pop makes the world go round!"`, return `"crackle"`.

Bonus: handle punctuation.

☐ Unique Words

Given a string, retain *words that occur only once*. Given `"Sing! Sing a song; sing out loud; sing out strong."`, return `"Sing! Sing a song; loud; strong"`. Punctuation is part of the word: `"Sing!"` is not `"Sing"`.

Bonus: ignore punctuation and capitalization. Ex.: given `"Sing a song! Sing a song; sing out loud and strong."`, return `"out loud and strong"`.

Chapter 10 – Strings, Part II

Let's revisit strings with *recursion* in mind. Recursion is often quite valuable, as shown in this chapter.

☐ String: Rotate String

Create a standalone function that accepts a string and an integer, and rotates the characters in the string to the right by that amount. Example: given `("Boris Godunov",5)`, you should return `"dunovBoris Go"`.

☐ Censor

Create a function that, given string and array of *'naughty words'*, returns new string with naughty words changed to "x" chars. Given `("Snap crackle pop nincompoop!", ["crack", "poop"])`, you should return `"Snap xxxxxle pop nincomxxxx!"` (after giggling a little bit).

Second: handle capitalization appropriately.

☐ String: ionIs Rotat (Is Rotation)

Create the function `isRotation(str1,str2)` that returns whether the second string is a rotation of the first. Would you change your implementation if you knew that the two were usually entirely unrelated?

☐ Bad Characters

Given two strings, the second string contains characters that must be removed from the first. Return string formed by removing any instances of those characters from the first string.

☐ Genetic Marker

Create a function that, given an array of strings and a string, returns a boolean whether the string is found anywhere in the array of strings. Note: strings found in the array might contain the '?' wild-card character, signifying that it can represent any character needed in order to complete a match.

☐ Optimal Sequence

You will be given an array of strings. All of these strings are the same length, and all contain only upper-case alphabetical characters or the '?' character. The '?' is a single-character wild-card; you can change it into any character needed. Return the sequence of words satisfying the following constraints:
1) From first word to last word, each column of letters must be in alphabetical order.
2) All question-mark characters must be expanded into their explicit values in the return array.
3) If more than one solution exists, return the one with lower overall alphabetical value.
4) If no solution exists, return `null`.

Examples: given the array `["EA?K","?RX?","GAG?"]`, return `["EAAK","GAGK","GRXK"]`.
For the array `["?F??","W??S","??X?"]`, your function should return `["AAXA","AFXA","WFXS"]`.
For an input of `["?UD","FI?","A?E"]`, return `null`.

Chapter 10 – Strings, Part II

This chapter we revisit strings, having mastered the fine art of *recursion*. Remember: recursion is not an answer to every problem; everything that can be solved with recursion can also be solved without.

☐ String: Dedupe

Remove duplicate characters (case-sensitive) including punctuation. Keep only the *last* instance of each character. Given `"Snaps! crackles! pops!"`, return `"Snrackle ops!"`.

☐ Index of First Unique Letter

Return the index of the first unique (case-sensitive) character in a given string. Ex.: `"empathetic monarch meets primo stinker"` should return 35 (`str[35]` is `"k"`).

☐ Unique Letters

Return only the unique characters from a given string. Specifically, omit *all* instances of a (case-sensitive) character if it appears more than once, respecting spaces and punctuation. Given `"Snap! Crackle! Poop!"`, return `"SnCrcklePp"`.

☐ Num to String

Create a function that converts a number into a string containing those exact numerals. For example, given `1234`, return the string `"1234"`. No, you may not use the `toString()` function.

Second: include fractional values as well. Given `11.2051`, return `"11.2051"`.

☐ Num to Text

Convert an integer into the English text for the number. Given `40213`, return `"forty thousand two hundred thirteen"`.

Second: include 4 fractional digits. Given `11.2051`, return `"eleven point two zero five one"`.

Chapter 10 – Strings, Part II

This chapter we revisit *strings*, having mastered the fine art of *recursion*. Remember: recursion is not an answer to every problem; everything that can be solved with recursion can also be solved without.

☐ String: Is Permtutaoin (Is Permutation)

Create function that returns whether second string is a permutation of first. For example, given `("mister","stimer")`, return `true`. Given `("mister", "sister")`, return `false`.

Bonus: handle uppercase/lowercase.

☐ String: All Permutations

Create a function that returns all permutations of a given string. Example: given `"team"`, return an array with the unique <u>24</u> strings including `"team"`, `"meat"`, `"tame"`, `"mate"`, `"aemt"`, `"tmea"`, `"etam"`, `"atme"`, etc. How can you know that you covered them all?

☐ String: Is Pangram

Return whether a string contains all letters in the English alphabet (upper or lower case). For `"How quickly daft jumping zebras vex!"`, return `true`. For `"abcdef ghijkl mno pqrs tuv wxy, not so fast!"`, return `false`.

☐ String: Is Perfect Pangram

Create a function that returns whether a given string contains all letters in the English alphabet (upper or lower case) *once and only once*. Note: ignore punctuation and spaces. Given `"Playing jazz vibe chords quickly excites my wife."`, return `false`. Given `"Mr. Jock, TV quiz PhD, bags few lynx."`, return `true`.

Sick of strings? How about stocks? Remember, recursion is *not* always the best way to solve problems.

☐ Best Time to Buy and Sell Stock

Using his machine learning prowess, Uthman can perfectly predict the closing price of one specific publicly traded stock. Before using his power for good, he will raise money in the stock market. Write `bestSingleBuySell(arr)` to return his maximal profit from one purchase and then sale, of just one share. The given `arr` holds the prices at which he can make his purchase and sale. Example: given the array `[6,4,6,5,9,7,6,12,`<u>`2,6,11`</u>`,2,4]`, return the maximal profit `9`.

Second: instead of a single buy/sell, let's say he can make a *series* of them, but can still only hold either one or zero shares at any time. Rework your function to maximize profit, and return that profit. Example: given the array `[6,`<u>`4,6`</u>`,`<u>`5,9`</u>`,7,`<u>`6,12`</u>`,`<u>`2,6,11`</u>`,`<u>`2,4`</u>`]`, return the maximal profit `23`.

Third: if he can make at most *two* transactions, now what is his best strategy? Rework your function. Example: given the array `[6,`<u>`4,6,5,9`</u>`,7,`<u>`6,12`</u>`,`<u>`2,6,11`</u>`,2,4]`, return the maximal profit `17`.

Fourth: what if he can make at most <u>K</u> transactions? Given `arr` and `K`, rework your function.

Chapter 10 – Strings, Part II

This chapter we revisit strings, having mastered the fine art of *recursion*. Remember: recursion is not an answer to every problem; everything that can be solved with recursion can also be solved without.

☐ Are Strings Loosely Interleaved

Given three strings, return boolean whether third string is a proper (no dupes) interleaving of first two. Given (`"dne"`,`"ail"`,`"daniel"`) return `true`. Given (`"dne"`,`"ail"`,`"dalein"`) return `false`. For (`"dne"`,`"ail"`,`"ddaanneeiill"`) return `false`.

☐ All Loosely Interleaved Strings

Given two strings, return an array containing all possible proper interleavings of those strings. Given (`"ab"`,`"yz"`), your function should return [`"abyz"`,`"aybz"`,`"ayzb"`,`"yabz"`,`"yazb"`,`"yzab"`]. **Second:** Ensure no duplicates in your returned result array.

☐ Make String Palindrome (Remove One)

Given a string, return index of the first character which, if removed, converts string into a palindrome. If string is already palindromic, return `-1`. Given `"bene"` return 0 (`"ene"`). Given `"dude"` return 3 (`"dud"`). Given `"bub"`, return `-1`. You can assume there will always be a solution, for the string provided.

☐ Make String Palindrome (Add One)

Given a string, return a character which, if added somewhere in the string, converts it into a palindrome. If string is already palindromic, return `""`. Given `"tutu"` return `"u"` or `"t"`. Given `"dude"` return `"e"`. Given `"dad"`, return `""`. You can assume there will always be a solution, for the string provided.

Chapter 10 – Strings, Part II

This chapter we revisit strings, having mastered the fine art of *recursion*. Remember: recursion is not an answer to every problem; everything that can be solved with recursion can also be solved without.

☐ String Encode

You are given a string that may contain sequences of consecutive characters. Create a function to shorten a string by including the character, then the number of times it appears. For `"aaaabbcddd"`, return `"a4b2c1d3"`. If result is not shorter (such as `"bb"`=>`"b2"`), return the original string.

☐ String Decode

Given an encoded string (see above), decode and return it. Given `"a3b2c1d3"`, return `"aaabbcddd"`.

☐ Shortener

Given string and desired length, return a maximally readable string of that length, using this process:
0) Remove any leading or trailing spaces (or conversely, pad on both sides out to the desired length),
1) Capitalize each word before removing spaces between words (starting from the back),
2) Remove punctuation, starting from the back,
3) Remove lower-case letters (vowels first), from the back,
4) Remove upper-case letters, from the back.

Given a string `"It's a wonderful life, Beth!  "`, desired outputs for the following lengths are:

33	`"   It's a wonderful life, Beth!   "`
26	`"It's A WonderfulLife,Beth!"`
22	`"It'sAWonderfulLifeBeth"`
17	`"ItsAWonderflLfBth"`
12	`"ItsAWndrflLB"`
3	`"IAW"`

☐ Weekend Challenge: Strings, Part II (Search with Regex)

Remember a few weeks ago when we recreated JavaScript's built-in `string` methods? Let's add a powerful new feature to `String.search(val)`. As you recall, this method searches `string` for a given `val` (another string), and returns the index position of the first match found (`-1` if not found).

Your weekend challenge: *regular expression* support! Below are a few examples how this should work:
`"dude".newSearch("[q-z]")` should return 1. `"dude".newSearch("(ud)")` should return 1.
`"dude".newSearch("[^a-e]")` should return 3. `"dude".newSearch("d$")` should return -1.

This is a *very difficult* (weekend-level) challenge and will require additional research. Are you up for it?

The "Bug-Laden 13" (#3)

What defects can you find in the below "Basic 13" submissions?

Print1To255()
Print all the integers from 1 to 255.

```
function print1to255()
{
var num = 1;
   while (num <= 255) {
      console.log(num);
   }
}
```

PrintIntsAndSum0To255()
Print ints 0-255, and with each the sum so far.

```
var sum = 0;
function printIntsAndSum0to255()
{
   for (var num =0;num <=255;num++)
   {
      sum += num;
      console.log(num," - sum:",sum);
   }
}
```

PrintMaxOfArray(arr)
Print the largest element in a given array.

```
function printMaxOfArray(arr)
{
   var max = arr[0];
   for(var idx = 1;idx < arr.length;
         idx++){
     if (arr[idx] > max) {
        max = arr[idx];
     }
   }
   console.log("Max value:", max);
}
```

PrintOdds1To255()
Print all odd integers from 1 to 255.

```
function printOdds1to255() {
   var num = 1;
   while (num <= 255) {
      num = num + 2;
      console.log(num);
   }
}
```

PrintArrayVals(arr)
Print all values in a given array.

```
function printArrayVals()
{
   for(var idx= 0; idx< arr.length;
         idx++) {
      console.log("arr[", idx,
                   "]=", arr[idx]);
   }
}
```

PrintAverageOfArray(arr)
Analyze an array's values; print the average.

```
function printAverageOfArray(arr)
{
   if (arr.length == 0) {
      console.log("[], no average.");
      return;
   }

   var sum = arr[0];
   for(var idx = 1;idx < arr.length;
         idx++) {
      sum += arr[idx];
      console.log(sum/arr.length);
   }
}
```

The "Bug-alicious" 13 (#3) – continued

ReturnOddsArray1To255()
Create & return array with odd integers from 1-255.

```
function returnOddsArray1to255() {
   var oddArray = [];
   for (var num = 1; num <= 255; num += 2) {
      var temp = num;
      oddArray.push(temp);
   }
   return oddArray;
}
```

ReturnArrayCountGreaterThanY(arr, y)
Given array, return the count that is greater than Y.

```
var numGreater = 0;
function returnArrayCountGreaterThanY(arr, y) {
   for (var idx = 0; idx < arr.length; idx++) {
      if (arr[idx]>y) { numGreater ++; }
   }
   console.log("%d are larger than %d", numGreater, y);
}
```

PrintMaxMinAverageArrayVals(arr)
Given an array, print max, min and average values.

```
function printMaxMinAverageArrayVals(arr) {
   if (arr.length == 0) {
      console.log("[], no min/max/avg");
      return;
   }
   var min = arr[0], max = arr[0];
   var sum = arr[0];
   for(var idx = 1; idx <= arr.length; idx++) {
      if (arr[idx] < min) { min = arr[idx]; }
      if (arr[idx] > max) { max = arr[idx]; }
      sum += arr[idx];
   }
   console.log("Max value:", max);
   console.log("Min value:", min);
   console.log("Avg:",sum/arr.length);
   return min, max, avg;
}
```

"Basic Forrest and His Friend Bugga Gump" (#3) – continued

SquareArrayVals(arr)
Given an array, square each value in the array.

```
function squareArrVals(arr)
{
   var numSquareValues;
   for (var idx = 0; idx < arr.length; idx++) {
      arr[idx] = arr[idx] * arr[idx];
   }
   return numSquareValues;
}
```

ZeroOutArrayNegativeVals(arr)
Given an array, set negative values to zero.

```
function zeroOutArrayNegativeVals() {
   for (var idx = 0; idx < arr.length; idx++) {
      if (arr[idx]<0) { arr[idx] = 0; }
   }
}
```

ShiftArrayValsLeft(arr)
Given array, shift values forward by one, drop the first values and leave extra '0' value(s) at the end.

```
function shiftArrValsLeft(arr) {
   for (var idx = 1; idx < arr.length; idx++)
   { arr[idx - 1] = idx; }
   arr[arr.length - 1] = 0;
   return arr;
}
```

SwapStringForArrayNegativeVals(arr)
Given array, replace negative values with 'Dojo'.

```
function swapStringForArrayNegativeVals(arr) {
   for (var idx = 0; idx < arr.length; idx++) {
      if (arr[idx] < 0)
         arr[idx] == "Dojo";
      }
   }
   return arr;
}
```

Chapter 11 – Trees

This chapter we explore trees, and in particular **binary search tree** (BST), an important data structure. The BST is optimized for quickly finding/retrieving elements. A BST is similar to a linked list, in that it stores data elements within node objects. Let's compare a *doubly linked list node* to a *binary tree node*.

```
function DLNode(value) {           function BTNode(value) {
   this.val = value;                  this.val = value;
   this.prev = null;                  this.left = null;
   this.next = null;                  this.right = null;
}                                  }
```

In a *doubly linked list*, each node has a value, plus pointers to two peers (*prev* and *next*). Similarly, in a **binary tree** each node has a **value**, plus pointers to two children, **left** and **right**. Just as with linked lists, these pointer attributes often reference another node, but can be null. Linked lists and binary trees always start with a single node; in a linked list we call it the head, in a binary tree we call it the root. The BST *structures the data* in a tree rather than a flat linear sequence.

A binary tree node can have a left child and/or a right child; each child might have left and/or right children of its own. An entire section of a family might descend from one sibling as opposed to another, similarly there are related subsets of a binary tree. These are (no surprise) called *subtrees*. We refer to all nodes stemming from the root node's left pointer as the root's left subtree, for example. By their basic definition, neither generic binary trees nor generic linked lists impose any specific order on where values must be located in them. There *is* a type of binary tree that adds structure, though. Read on.

The **binary search tree** adds a requirement that for every node, all nodes in its left subtree must have smaller values. Similarly, its right subtree must contain only values that are greater than or equal to its value. This constraint holds for every node in the subtree, not just the direct children. These rules determine exactly where new children are placed in a BST. If "Grandparent" node<50> has a right child with the value 75, then children of node<75> are appropriately constrained not only by their parent, but by that grandparent as well. Specifically, the entire left subtree of node<75> must have values between 50 and 75.

BST nodes without children are considered *leaf* nodes. Depending on its values, no node is required to have two children. Even in a tree containing many values, the root node might have a *left* or *right* pointer that is null (e.g. if the root contains the smallest or largest value in the tree, respectively).

The Binary Search Tree is an example of an *Ordered* data structure, because the values are stored in a way that allows us easily to get from one value to the next-largest value or next-smallest value.

Chapter 11 – Trees

Let's build a basic Binary Search Tree. These challenges start with the following reference definitions:

```
function BTNode(value) {
   this.val = value;
   this.left = null;
   this.right = null;
}
```

```
function BST() {
   this.root = null;
   // add methods here...
}
```

☐ BST: Add

Create an `add(val)` method on the `BST` object to add new value to the tree. This entails creating a `BTNode` with this value and connecting it at the appropriate place in the tree. Unless specified otherwise, BSTs can contain duplicate values.

☐ BST: Contains

Create a `contains(val)` method on `BST` that returns whether the tree contains a given value. Take advantage of the BST structure to make this a much more rapid operation than `SList.contains()` would be.

☐ BST: Min

Create a `min()` method on the `BST` class that returns the smallest value found in the `BST`.

☐ BST: Max

Create a `max()` `BST` method that returns the largest value contained in the binary search tree.

☐ BST: Size

Write a `size()` method that returns the number of nodes (values) contained in the tree.

☐ BST: Is Empty

Create an `isEmpty()` method to return whether the BST is empty (whether it contains no values).

Chapter 11 – Trees

You may have already realized that all Binary Search Trees are not equivalent. The arrangement of the nodes in the tree have a real effect on its efficiency. In referring to a tree's shape, we use the terms *depth* (also known as *height*) and *balance*, and a few chapters down the road we will work with trees of certain shapes that we refer to as *full* and *complete*. Let us explore these terms further.

Binary Tree Depth

A tree's **depth** is the length from root to farthest leaf including both. If we add nodes to a BST in random order, the tree grows in a relatively *balanced* manner – left and right subtrees will be about the same size, with mostly equal depth. If we add elements in *sorted* order, the tree becomes *unbalanced*, resembling a linked list in shape, and depth might approach the total number of elements. Even balanced trees often have a few "holes" where non-leaf nodes have one child that is NULL. However, the fewer the holes, the fuller a BST is. Using the tree metaphor, a full BST is a very "bushy" tree, rather than thin and spindly. More nodes, contained in the same number of layers, makes for a better tree. Stated differently, given two binary trees with the same number of nodes, the one with less depth is always more efficient. Why is this?

Our answer lies in the reason that finding values in BSTs is so much quicker than finding them in SLists. Every node in a binary tree has branches, so there isn't a single path to follow from beginning node to end node. Furthermore, because BSTs are ordered, we always choose the correct direction at every fork. Instead of searching all values, the longest search is only the depth of the tree. This is why shallow, full trees are best. As data structures go, BSTs *rock* for fast retrieval and maintaining order.

Today, add these additional methods to our `BST` class implementation:

☐ BST: Height

Build a `height()` method on the `BST` object that returns the total height of the tree – the longest sequence of nodes from root node to leaf node.

☐ BST: Is Balanced

Write `isbalanced()` method to indicate whether a `BST` is balanced. For this challenge, consider a tree balanced when *all* nodes are balanced. A `BTNode` is balanced if heights of its left subtree and right subtree differ by at most one.

☐ Array to BST

Given an array that is sorted in ascending order, return a `BST` object that is height-balanced.

☐ Closest Common Ancestor

Given a `BST` and two contained values, return the value of the *closest common ancestor* node. For each node, the chain up to `root` (including `self`) represents that node's ancestry. Return the value of the node in both ancestor chains that is closest to both.

Chapter 11 – Trees

Binary Search Tree Traversal

Binary search trees are mostly used for their ability to fast-find, but sometimes we need to enumerate all their values. Here are three examples that illustrate why we might want different *orders* for listing the tree node values. 1) If we need to temporarily convert a BST to a different data structure, we may want it to list its values in numerical order. 2) If we want to duplicate a tree, we need to build it from the parent nodes downward, so we want to list parent nodes before child nodes. 3) If tree nodes might not represent values, but, say, components in a manufacturing process, where a component can only be assembled once its 'child' subcomponents are built, then we might want to list both child nodes before their parent node. These three examples are called ***in-order***, ***pre-order***, and ***post-order*** traversals, respectively. The terms pre-order and post-order refer to when a node is enumerated, compared to its children – if it is enumerated first, then this is *pre-order*; if it is enumerated last, then this is *post-order*. Enumerating a left child first, then the node itself, then the right child, is *in-order*.

☐ Traverse BST Pre-Order

Create `bstPreOrder(BST)` that prints the BST's values, traversed pre-order.

☐ BST to Array

Create `bst2Arr(BST)` that outputs an array containing a BST's values, traversed in-order. **Second:** create both `bst2ArrPre` and `bst2ArrPost` for those traversal methods. **Third:** refactor to minimize code.

☐ BST: Minimum Height

Build `minHeight()` method on `BST` that returns the *minimal* height – the shortest sequence of nodes from root to any leaf. How does the code compare to that of `height()`?

☐ Traverse BST Post-Order

Create `bstPostOrder(BST)` that prints the BST's values, traversed post-order.

☐ BST to List

Create `bst2List(BST)` that outputs a singly linked list containing the BST values in-order. **Second:** create both `bst2ListPre` and `bst2ListPost` to traverse in those ways. **Third:** refactor to minimize code.

☐ Traverse BST Pre-Order, No Recursion

Given a `BST` object, `console.log` its values in pre-order, *without using recursion*.

Chapter 11 – Trees

Self-Instantiating Classes

Implement today's challenges into the BST class below. Notice anything new? Why would we add this?

```
function BTNode(value) {
   if (!(this instanceof BTNode))
   { return new BTNode(value); }

   this.val = value;
   this.left = null;
   this.right = null;
}
```

```
function BST() {
   if (!(this instanceof BST))
   { return new BST(); }

   this.root = null;
}
```

Answer: the additions to our `BTNode` and `BST` classes are `instanceof` checks, which make it so that these objects can be created with the following code:

```
var myBrandNewBST = BST(); // no new needed
var aNewNode = BTNode(42); // no new
```

Fabulous. Now, back to work. Today, add these additional methods to our `BST` class implementation:

☐ BST: Remove

Remove a given val. Return `false` if not found.

☐ BST: Is Valid

Construct an `isValid()` method on the `BST` object to determine whether tree has valid structure. Specifically, ensure that all nodes and values are located in the appropriate left or right subtrees. This might be trickier than it seems at first glance. What are a few helpful "invalid tree" test cases?

☐ BST: Remove All

Clear all values from the tree.

☐ BST: Add Without Dupes

Add a given value *only if it is not already found*. Return true if added, false otherwise. Remember our Set Theory: this changes our BST from an ordered multiset to an ordered set.

Second: What other methods need changing, if we want our BST to be a true 'set'? Build those.

☐ Traverse BST Reverse-Order

Create `bstReverseOrder(BST)` that prints the `BST`'s values, traversed in reverse order.

Chapter 11 – Trees

Add these methods that (might) benefit from *in-order traversal*.

An alternate way to implement these is to add an attribute `.parent`. If you add this attribute, consider how you would need to change the other `BST` methods you've built to date.

☐ BST: Val Before

Create a `BST` method that, given a value that may or may not be in the tree, returns the value that is most immediately smaller. Examples: for tree {2,5,8}, `valBefore(3)` returns 2, and `valBefore(8)` returns 5.

☐ BST: Val After

Write a method on the `BST` class that returns the value immediately following the given one, even if that given value is not contained in the tree. Examples: for tree {2,5,8}, `valAfter(3)` returns 5; `valAfter(8)` returns `null`.

☐ BTNode: Node Before

Create a `BTNode` method that, given a node that is in the `BST`, returns *a pointer to the node* with the most immediately smaller value. Examples: for tree {2,5,8}, `nodeBefore(node5)` returns the node containing 2; `nodeBefore(node8)` returns the node containing 5.

☐ BTNode: Node After

Parallel to `nodeBefore`, write a `BTNode` method that returns the node immediately following the given node (which is guaranteed to be in the tree). Examples: for tree {2,5,8}, calling `nodeAfter(node2)` returns the node containing 5; `nodeAfter(node8)` returns `null`.

☐ BST: Closest Value

Create `BST` method `closestValue(val)` to return the value contained in a `BST` that is closest to the given `val`. This could be the exact value (if tree contains it), or one that is greater or less than `val`. Take care: there is no guarantee that closest value is direct parent, grandparent, child, grandchild, etc.

☐ Tree Path Contains Sum

Given a binary tree (not necessarily a BST) containing numbers and a sum, can you determine whether the tree has a root-to-leaf path that, if you add up those nodes values, equals sum? Return a boolean. If a particular node has (for example) a left child but no right child, you can consider it a leaf.

Second: instead of returning a boolean, return an *array* of all the root-to-leaf paths that equal sum.

Chapter 11 – Trees

Making BST a Fully Navigable Data Structure

In order to move from one node to its successor, sometimes we will need to traverse to a node's parent. How costly would it be to add a `.parent` pointer to our `BTNode` class? Would we need to make any changes to the `BST` class itself?

Answer: the `BST` methods `add()`, `isValid()`, `remove()` and `addNoDupes()`, as well as the `BTNode` method `isValid()`, plus both <u>constructors</u> would need to change to incorporate `.parent` into `BTNode`. For example, the `BTNode` constructor would need to include `this.parent = null;`. Secondly, the `BTNode.isValid` method would need to ensure that `if (this.left)`, then `(this.left.parent == this)`. Also, `a.isValid` should ensure that `this.root.parent` is always null. Even more complex, though, are the required changes to the `add` and `remove` methods, where we need to account for both sides when making a change to the `BST` (not unlike when making changes to a `DList`!).

☐ BST With Parent

Create a `BTNode2` data structure (and the necessary changes for an accompanying `BST2`) that adds a `.parent`. When is it more optimal? Is it worth the trouble? Work out the changes to prove it to yourself!

☐ Sum of BST Root-Leaf Numbers

Given a binary tree (not necessarily a BST) that contains values between 0 and 9, we consider the digits encountered in order when traversing from root-to-leaf to be that path's *root-leaf number*. The root-leaf path 4->2->3 represents the root-leaf number 423. Find the sum of all root-leaf numbers found in the provided binary tree.

☐ Left-Side Binary Tree

Given a binary tree, create and return an array containing the values that you would see if you metaphorically *stood to the left of the tree and looked sideways at it*. You will see the root, of course, plus only the leftmost of children at each level.

Chapter 11 – Trees

With short answer questions, you can demonstrate *technical depth* as well as *clarity of communication*. How would you answer the following, if asked in an interview?

☐ Short Answer Questions: Trees

What is a binary tree? Are they too complex to use?
Is there more than one kind of binary tree? Can you describe them?
What is the most common binary tree? Why would I use this type of binary tree?
Compared to other data structures, what advantages does it have? What disadvantages?

What is a BST? What is the difference between a binary tree and a BST?
How are BSTs represented in code?
If BSTs consist of BSTNode objects, then how are BSTNodes represented in code?
Why might it be better to be handed a BST object instead of the head BSTNode?
What is the sequence of steps needed when adding a value to a BST?
Likewise, what steps are needed when removing a value from a BST?
Finally, what steps are needed when searching for a value in a BST?
How would one check whether a BST is valid?
For a BST containing the following methods – add, remove, min, max, removeMin, removeMax, contains, prevVal, nextVal, size – which are considered relatively *fast*? *How* fast?
Likewise, which methods are considered slow? *How* slow?

Chapter 12 – Sorts

Why do we study the specific topic of *sorting*? Because sorting is an area where algorithm choices have significant and obvious ramifications for how well that code performs. Learning about sorting algorithms will equip you with techniques that you can use to analyze any set of code.

How do we judge *code quality*? There are many ways one might assess software. For most, a first thought is simply: *in good software, the features work*. That's reasonable, of course, but many aspects go into *whether something works as expected*. In addition to basic functionality, here are a few others. Is it resilient to unexpected inputs or malicious intent? Does it run in diverse environments, such as device form factors and/or different browsers? Is it trustworthy with users' confidential data? Are string messages handled appropriately so that the code can easily be localized into worldwide languages? Can it be easily configured and serviced by those maintaining and updating it post-release? Is it accessible for customers with visual/auditory disabilities? Is the source code understandable (not just by one, but also broadly across the team)? How well documented is the source (or the overall product)? How rapidly/easily can it be extended for new features? Product excellence has many dimensions.

In many situations, what trumps most of these factors is software <u>*performance*</u>. This can also mean many things, but primary measures of software performance are *run time* and *resource consumption* (*time and space*, if you will). Everyone that works with software has experienced software that is frustratingly slow. Even small time optimizations can make a product feel more snappy and responsive. Regarding resource consumption, this can be permanent storage (storage, database), memory (heap, call stack), network bandwidth, or even power – after all, no one likes an app that drains their battery. Depending on product requirements, any or all of these may be important. That said, classic software analysis focuses on 1) run time and 2) memory consumption, when it comes to evaluating algorithms.

Certain algorithm texts refer to "asymptotic behavior" of an algorithm. This simply means the behavior of an algorithm as the (input) data set gets extremely very large. Almost any sorting algorithm will suffice if we are sorting only ten elements, but if we must sort 4 billion numbers, then algorithm choice matters. Later this chapter, you will learn more about how we measure algorithms and what leads to high-performance. Sorting algorithms are not the only software whose performance should be analyzed, nor generally the most important. However, studying them is an excellent proxy for other software elsewhere. Have fun this chapter!

Chapter 12 – Sorts

When comparing run times and memory consumptions of two piece of software, we must be careful. What if one is in PHP, and the other is in C or even machine assembly language? What if we run one on an Apple Watch, and the other on a massive IBM 64-processor server with 512 GB of RAM? (To bend the "apples and oranges" metaphor, this would literally be comparing *Apples and [Big] Blues*.) To factor out these differences and focus only on the algorithm, performance analysis is always relative, not absolute. That is to say, we should compare the algorithm, in *that language* within *that environment*, only to *itself*, when given different types and sizes of inputs. Specifically, by what percentage does run-time change when we double the input size? By what factor does memory consumption grow, if we make our input ten times bigger? As input sizes get larger, extraneous factors melt away, leaving only critical ones that ultimately constrain whether our software can handle 100 simultaneous users, or 1,000, or even 100,000.

We start with the first sorting algorithms programming students learn – Bubble and Selection.

☐ Array: Bubble Sort

For review, create a function that uses BubbleSort to sort an unsorted array in-place.

☐ Array: Selection Sort

For review, create a function that uses SelectionSort to sort an unsorted array in-place.

☐ SList: Bubble Sort

Create a function that uses BubbleSort to sort a linked list. The list nodes contain `.val`, `.next` and other attributes you should not reference.

☐ SList: Selection Sort

Create a function that sorts a singly linked list using selection sort. Nodes contain `.val`, `.next` and other attributes you should not reference.

☐ Multikey Sort

For this challenge, you will sort an array, however the items in the array are not simple numbers. Given an array of objects, where each object contains a `.firstName` and a `.lastName`, sort the array by both last name (primary) and first name (secondary). Lee Abbey should be sorted before Aaron Carnevale, and Aaron Carnevale should be sorted before his brother Giorgio Carnevale.

Chapter 12 – Sorts

Big-O Notation

Previously we mentioned that when analyzing algorithms, comparisons must be relative, when given different inputs. Specifically, as we increase the input size by 10, how does the time needed to run the algorithm change? How does memory consumption change? Generally, there are only a few growth rate types. The mathematical convention that represents these growth factors is called Big-O notation.

Side note: really hard-core algorithm analysis experts talk not only about Big-O but also *Big-Omega* and *Big-Theta*. In brief, Big-O describes *worse-case* performance ("performance will never be any worse than …"); Big-Omega *best-case* ("in the ideal situation, performance might be as good as …"); Big-Theta *average case* ("on average across a broad range of inputs, performance will be …"). Their values can differ, but for many analyses you can think of them as the same. Further, when best-case and worst-case differ, most people talk mostly about Big-O and secondarily mention "best-case".

What does Big-O notation indicate? It conveys how an algorithm will perform, as input sizes grow large. As we multiply our input by factor N, how do our run time and memory consumption change? In practice, we would first measure the time and memory consumed when running with an input of specific *size*; then measure the same when given an input of "size x N" – this ratio, in terms of N, is our Big-O.

Consider `FindMax()` that returns an array's lowest value. If we double array length, we expect `FindMax` to run twice as long. If we multiply array length by N, run time should multiply by exactly N as well. Hence we say the time complexity of this algorithm is `O(N)`, or verbally "for run-time, it has a Big-O of N." Looking at memory consumption, the only memory needed is local storage of a `FOR` loop index, and a local variable to track the min value. This is the case *regardless* of the array's length, so as we multiply array length by N, our additional memory requirements are constant (i.e., multiplied by 1). Hence the algorithm's memory complexity is `O(1)`, or verbally "for memory, Big-O is 1." If our algorithm needed to make a copy of the array, then the Big-O for memory would be `O(N)`. One last thing: with recursion, we also factor in the additional stack space as we recurse. We'll briefly touch on that later.

☐ Array: Insertion Sort

Create a function that InsertionSort to sort an unsorted array in-place. What is the run-time complexity? What is the space complexity?

☐ SList: Insertion Sort

Use InsertionSort to sort singly linked lists. Only reference `ListNode` attributes `.val` and `.next`. What are the run-time and space complexities?

☐ Array: Combine

Create function `combineArrs(arr1,arr2)` that sorts two already separately sorted arrays, placing the result back into the first provided array. Can you work completely in-place?

☐ SList: Combine

Create a function that combines two already-sorted linked lists, returning a sorted list with both inputs. List nodes contain `.val`, `.next` and other attributes that you should not reference.

Chapter 12 – Sorts

When discussing sorting algorithms, we talk mostly about *run-time* performance – *how does Time Needed change, as input size grows?* But Big-O can also refer to resource consumption: memory, storage or network bandwidth – most commonly, RAM. The memory consumed by an algorithm is either heap or call stack or both. These correspond to 1) copying an input or 2) making recursive calls. Clearly, all things equal, an algorithm shouldn't make a copy of the input. After all, we might receive an array containing 4 billion values! Also, call-stacks are not unlimited; it doesn't take much to "blow our stack". Everything solved with recursion is solvable without. More on `O(space)` later.

So, which sorting algorithm is *truly* best? Again, the only correct answer is "depends on situation." However, there are numerous characteristics that describe sorting algorithms, and we will discuss one each day through the rest of the chapter. Today we discuss what makes an algorithm *Adaptive*.

Adaptivity

For many algorithms, the input data's configuration (e.g. randomized, mostly sorted, reversed) makes a big difference in performance. Even when handed already-perfectly-sorted data, SelectionSort makes the same number of comparisons as if values were in random order. There is almost zero difference between its best-case performance and worst-case performance. (Good news: predictable! Bad news: $O(N^2)$!) So, SelectionSort does not *adapt* to data that is already partially or fully sorted.

On the other hand, InsertionSort and BubbleSort show huge differences between best-case and worst-case run time. You can even see this in the code, whenever we have a "fast finish" check that breaks out early if we make a complete pass without needing any swaps. We call these algorithms *Adaptive*.

When is this important? Consider a huge quantity of existing, already-sorted data, where you must add a small number of new, unsorted values. With InsertionSort, we can quickly sort these new values into place with little penalty from the magnitude of existing data. Big win!

☐ SList: Merge Sort

Use `combineLists(list1,list2)` to build the `mergeSortList(list)` algorithm for an unsorted singly linked list. What are run-time and space complexities of your solution?

☐ Array: Partition

Partition unsorted array in-place. Use `arr[0]` as pivot val; return idx of pivot. Input `[5,4,9,2,5,3]` becomes `[4,2,3,5,9,5]`, return `4`.

Second: for pivot, use median of *first, last, mid*.
Third: partition a *subset*, given *start* and *end*. Exclude end; default values are 0 and arr.length.

☐ SList: Partition

Partition a singly linked list. Use first element as pivot; return the new list. List nodes contain `.val` and `.next`; do not reference other attributes. For example, if you are given the following linked list: { 5=>1=>8=>4=>9=>2=>5=>3 }, you should return: { 1=>4=>2=>3=>5=>8=>9=>5 }.

Chapter 12 – Sorts

We've discussed what it means when an algorithm <u>adapts</u>: can it take advantage of partially-sorted inputs to run faster? Today we discuss *stability*. What is it, and why does it matter?

Stability

In most of our sorting work so far, we have dealt with simple collections of single values, such as an array of 15 numbers. In real life, however, data is rarely that minimal, and never that simple. Much more likely would be a linked list or array containing many thousand records, and each record contains 5-10 different fields. To sort these records, we may need to reference multiple fields (for example: sorting customer events by last name, then first name, then event date). One strategy, when sorting by multiple fields, is to sort first by the least important factor (date), then by more important factors (first name), ending with the most important (last name).

However, this multi-pass strategy *only* works if our sorting algorithm is able to retain the existing order, when finding duplicate values during subsequent passes. Some algorithms, such as selection sort and quick sort, swap elements across significant parts of the input array, and hence do not guarantee to keep duplicate values in their original sequence; they *destabilize* any preexisting ordering. If we have already sorted "Buster Jones" ahead of "David Jones" based on first name, we don't later want to carelessly put David Jones ahead of Buster Jones just because their last names are identical. With selection and quick sorts, this unfortunately might happen!

On the other hand, insertion sort and bubble sort only swap adjacent elements, so existing sequence is preserved when they encounter duplicate values. Insertion sort and bubble sort are <u>Stable</u> sorting algorithms; they hold any previous order *stable* when doing their work. Again, this becomes a factor mainly when doing successive sorting passes, such as sorting by multiple fields (e.g. userID, date). However, stability doesn't mean looking at additional fields to *break ties*; it means that in case of a tie, the *value that was previously first, stays first*.

☐ Array: Quick Sort

Create a function that uses yesterday's `partitionArray()` to sort an array in-place. With yesterday's code plus a very few new lines, you will implement QuickSort! What are the run-time and space complexities of your `quickSortArr` implementation?

☐ Array: Merge Sort

Use the `combineArrs()` function above to construct `mergeSortArr()` for an unsorted array. What are the run-time and space complexities of your `mergeSortArr` solution?

☐ Array: Partition3

Previous `partition()` implementations do not group duplicates of the pivot together. Create `partition3()` to keep pivot elements together; return an array containing indices for *first pivot* and *first greater*. Change [5,1,8,4,9,2,5,3] to [1,4,2,3,5,5,8,9] and return [4,6]. Note: other 5 moved next to pivot.

Second: pick a more optimal pivot.
Third: partition only a *portion*, with *start* and *end*.

Chapter 12 – Sorts

As mentioned before, when analyzing software performance, we look at runtime performance (duration to run to completion), but also its consumption of other resources. Will it require a huge amount of disk storage? Is it excessively chatty on our network? Does it mercilessly drain our battery in mere minutes? An important factor, and sometimes easiest to quantify, is extra *memory* (in addition to input) it requires. RAM consumption could be *heap* (e.g. allocate space to copy our array!), or *call stack* (recursively call ourselves, once for every node!). Either way we might run out of memory, at which point depending on where our code runs, it will slow to a crawl (best-case) or crash (worst-case, common).

Memory Analysis

From a call stack perspective, we simply cannot use recursion unless we limit the depth of any single chain of recursion. For example, if we have a BST with 1,000,000 elements, nonetheless the tree (on average) will only be 20-25 elements deep, so recursively traversing a BST consumes a tolerable amount of stack space. Specifically, we would say that it requires `O(logN)` stack space. (Why? Think of log as the inverse of exponents. Each time our tree goes one level deeper, it doubles in size. How many levels do we need to handle one million? Well, 2 raised to the 20 power is ~ 1 million. In other words, the log2 of 1 million is 20, so on average a BST of size N would be logN nodes deep.)

What about heap space, then? What if we don't make a copy of the data, but we do maintain a bunch of local variables, maybe a dozen? Not a problem! In the big picture, don't worry much about local variables – their 100 puny bytes are insignificant compared to ~~the power of the force~~ the magnitude of copying even just half of the potentially-huge input data we are sent. An ideal algorithm, then, is one that requires no additional copy of the input data at all. If an algorithm can operate successfully with no additional heap requirements, but only the space of the input data it is handed, then we call that algorithm in-place. Running in-place does not mean that the algorithm is automatically `O(1)` for memory, because if it is recursive it will still consume stack space. However, running in-place is a huge win in many scenarios, particularly on mobile devices with limited memory.

☐ Smarter Sorting

For Yi's data science dissertation, she needs a distribution graph containing billions of data points. Amazingly, she found an array containing IQs for every person on earth, and now *you must sort it*. All values are between 0 and 220, and the array is 7 Billion elements long. What are your run-time and space complexities?

☐ Quick Sort 3

Create a `QuickSort3` function that uses `Partition3` to sort an array in-place. Can you devise specific arrays that are sorted much faster with `QuickSort3` than with `QuickSort`?

☐ Master Invoice List

Tran's House of Trains™ is a booming online hobby store. Each department head already has a list of invoices for that group, sorted by timestamp that day. They need to put these lists together for their chief executive, Chris. What do you recommend, and what is the performance of this solution? Write a function that will do the work needed.

Chapter 12 – Sorts

☐ Urban Dictionary Daily Add

On his off days, Kris volunteers at UrbanDictionary.com, because it makes him feel hip and fresh. Their collection is about 8 million words, and they receive 2000 new words a day. Because they want to keep their data hip and fresh, they incorporate any new words within minutes of submittal, re-sorting their entire collection every five minutes. Kris notices that only about 7 words are added each time they sort. He's thinking selection sort (their current design) might not be the best choice. What do you think?

☐ Pancake Sort

Christopher Burns has successfully defied his last name, cooking a wonderful breakfast for the entire Dojo without singeing a single flapjack. Now *you* have a large stack of pancakes of varying sizes, ready to serve. You believe you should first *sort* them from smallest (on top) to widest (on bottom), as syrup pours best that way – plus, it reminds you of the Towers of Hanoi (Minh's favorite recursive problem).

Your only tool is a spatula that you can insert below any pancake, to flip it and all pancakes above. Pancake sizes are represented in an array: for example, 4 pancakes *already* stacked from smallest to biggest would be `[1,2,3,4]`. If you insert the spatula between second and third pancakes, then flipped, the stack would now be `[2,1,3,4]`. Given an arbitrarily large stack of **N** pancakes, how many spatula flips will it take to sort the pancakes into width-order? Design a high-performance algorithm, because everyone is getting hungry....

☐ Radix Sort

For an array 7 million long with values from 0 to 4 billion, how rapidly can you radix-sort it in-place? You can create a new array as large as the original. What are the run-time complexity and the space complexity of this solution, and does it depend on the values you are sorting?

☐ Belt Sort

Given array of objects representing students, where each student object has `.belt` attribute, sort in-place so all students with same belt are adjacent, in order "none", "yellow", "red", "black", "double-black", "triple-black" and "triple-black plus blue". Dojo students (or their belt records) are not just numbers, so naïve sorts might not work....

☐ Wiggle Sort

A sequence of numbers is "wiggle-sorted" if the differences between each successive value always alternates between positive and negative. Equal values should not be adjacent. Given an array of numerical values, wiggle-sort the array. What is the Big-O of your run-time performance?

☐ Median of Unsorted Array

Create a function that determines the median of an array of unsorted values. When Sosho claimed he could 'name that tune' in just $O(N)$, the Dojo was all aflutter. Any solution is fine, but doing this in $O(N)$ has been agreed-upon across the industry as an 'interesting problem'.

Chapter 12 – Sorts

Sorting Review

We discussed numerous aspects that different parties might consider important in judging a piece of software "good". These include correctness, resiliency to bad inputs, security against hackers, being easy and fun to use, extensibility to accommodate future features, clarity of being understood by other engineers, whether the software is easily internationalized to 100+ spoken languages around the world, how easily it can be deployed or updated, etc. Depending on your role, "good" software means different things. For most, though, performance is in your top 3 most important factors.

We focus on performance of *sorting algorithms* because there are multiple diverse ways to sort data, and most algorithms have at least one redeeming factor making it valuable in some situation. We need to know when to choose that particular algorithm, based on the problem's requirements.

For algorithm performance, we factor out hardware specifics and programming language, only comparing an algorithm to itself, with some other larger input data. The head start from having a faster programming language is insignificant compared to the power of a superior algorithm (if our data set is big enough). As our input data grow larger by N, by what factor does runtime grow? By what factor does memory requirement grow? This type of analysis is called Big-O notation.

We focused primarily on the Big-O of an algorithm's *runtime* (how long it takes to run), but also memory usage. Runtime complexity is often understood by looking at nesting of loops. `O(N²)` algorithms such as bubble sort are considered slow. The basic algorithms used to teach sorting are all `O(N²)` because, essentially, they compare every value to every other value (N x almost-N). However, some algorithms have optimizations that lead to significant differences between average run-time and best-case runtime. More sophisticated algorithms use "divide and conquer" schemes that quickly cut the problem space so that each value is not compared against every other. In this way, they roundly defeat `O(N²)` algorithms – their average performance is `O(NlogN)`. That said, they might have weaknesses, such as specific input data that trigger horrible worst-case performance (quick sort).

We discussed specific characteristics of sorting algorithms, and when they might be important. These include being **adaptive** (taking advantage of partially sorted data), **stable** (retaining existing sequence of duplicates), **in-place** (not using space beyond the input data). None of the `O(NlogN)` algorithms are adaptive, and although merge sort is the only one that is stable, it is also the only one *not* in-place. Memory usage might be *heap* (from copying input data), or *stack* (from recursive "divide and conquer" calls). On mobile devices memory is often scarce; operating in-place is usually critical.

In special situations, you can use unusual sorting algorithms such as CountingSort or Radix, which miraculously sort simple values in `O(N)` but cannot accommodate additional data. Understanding the various characteristics of these algorithms is what enables you to choose the right tool for the right job.

The "Bug-Infested 13" (#4)

Some of these "Basic 13" submissions have bugs; can you find them?

Print1To255()
Print all the integers from 1 to 255.

```
function print1to255() {
   for (var num=1;num <=255;num++) {
      console.log(num);
}
```

PrintIntsAndSum0To255()
Print integers from 0 to 255, and the sum so far.

```
function printIntsAndSum0to255()
{
   var sum = 0;
   for (var num=0; num<=255;
      sum+=num,num++)  {
      console.log(num+" - sum:"+sum);
   }
}
```

PrintMaxOfArray(arr)
Print the largest element in a given array.

```
function printMaxOfArray(arr)
{
   if (arr.length == 0) {
      console.log("[], no max val.");
   }
   var max = arr[0];
   for (var idx=1; idx < arr.length;
      idx++) {
     if (arr[idx] > max)
     { max = arr[idx]; }
   }
   console.log("Max val:", max);
}
```

PrintOdds1To255()
Print all odd integers from 1 to 255.

```
function printOdds1to255() {
   for(var num = 1;num<= 255;num+=2)
   { print(num); }
}
```

PrintArrayVals(arr)
Print all values in a given array.

```
function printArrayVals(arr)
{
   for (var idx=0; idx < arr.length;
      idx++)
      console.log("["+index+"]="+arr);
}
```

PrintAverageOfArray(arr)
Analyze an array's values and print the average.

```
function printAverageOfArray(arr)
{
   if (arr.length == 0) {
      console.log("Empty, no avg.");
      return;
   }

   var sum = arr[0];
   for(var idx=1; idx<arr.length-1;
      idx++) {
      sum += arr[idx];
   }
   console.log(sum/arr.length);
}
```

"Ain't Too Proud to Bug" (#4) – continued

ReturnOddsArray1To255()
Create & return array with odd integers 1-255.

```
function returnOddsArray1to255(arr){
   var oddArray = [];
   for(var num=1; num<=255;num+=2) {
      oddArray.push(num);
   }
   return oddArray;
}
```

ReturnArrayCountGreaterThanY(arr, y)
Given array, return count greater than Y.

```
function numGreaterThanY(arr, y) {
   var numGtr;
   for (var idx=0; idx<arr.length;
        idx++) {
      if (arr[idx] > y) { numGtr ++;}
   }
   console.log("%d > %d",numGtr,y);
   return numGtr;
}
```

SquareArrayVals(arr)
Given an array, square each value in the array.

```
function squareArrVals(arr)
{
   for ( var idx = 0;idx<arr.length)
                   idx++)
   {
      arr[idx] = arr[idx] * arr[idx];
   }
}
```

ZeroOutArrayNegativeVals(arr)
Given an array, set negative values to zero.

```
function zeroOutArrNegativeVals(arr)
{
   for ( var idx = 0;
         idx < arr.length; idx++) {
      if (idx < 0)
      { arr[idx] = 0; }
   }
}
```

ShiftArrayValsLeft(arr)
Given array, shift values forward. Drop first value(s) and leave extra '0' value(s) at end.

```
function shiftArrValsLeft(arr)
{
   for (var idx = 1;
        idx < arr.length;idx++) {
      arr[idx - 1] = arr[idx];
   }
   return arr;
}
```

SwapStringForArrayNegativeVals(arr)
Replace negative array values with 'Dojo'.

```
function swapStrForArrNegVals(arr) {
   for (var idx=0; idx < arr.length;
        idx++){
      if (arr[idx] < 0) {
         arr[idx] = "Dojo";
      }
   }
   return arr;
}
```

"Bilbo Buggins and the Unexpected Defects" (#4) – continued

PrintMaxMinAverageArrayVals(arr)
Print max, min and average array values.

```
function printMaxMinAverage(arr) {
   if (!arr.length) {
      console.log("[], no workie!");
      return;
   }
   var min, max, sum;
   min = max = sum = arr[0];
   for(var idx=1; idx<arr.length;
         idx++) {
      if(arr[idx]<min) {min=arr[idx]}
   }
   for(var idx=1; idx<arr.length;
         idx++) {
      if(arr[idx]>max) {max=arr[idx]}
   }
   for(var idx=1; idx<arr.length;
         idx++) { sum+=arr[idx]; }
   console.log("Max val:", max);
   console.log("Min val:", min);
   console.log(sum/arr.length);
```

```
function printMaxMinAverage(arr) {
   if (arr.length == 0) {
      console.log("[]:No MinMaxAvg");
      return;
   }
   var min = arr[0];
   var max = arr[0];
   var sum = arr[0];
   for(var idx=1;idx<=arr.length;
         idx++){
      if(arr[idx]<min) {min=arr[idx];}
      if(arr[idx]>max) {max=arr[idx];}
      sum += arr[idx];
   }
   console.log("Max value:", max);
   console.log("Min value:", min);
}
```

```
function printMaxMinAverage(a)
{
   if (a.length == 0)
   {
      console.log("[]:no MinMaxAvg");
      return;
   }
   var min,max,sum;
   min = max = sum = a[0];
   for(var idx=1;idx<a.length;idx++)
   {
      if(a[idx]<min)  {min=a[idx];}
      else
         if(a[idx]>max) {max=a[idx];}
         else {sum+=a[idx]}
   }
   console.log("Max:", max);
   console.log("Min:", min);
   console.log("Avg:",sum/a.length);
}
```

```
function printMaxMinAverage(arr)
{if(arr.length==0){console.log("Null
arr, no min/max/avg");return;}var
min=arr[0];var max=arr[0];var
sum=arr[0];for(var
idx=1;idx<arr.length;idx++){if(arr[
idx]<min){min=arr[idx];}if(arr[idx]>
max){max=arr[idx];}sum+=arr[idx];}
console.log("Max:",max," Min:",min);
console.log("Avg
value:",sum/arr.length);}
```

134

Chapter 13 – Sets and Priority Queues

Sets and Multisets

Whether working with a deck of cards or results from a database query, we constantly work with *sets* – a mathematical term for collections of values that we group together. Just as there are many reasons to group values together, likewise there are different types of sets, each useful in certain situations. Specifically, you might care how a set handles *duplicates*, and whether it keeps values *ordered*.

By default, **sets** do not contain duplicate values; adding value 42 to the set ("Zork", "grue", 42), you still have ("Zork", "grue", 42). Ex.: when gathering nominations for Best Restaurant in Town, the nominee list is a *set*. There can also exist sets that contain duplicate values; these are **multisets**. In collections of this type, duplicate values matter: multiset (1, 1, 1, 3) and multiset (1, 1, 3, 3) are *not* equivalent. Example: after a public vote for favorite restaurant, during the vote-counting process we could use a multiset, such as (Joe's, Joe's, Mel's, Joe's, Joe's...).

For some sets, the order matters (such as words in a dictionary). This type is called an **ordered set**. For others (e.g.: members of a club), it doesn't: these are **unordered sets**. More on these tomorrow!

What can we do with these different flavors of set? You might *add* an element, *remove* one, or check whether the set *contains* a certain element, and if so how many. With *ordered* sets, we can also retrieve *first* or *last* element, and from any element get *next* or *previous*. These are standard operations for any data structure that we use to collect values, such as an array or a singly linked list.

Throughout the chapter, remember these set types:

    Set   *Multiset*   *Ordered*   *Unordered*

☐ Interleave Arrays

Given two unsorted arrays, create a new array containing the elements of both, resulting in an *unsorted merge* of all values. When populating the new array alternate (interleave) values between the two arrays until one is exhausted, then include all of the other. Example: given `[77,22,11,22]` and `[2,6,7,2,6,2]`, return `[77,2,22,6,11,7,22,2,6,2]`.

☐ Merge Sorted Arrays

Efficiently merge two already-sorted arrays into a new sorted array containing the *multiset* of all values. Example: given `[1,2,2,2,7]` and `[2,2,6,6,7]`, return new array `[1,2,2,2,2,2,6,6,7,7]`.

☐ Minimal Three-Array Range

Given three separately-sorted arrays, determine the value from each array that creates the smallest range, and return the min and max of that range. All three of the arrays must have a value within the range. Example: given `([1,2,4,15],[3,10,12],[5,10,13,17,23])`, return `{min:3,max:5}`.

Chapter 13 – Sets and Priority Queues

Set Operations

Yesterday we discussed different characteristics of a _set_. By default, sets contain no duplicates, but a type that can is called a _multiset_. A normal set does not track the counts of values, but a multiset does.

Sets that keep elements in strict order are _ordered_ sets (or _ordered multisets!_). Those that don't are _unordered_ sets/multisets. There are costs associated with removing duplicates or maintaining a set's order, so if we add values without sorting or removing duplicates, we have an unordered multiset.

When working with more than one set, we can combine them in various ways. We can simply **merge** two sets, resulting in a multiset that includes all values from both sides. Merging always results in a multiset, because every duplicate is kept. A second option is to get the **union** of sets A and B, which would include all values from one set, plus anything from the other set that we haven't already included. Conceptually, this equates to a logical OR: to be included in this union, an element must be found in one set _or_ the other (or both). A third type of set combination is an **intersection**, conceptually similar to a logical AND. To be included in an intersection, an element must be found in one set _and_ the other.

A _merge_ is simply the sets, together.
A _union_ contains values in either set: [1,3,1,2,6]

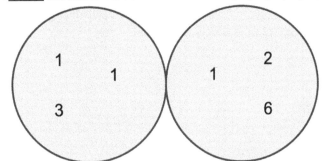
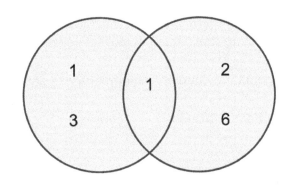

An _intersection_ contains only values in both sets: [1]

Shown above, for _multisets_ these operations affect _value counts_ accordingly. For multisets containing the same value ('1' above), union retains the higher count (3 '1's are retained); intersection retains the lower count (2 '1's are retained). Given ordered multisets [1,1,1,3] and [1,1,2,6]: the _merger_ is [1,1,1,1,1,2,3,6]; the _union_ is [1,1,1,2,3,6]; the _intersection_ is [1,1]. Lastly: if a set contains all the values of another set, like [1,2,2,3] and [2,3], the second is a **subset** of the first.

☐ Intersect Sorted Arrays

Efficiently combine two sorted arrays into an array containing the sorted _multiset intersection_ of the two. Example: given [1,2,2,2,7] and [2,2,6,6,7], return [2,2,7].

☐ Intersect Sorted Arrays (dedupe)

Efficiently combine two sorted multiset arrays into an array containing the sorted _set intersection_ of the two. Example: given [1,2,2,2,7] and [2,2,6,6,7], return [2,7].

Chapter 13 – Sets and Priority Queues

As you proceed through this chapter, put yourself in a technical interview mindset with these concepts:

*Don't panic   Think out loud Clarifying questions   Error and corner cases   Example inputs
      Diagrams   Admit when its suboptimal (but keep going) "What are we optimizing for?"*

Throughout these challenges, remember the basic set operations and characteristics:

Merger   Union Intersection   Set / Multiset Ordered / Unordered   Subset

☐ Union Sorted Arrays

Efficiently combine two already-sorted arrays into a new sorted array containing the *multiset union*. Example: given [1,2,2,2,7] and [2,2,6,6,7], return [1,2,2,2,6,6,7].

☐ Union Sorted Arrays (dedupe)

Combine two sorted arrays into a new sorted array containing the *union set* (i.e. remove duplicates). Example: given [1,2,2,2,7] and [2,6,6,7], return [1,2,6,7].

☐ Intersection Unsorted Arrays (in-place)

Intersect two <u>unsorted</u> arrays, putting the *unsorted multiset* result 'in-place' into the first. Running 'in-place' also means you cannot create any data structure to hold values, such as an associative array. Given [2,7,2,1,2] and [6,7,2,7,6,2], you could change the first to [7,2,2] in any order.

☐ Intersection Unsorted Arrays

Intersect two arrays to create an *unsorted multiset*. You can use an additional data structure type if it is helpful. However, don't alter the arrays; return a new one. Given the arrays [6,7,2,7,6,2] and [2,7,2,1,2], return a new array containing [7,2,2] in any order. Is 'non-in-place' easier? Faster?

☐ Union Unsorted Arrays

Return a new *unsorted union multiset* of two arrays; do not alter the originals. For [2,7,2,1,2] and [6,7,2,7,6,2], you could return [7,2,7,2,2,1,6,6]. How efficient can you be, for *long* arrays?

Chapter 13 – Sets and Priority Queues

This chapter we dive further into Set Theory. Put yourself into the mindset of a technical interview during this chapter's algorithm challenges, using the following concepts:

merger *union* *intersection* *set / multiset*
ordered / unordered *in-place* *stable* *subset*

If needed, refer to previous "Union Unsorted Arrays" solution for starting points to these challenges:

☐ Union Unsorted Arrays (in-place)

Put *union multiset* of two unsorted arrays into the first. Given (`[2,7,2,1]`,`[6,7,2,6]`), change the first to include (in any order) the elements `[2,7,2,1,6,6]`.

☐ Union Unsorted Arrays (no duplicates)

Return the *union set* (remove any duplicates) of two unsorted arrays. Given (`[2,7,2,1]`, `[6,7,2,6]`), return (in any order) `[2,7,1,6]`.

☐ Subset Sorted Arrays

Given two sorted arrays, return a boolean whether the second is a subset of the first. Can you use their sorted nature to your advantage?

☐ Subset Unsorted Arrays

Given two *unsorted* arrays, return whether second is subset of first. Solve in `O(N)` runtime.

Second: can you solve this in-place? How does this affect your runtime performance?

Set Theory Recap

We explored Set Theory, including Sets vs. Multisets, Ordered vs. Unordered, and set operations such as Merge, Union, Intersection and Subset. Along the way we discovered universal principles, such as:
- Ordered sets should be managed by iterating them concurrently, matching up values.
- Unordered sets can be managed with associative arrays, where set members become keys, and values are booleans (for an Unordered Set) or counts (for an Unordered Multiset).

Looking for a break from Unions and intersections? Here's something completely different.

☐ My Very Own Square Root

Write your own square root function. You may not use math functions or operators except for *, the built-in multiplier. Given an *integer*, you should return an *integer*.

Second: accept and return *floating-point numbers*, accurate to two decimal places.

Next, we will revisit our old friend the *queue*, but with a wonderful twist!

Chapter 13 – Sets and Priority Queues

Queues and Stacks are easy to construct, and values can be quickly added and removed. They are *optimized* for quick addition – and quick removal as well, *if you want values in order they were added* (or *reverse* for Stacks). They are **not** optimized for search: elements are stored linearly, per insertion time, without regard for values themselves. We might (for example) iterate all values to find the lowest.

Priority Queues

What if, instead, we created a data structure that acted like a Queue, but *did* care about values instead of insertion time. This data structure would maintain its elements in *value* order, regardless of the order in which they were added. We could extract (pop, dequeue) an element at a time, and always get the lowest value. This is valuable as (for example) a way to prioritize a list of to-do items so that when we take an item from the Queue, it is always the most important one. In fact, OS subsystems such as networking and storage work in this way: diverse I/O requests are continually added to a prioritized queue, and the system extracts (and satisfies) them in priority order. Let us build this *Priority Queue*.

☐ SList: Priority Queue

We want to create a Queue data structure that keeps its elements in sorted order, so that when we call pop(), we get the first element in *sorted* order (rather than sequential order, like a regular FIFO queue).

Create a `PriQueue` *data structure by making changes to* `SLQueue` *and* `SLNode`:
A `PriQNode` class should be identical to `SLNode`, plus `.pri`, which is set by an additional argument passed to the constructor. The `PriQueue push()` method should accept both value and *priority*, and priority should be used to add the node at the right spot (instead of at queue's end).

☐ Sequencer

Using a singly linked list priority queue object, build a system that orders and "plays" messages uses the system timestamp (get this by calling `Date.now()`). Create two functions that are used as follows:

```
sequenceMessage([2000000000000, "Msg 4"]);
sequenceMessage([1453506544890, "Msg 2"]);
sequenceMessage([1453506544900, "Msg 3"]);
sequenceMessage([1000000000000, "Msg 1"]);
   // assume current time is now 1453506544898
playMessages();           // "Msg 1", then "Msg 2" are logged to console
   // ...assume time passes, and now current time is now 1453506544915
playMessages();           // "Msg 3" is logged to console
```

Your `sequenceMessage(arr)` will be sent a two-element array, containing a timestamp and a string. The timestamp is in milliseconds, and corresponds to values obtained by `Date.now()`. Sort messages by ascending timestamp. When `playMessages()` is called, `console.log` (in order) the strings of messages with timestamps in the past, and remove them from your list.

Chapter 13 – Sets and Priority Queues

Heap Data Structure

The mythical *manticore* had lion's body, human head, and scorpion tail. Priority queues are commonly constructed with *minheaps*, with similarly unusual characteristics (not heap where memory allocations occur, although regrettably the same word). Not to be outdone by manticores, heaps act like queues, manage data like trees, and are stored in arrays. Rather than extraordinary speed in a few aspects, heaps strike a balance: great insertion, good deletion, and great extraction (in monotonic priority order).

How does this creature do it? A heap isn't fully sorted. It knows the lowest value, and can quickly rearrange to stay "sorted just enough" for the next ask. Insertion similarly does *just enough* to stay "somewhat sorted" without extra work. These "lazy" heaps work this way: *first*, data are arranged in binary nodes. *Second*, minheap node must have a value less / equal to its children's. *Third*, minheaps are *complete* trees: all nodes have two children except at deepest level, where nodes populate from leftmost extending right. That's it! Here we assume a *minheap*, although we easily invert rules for *maxheap*. The only behavior difference: maxheaps extract values largest to smallest, not lowest-first.

Here's the next interesting detail: instead of using actual binary tree nodes, a minheap puts values into an array, using array indices to track parent-child relationships between values. Specifically, value at index N has children at indices 2N and 2N+1, and its parent can always be found at N/2. The root of the heap is located at index 1 (index 0 usually holds some other value). Thus, tree traversal from arbitrary nodes is quick. With this in mind, four of the basic data structure methods (`size()`, `isEmpty()`, `top()`, `contains(val)`) are trivial. The performance of `contains(val)` is horrid (effectively, it must search the entire underlying array). The `insert()` and `extract()` methods are more interesting.

For `insert(val)`, we know that our tree's size will grow by one. Because our tree is *complete*, we know where this new *node* will be added (our `Array.length` will grow by one). Although that likely isn't where it belongs, we put the *new* value there to start. We then undergo a "promote" process for node, comparing it to parent. If value is less than parent's, we swap them and try to promote it again (comparing to its new post-swap parent). Once it can no longer be promoted, insertion is complete.

Build the following methods on a new class called a `MinHeap`:

☐ Heap: Constructor

Create a `MinHeap` constructor function.

☐ Heap: Size

Return the number of values in the `MinHeap`.

☐ Heap: Contains

Return whether a given val is within the heap.

☐ Heap: Is Empty

Return whether the heap is empty.

☐ Heap: Top

Return (not remove) the heap's minimum value.

☐ Heap: Insert

Add the given value to our heap.

Chapter 13 – Sets and Priority Queues

Let us continue our development of the `MinHeap` data structure. Previously, we developed the ability to add elements. Now we will build a method to remove the top element – we'll call it `extract()`.

For this discussion, keep in mind that although we are storing the element values in an array, we are still thinking about the collection of values as a binary tree. With this in mind, below I refer to values and nodes. By nodes, I just mean the array index where the value is found.

For `extract()`, we know that our tree size will shrink by one node. Because it is always a *complete* tree, we know that the node to be removed is the *last* node. In other words, our array will become shorter, by one. We also know which *value* needs to be removed from our array, and it is the *first* value, not the last value. To use a metaphor, we remove the first person, and the last chair. So, our challenge, when we extract a value from our heap, is how to *minimally* rearrange values in the tree so that all the remaining nodes are occupied by the remaining values, in a way that satisfies all the heap rules. Doing this in a minimal way is the hallmark of a heap.

We start by considering the last value in the heap – the one sitting in the array index we want to remove. We give that value an unusual opportunity: we move it to the *root* for a short time. From there, we will put the value through a "demote" process to shift it downward in the tree to a more suitable spot. What does this "demote" process entail? After swapping the value into the root spot, we first compare it to its two new children. If either of them has a lower value than it does, we swap it with the lower one, then repeat this "demote" process with that same value in its new spot, until it has no children with lower values (this might not happen until it has no children at all!). Once it can no longer be demoted, the extraction process is complete.

With `extract()`, our basic data structure implementation is complete. Additionally, we would like the ability to pass in an array and have the Heap adopt that array as its own, quickly repairing it to a state of compliance with the Heap rules. First, change the Heap constructor to optionally accept an array. Also create the `heapify` method that accepts and repairs this array after the Heap has been created.

☐ Heap: Extract

Create a `MinHeap` method that removes the heap's minimum value and returns it.

☐ Heap: Heapify Array

Create a heap method that accepts an array as its own, and turns it into a rule-abiding `MinHeap`.

☐ Heap Sort

Lance discovers with glee that if one heapifies an unsorted array, then extracts values, the array is sorted in $O(N \log N)$ time – as fast as quick sort or merge sort, the usual winners in generalized sorting! He views this as solid proof that the Heap truly is "the crown prince of data structures." Write a *standalone* function `heapSort(arr)` that accepts an unsorted array and uses a heap to sort it.

Second: do this in-place without creating a second array.

Chapter 13 – Sets and Priority Queues

☐ Median of Data Stream

With a separate function `addValue(val)`, you will be given a continuous stream of data, one value at a time. At any moment, with reasonable performance you need to be able to return the median value. (What is reasonable performance?) Recall that the median of an even number of elements is the average of the two middle values.

Before next chapter, here are a few other Queue/Stack problems to keep you thinking. Have fun!

☐ Queue from Two Stacks

Using only Stack objects (not other data structures such as linked lists or arrays), implement a Queue.

☐ Priority Queue from Two Stacks

Using only Stack objects (not other data structures such as lists or arrays), implement a Priority Queue.

☐ Comparing Stacks/Queues to Other Data Structures

By now we have studied a few different data structures: array, `SList`, `DList`, `BST`, `SLQueue`, `CirQueue`, `ArrStack`, `Deque`, `PriQueue`. Each of these could be built as a *set* instead of a *multiset* (rejecting duplicate values instead of accepting them). We will not require you to build all the possible variants, but below we list them for completeness. Those that are bolded are ones you've already built previously; those underlined are highly recommended. In most cases, creating these will require only small adjustments to code you've already written.

Array (random-access multiset)
Array without duplicates (random-access set)

SList (forward-iterated insertable multiset)
SList without duplicates (forward-iterated insertable set)

DList (double-iterated insertable multiset)
DList without duplicates (double-iterated insertable set)

Binary Search Tree (ordered multiset)
Binary Search Tree without duplicates (ordered set)

SLQueue (sequential multiset)
SLQueue without duplicates (sequential set)

CirQueue (sequential multiset)
CirQueue without duplicates (sequential set)

SLStack (sequential multiset)
SLStack without duplicates (sequential set)
ArrStack (sequential multiset)
ArrStack without duplicates (sequential set)

Deque (double-sequential multiset)
Deque without duplicates (double-sequential set)

PriQueue (forward-ordered multiset)
PriQueue without duplicates (forward-ordered set)

Next chapter we'll build these:
Associative Array (unordered multiset)
Associative Array without duplicates (unordered set)

Chapter 13 – Sets and Priority Queues

With short answer questions, you can demonstrate *technical depth* as well as *clarity of communication*. How would you answer the following, if asked in an interview?

☐ Short Answer Questions: Sets and Priority Queues

What is a Set data structure? What is an example of this, in the natural world?
By default, is a set Ordered or Unordered?

What is a Map data structure? What is an example of this, in the natural world?
Generally, how do sets and maps differ?

By default, do maps allow multiple keys with the same value?
Generally, how are sets and multisets different?

What is one good way to implement an unordered map?
What is one good way to implement an ordered multimap?
What is one good way to implement an ordered set?
What is one good way to implement an unordered multiset?

What is a Heap? How do they work generally?
What are the advantages of using a Heap? What are the disadvantages?
What happens 'under the hood' when a value is added to a Heap?
Likewise, what's the sequence of events when removing a Heap value?
How can I check whether a Heap is valid?
What is the difference between a MinHeap and a MaxHeap?

For a MinHeap data structure that has the following methods – push, pop, min, max, removeMin, removeMax, contains, prevVal, nextVal, size – which of these are relatively *fast*? *How* fast?
Conversely, which of these methods would be considered relatively slow? *How* slow?
When would a heap be considered 'full'?

What is a Priority Queue, and is it at all different than a Heap? How?
When would you use a BST instead of a Priority Queue?
When would you use a 'regular' Queue instead of a Priority Queue?

What is HeapSort, and how does it work?
What are the Big-O requirements (run-time and space) for HeapSort?

Chapter 14 – Hashes

Have you ever wondered how *key-value* data structures work? You have already worked with these, as they are prominent in most programming languages. Regardless of the number of key-value pairs, they can "instantly" retrieve values (`O(1)` run-time perf!). How do they do this, even when highly loaded?

This chapter we investigate a new data structure – one used "under the covers" to construct the collection of unordered key-value pairs known in PHP as associative arrays, in Python / Swift / C# as dictionaries, in JS as objects (minus methods, prototypes, etc.), and in C++ STL as maps. Ruby and Java have the most appropriate name for this unordered key-value data structure: Ruby calls them hashes, and Java calls them hashtables. Why? Because a *hash* function gives this data structure its quick-check, quick-retrieval feature, even when containing lots of data.

Consider the *array* data structure, which is quick-retrieval. Every array element can be immediately reached with a single index dereference. *If you know the index*, you can directly access its value: `arr[idx]`. This strength is also its main weakness: you *must* know index in order to access element.

The word "associative" is used with these because they *associate* a certain key with a certain value. If we use an associative array to track a specific user, we might have this: `{ name: "Marino", age: 27, IQ: 144, languages: ['Italian', 'English'], height: 181 }`. Here, we directly access the user's age (for example) by referencing the key: `myUser['age']` or `myUser.age`. If associative arrays didn't exist yet, how would we construct them using only traditional (numerical) arrays?

Traditional arrays associate *numerical* indices with values. The index is a key. Continuing our example to store user information in an array `["Marino",27,144,['Italian','English'],181]`, we can quickly access user age (27) or name ("Marino"), because we know the one and only one place in the array where we always find user age (at index `[1]`) or name (at index `[0]`). We get the benefit of quick-retrieval only if 1) for each piece of information, we have a specific index where we always store it, and 2) we remember that decision (e.g. that `[0]` corresponds to name, `[1]` to age, etc). Can we make this automatic, while retaining quick-retrieval? Yes. A *hash function* can automatically pick indices for us.

Hash functions take inputs (generally strings) and generate large, seemingly random (but repeatable) numbers, called *hash codes*. To generate a unique index for each key, we use its hash code as the index – this way each key has a reproducible index in our array where its value will be stored. Note: hash codes could be huge (or negative). To fit into our array, we limit them to a manageable range.

We solve this by constraining our array to a certain capacity, and *modulo*ing the hash codes so that they fit into that range. To store the key/value `{ name: "Marino" }` into our 'map', we get the hash code of the key `name`, `mod` that hash code to get an index that fits within the capacity of our array, and save "Marino" at that index. To retrieve the value for key `name`, we hash the key, `mod` the hash code to get an index within bounds of our array, then retrieve value at that index. We can store vast numbers of key/value pairs and still quickly retrieve values, without iterating through keys or values *or* having to remember which index corresponds to which key. It's a beautiful thing.

Chapter 14 – Hashes

We now know all we need to build the associative array data structure, also called *unordered_map*. It's a **Map**, because keys map to values (if it had single values, not key-value pairs, we call it a *set*). It's **Unordered**, because (unlike BST or Queue) we do not maintain any order or sequence for elements. Our hash is sufficiently random we know nothing about keys that are hashed to adjacent buckets.

With any data structure, after creating a simple constructor (`HashMap()`), we build methods for adding data to the structure and for checking whether a value is found in the structure – `add(key, value)` and `contains(key)`. Let's also build `isEmpty()`, which suggests we add `numKeys` to our constructor.

Here's our flow, where a call to **Add()** converts **Key** to **HashKey** to **ModHash**, changing the **Array**):
add("myKey",42) → "myKey" → -1853110172 → 2 → [undefined,undefined,42]
add("aKey","foo")→ "aKey"   → -851179773   → 1 → [undefined,"foo",42]

Our challenges use these reference definitions:

```
function HashMap(capacity) {
   this.capacity = capacity;
   this.table = [];
}

// We use this line to hash a string...
var myHashCode = myString.hashCode()
// ...based on this implementation:
String.prototype.hashCode = function()
{
   var hash = 0;
   if (this.length == 0) return hash;
   for (i = 0; i < this.length; i++) {
      char = this.charCodeAt(i);
      hash = ((hash<<5)-hash)+char;
      hash &= hash; //Convert-->32b int
   }
   return hash;
}

// JS % acts oddly for negatives,
// so we define our own this way...
function mod(input, div)
{ return (input % div + div) % div; }

// ... and we use it this way:
var myIdx = mod(myHashCode,arrSize);
```

☐ Hash: Add

Create an `add(key, val)` method on `HashMap` to add a new key and value to the map. This entails hashing key, mod'ing it into the size of your array, and placing the value there.

Second: If two values hash to the same index, it causes a *hash collision*. Then, you should use a secondary array or `SList` instead of overwriting (losing) values. Do you still have to worry about hash collisions if you have a *set*, not a *multiset*?

☐ Hash: Is Empty

Dude, what if you use a `HashMap` to find your *hash cache*, but someone stole it all? Bummer. Return whether this `HashMap` is empty. This is a one-liner but requires changes elsewhere.

☐ Hash: Find Key

Create a `find(key)` method to return value for given key. If key is not found, return `null`.

Second: if you altered `add(key,val)` to handle collisions, extend `find(key)` accordingly.

Chapter 14 – Hashes

So far, our *hash* structure can add and retrieve key-values, and indicate *emptiness*. These correspond to classic methods `add`, `contains` and `isEmpty`. What about the others (`remove`, `size`, `front`)?

First, `front` has no meaning in a key-value data structure. We don't keep keys or values in any order, other than how our hash code handles them – and this is not an order we expose to the user, since we might change our hash someday. Second, `size` is only partially relevant in a key-value data structure. A hash is similar to a circular queue: it has *capacity* (the unchanging number of available buckets), as well as the number of elements added so far. Unlike a `CirQueue`, a hash can map many elements to one bucket. Accordingly, "full-ness" is not *how many elements*, but instead the *ratio of elements to available buckets*. We call this the load factor. Finally, `remove` is just what you might expect: it accepts a key, and if that key is present, it removes the key-value from the data structure, returning the value.

Today we will create these exact methods and add them to our `HashMap` class implementation:

☐ Hash: Remove

Create `HashMap` method `remove(key)` that finds key, removes key/value pair, and returns the value (or `null` if key not found in our map).

☐ Hash: Grow

Write a method `grow()` to increase the internal array of buckets by 50% (20-element array would become 30 elements). Afterward, rehash all keys, since your **mod** factor has changed....

☐ Hash: Add

Create `addMap(HashMap)` that accepts another `HashMap` of key-value pairs and adds each pair to the existing map. For duplicate keys, new values overwrite old ones.

Second: incorporate a boolean input indicating whether new keys should overwrite existing.

☐ Hash: Load Factor

We may eventually want to grow our array size. Create `HashMap` method `loadFactor()` to return an elements/buckets ratio to monitor this.

☐ Hash: Set Size

Write a method `setSize(newCap)` to set the capacity of the internal bucket array to a specific length. As with `grow()`, after changing the array length, you must rehash all keys.

☐ Hash: Select Keys

Create method `selectKeys(keyArray)` to accepts an array of keys. Reject those keys in the existing map that are NOT in that array. If your map contains `{"cool":"Pariece", "smart":"Pariece", "tall":"Kareem"}`, then `map.selectKeys(["cool","smart"])` should change map to `{"cool":"Pariece", "smart":"Pariece"}`.

Hash Collisions

Collisions are a way of life in hashes. Consider this: as soon as you add a second value to your hash, there is a potential hash collision. Even without the **mod** operation, there is the theoretical possibility that two values will hash to the same value. This isn't likely, but always plan on collisions!

Chapter 14 – Hashes

Any two keys might hash to the same array index. For a hash to retrieve correct key-values, this means
   1) We must store an array at each index, not just a single value, and
   2) We must store the key along with the value, so we know which value to return.

Here's our flow: HashKeys   ModHash   Array
`add("myKey",42)` → -1853110172 → 2 → `[ [],[],[["myKey",42]] ]`
`add("aKey","foo")` → -851179773 → 2 → `[ [],[],[["myKey",42],["aKey","foo"]] ]`

Let's examine our array. It is a collection of *buckets*. A bucket is an array of key-values hashed to that index, such as `[["myKey",42],["aKey","foo"]]`. We iterate this shorter array to get key-values.

Hash tables are sometimes referred to in classical algorithm texts as **unordered maps**. In a map, there can be duplicate *values* (if different keys map to the same value), but there can be no duplicate *keys*. To store multiple equivalent keys one needs a *multimap*: a map that allows duplicate keys. Today you will make the changes needed to convert a `HashMap` into a `hashMultiMap` (or *unordered multimap*).

☐ Making Maps into Sets or Multimaps

We have previously mentioned both maps and sets. Sets are unordered collections of data, without any identifying label or index. You could think of a set as a map that has only keys. Today, we will change our `HashMap` data structure into a `HashSet` data structure, and even a `HashMultiSet` data structure.

Below are `HashMap`'s attributes/functions. Referencing previous solutions, *which class attributes / methods need changing to create an unordered_multimap? An unordered_set? Unordered_multiset?*

Needs to be changed to create:	unordered_set	unordered_multimap	unordered_multiset
`constructor(size)`	☐	☒	☒
`this.capacity`	☐	☐	☐
`this.table`	☐	☐	☐
`this.numElements`	☐	☐	☐
`this.add(key, value)`	☒	☒	☒
`this.find(key)`	☒	☒	☒
`this.isEmpty()`	☐	☐	☐
`this.remove(key)`	☒	☒	☒
`this.loadFactor()`	☐	☐	☐
`this.grow()`	☐	☐	☐
`this.setSize(newSize)`	☒	☐	☒

With this, refactor `HashMap`, resulting in related classes for `unordered_map` and `unordered_set` variants. For multiset and multimap, use a constructor `allowMulti` flag rather than a separate class.

Chapter 14 – Hashes

Referencing previous solutions, which attributes or functions need changing to change *unordered_map* to *unordered_multimap*? To create an *unordered_set*? An *unordered_multiset*?

unordered_multimap (from unordered_map)
`constructor`:
 `this.multi = allowDupes || false;`

`this.add(key,val)`: add an "`if (!this.multi)`" around *check-if-key-exists*.

`this.find(key)`: create `results[]`. If `(multi)`, push val for (dupe) keys found. Return results.

`this.remove(key)`: create `results[]`. If `(multi)` splice (>1) k/v found. Return results.

Others: no change (`capacity`, `isEmpty`, `numElements`, `loadFactor`, `grow`, `setSize`).

Summary of Map/Set Data Structures:
- **Maps** contain keys and values.
- **Sets** contain keys only.
- **Maps & Sets** have no duplicate keys: adding already-existing keys will overwrite previous values.
- **Multimaps & Multisets** allow duplicate keys: `find()` returns an array of values; `remove()` deletes all instances of key.
- **Unordered** data structures use hashing for rapid retrieval, but lose any sequence or order: `nextVal()`, `prevVal()`, `min()`, `max()`, `top()`, `front()` or `back()` are expensive for unordered data structures and generally not seen.
- **Ordered** data structures use sequencing (Stack, Queue) or sorting (BST, heap) to retain order, but retrieval is impacted.

unordered_set (changes from unordered_map)
`this.add(key)`: keys only – if key found, don't replace val; otherwise, push *key* (not [key, val]).

`this.find(key)`: keys only – if found, return `true` (not val); otherwise, return false.

`this.remove(key)`: keys only – if key found, remove and return `true` (not val), else `false`.

`this.setSize(newSize)`: keys only – when rehashing, `add(key)`, not `[key, val]`.

No change: `constructor`, `capacity`, `table`, `isEmpty`, `numElements`, `loadFactor`, `grow`.

unordered_multiset (from unordered_set)
`constructor`:
 `this.multi = allowDupes || false;`

`this.add(key)`: add "`if (!this.multi)`" around the *check-key-already-exists* loop.

`this.find(key)`: use `numFound`: if `(multi)`, `numFound+=count`. Return `numFound`.

`this.remove(key)`: use `numFound`: if `(multi)`, splice (multiple). Return `--numFound`.

`this.setSize(newSize)`: keys only – when rehashing, `add(key)`, not `[key, val]`. Others: no change (`capacity`, `table`, `numElements`, `isEmpty`, `loadFactor`, `grow`, `setSize`).

You have seen how *interface* (unordered map) is decoupled from underlying *implementation* (hash of arrays). In the same way that we examined *unordered* sets & maps, you could dive into *ordered* sets & maps. Ordered data structures care about *sequence*, so we could implement them with BSTs or heaps.

Chapter 14 – Hashes

With short answer questions, you can demonstrate *technical depth* as well as *clarity of communication*. How would you answer the following, if asked in an interview?

☐ Short Answer Questions: Unordered Data Structures

Describe what is meant by an *unordered* data structure.
Is there more than one type of unordered data structure? Why would I use each of these?
How are *unordered maps* commonly implemented? What is the underlying structure's name?
What is the sequence of steps taken, when adding a value to an unordered set?
What is the sequence when checking whether a given key exists in an undered map?
Likewise, what steps are taken when removing a value from an unordered set?
How would one check the validity of an unordered map?
For an *unordered set* containing the following methods – add, remove, min, max, removeMin, removeMax, contains, prevVal, nextVal, size – which methods are considered *fast*? *How* fast?
Likewise, which of these are considered relatively *slow*? Why are they slow? *How* slow?
Is there such thing as an 'unbalanced' unordered map? What should we do at that point?
Can unordered maps get 'full'? What should we do at that point?

☐ Short Answer Questions: Ordered Data Structures

Describe what is meant by an *ordered* data structure.
Is there more than one type of ordered data structure? Why would I use each of these?
How are *ordered maps* commonly implemented? What is the underlying structure's name?
What is the sequence of steps taken, when adding a value to an ordered set?
What is the sequence when checking whether a given key exists in an dered map?
Likewise, what steps are taken when removing a value from an ordered set?
How would one check the validity of an ordered map?
For an *ordered set* containing the following methods – add, remove, min, max, removeMin, removeMax, contains, prevVal, nextVal, size – which methods are considered *fast*? *How* fast?
Likewise, which of these are considered relatively *slow*? Why are they slow? *How* slow?
Is there such thing as an 'unbalanced' ordered map? What should we do at that point?
Can ordered maps get 'full'? What should we do at that point?

Chapter 14 – Hashes

☐ Blue Belt Exam

Today is a belt exam in Algorithms, leading to the rare, much-coveted Blue Belt.

Good luck!
Remember our super suggestions, good guidance, terrific tips, and perfect pearls of wisdom!

Chapter 15 – Trees, Part II

Returning to the important Binary Search Tree data structure, we now build on top of our previous work, with second-level topics such as completeness, traversal, repair, partition, and balance.

Full Trees and Complete Trees

We have previously discussed whether a BST is balanced. A BST that is roughly balanced retains its excellent performance, whereas if it grows unbalanced, its performance can rapidly deteriorate. Two types of trees that take this to the extreme are **Complete** and **Full** trees.

Full trees are perfectly balanced. If each step further away from the root node is represented by a *layer* of nodes at that level, then every layer that exists in the BST is entirely filled with nodes. In other words, each leaf node's path to the root has the same length. As a side effect, every full BST contains a number of nodes that is one less than an integer power of two (i.e. 1, 3, 7, 15, 31, 63, etc). A *full* tree is the strictest type of balanced tree possible!

Complete trees are just like full trees, with one possible exception. In a complete tree, it is acceptable for the bottom layer to be less than entirely filled, <u>so long as all nodes in that layer are as leftmost as possible</u>. Completeness is a superset of fullness; that is, all full trees are also considered complete. A *complete* Binary Tree is as balanced as a tree with that number of nodes can be. Completeness is also *very* expensive to maintain, and for this reason complete BSTs are rarely used in production, since the costs of keeping a BST truly complete are *much* higher than the costs of adjusting it only when it becomes significantly unbalanced. In practice, complete binary trees are normally only seen in non-BST situations, such as the 'Binary Tree projection' we see in the Heap data structure, where we interpret the underlying array index positions as `BTNode`s in a hypothetical binary tree.

☐ BST: Is Full

Chekov keeps his data perfectly clean. I mean, *per-fect-ly* clean. He doesn't just keep them balanced. He keeps a *full* BST at all times. Given a pointer to a BST object, return whether the BST is a *full* tree.

☐ BST: Is Complete

His cousin Pikov is a bit less neurotic. He does still keep everything highly balanced. He keeps his BSTs complete at all times. Given a BST object, return whether that BST is *complete*.

☐ BST Discussion

What is the advantage of Chekov's approach? What is the advantage of Pikov's approach? What about their crazy uncle Dropov, who never balances his BSTs at all – is he being negligent? Maybe there isn't a single 'right' answer. So how do we know what approach is best for the situation at hand?

Chapter 15 – Trees, Part II

Repairing a Binary Search Tree

If it is possible with `isValid()` to detect whether a `BTNode` is in an incorrect location, then it should also be possible to repair an invalid `BST`. Unfortunately, once we find an invalid node, we have no guarantee about the nodes below it – so our only recourse is to reinsert all of the subtree nodes (not just the one node we found to be invalid).

☐ BST: Repair

Sometimes it is hard to find good help. Oscar is working with a third-party library that receives data from outside sources and sorts it into a binary search tree. Oscar is positive the library has bugs, because sometimes the BSTs it produces don't meet the requirements of a `BST`. Given a potentially invalid `BST` object, create a standalone function `bstRepair(BST)` that rearranges nodes as needed to make it valid. Return `true` if you repaired the `BST`, or `false` if this was not needed.

☐ BST: Smallest Difference

Given a valid `BST`, return the smallest difference between any two values in the tree. What are the run-time and space complexities of your solution? Would it be less efficient if `BST` was very unbalanced?

☐ SList: Smallest Difference

Given sorted singly linked list, return the smallest difference between values. What are the run-time and space complexities of your solution?

☐ BST: Closest Value (again)

Given valid `BST` and number, return the tree value closest to that number. What are the run-time and space complexities of your solution?

☐ Array: Closest Value

Given sorted array and number, return the array value closest to that number. What are the run-time and space complexities of your solution?

☐ SList: Closest Value

Given sorted `SList` and number, return the list value closest to that number. What are the run-time and space complexities of your solution?

☐ DList: Closest Value

Given sorted `DList` and number, return the list value closest to that number. What are the run-time and space complexities of your solution?

For this particular problem, which of the data structures mentioned above will most likely lead to optimal performance in finding the closest value, across a diverse data set? How would you pre-process the values – potentially storing them in a different data structure – if optimal run-time performance was your primary goal, and you were willing to consume significant amounts of memory in order to achieve it?

Chapter 15 – Trees, Part II

BST Partitioning

Sometimes it is necessary to divide a BST into two. To accomplish this, we might want to split the BST around a specific value, or we might simply approximate a value that would put around half the values on one side and around half on the other. Similar to how we might divide, or *partition*, a linked list into two separate linked lists, likewise when we partition a BST we want the result to be two different non-overlapping BSTs, where every node in the previous BST is contained in one of the resultant BSTs.

☐ BST: Partition Around Value

Create a method `BST.partition(value)` where a `BST` object partitions itself around the given value (whether or not that value is found in the tree). The `BST` should change itself appropriately, as well as return a new tree object containing all other nodes. Remember, the ranges of the two `BST` objects should not overlap (the `max()` of one should be less than the `min()` of the other).

☐ BST: Partition Evenly

Create a standalone function that, given a valid BST, partitions the tree evenly into two distinct BSTs. As in the previous challenge, change the given BST to become one of the resultant BSTs, and return the other. The two resultant trees should be valid and non-overlapping.

Second: if we don't pay attention to balance, the two resultant BSTs might be tall and thin. To improve performance, make both subtrees a bit more balanced before returning them.

☐ BST: Reverse

Create a standalone function that accepts a `BST` object and reverses it. A reversed `BST` has its highest values in leftmost children, and its lowest values in rightmost children (root would be unchanged).

Chapter 15 – Trees, Part II

Repairing a More Complex Binary Search Tree

Refer to the `BST2` and `BTNode2` data structures, from our earlier BST chapter. We based `BTNode2` on `BTNode`, simply adding a `.parent` pointer; a `BST2` is merely a `BST`, plus necessary code to use and maintain `.parent` in the `BTNode2` objects it contains. As a result, invalid `BST2`s include not only those with incorrectly located nodes, but also those with defective pointer values (e.g.: a child's `.parent` doesn't point back, or node pointers create a loop!).

☐ BST: Kth-Biggest

Given a valid Binary Search Tree, find the Kth-largest element contained in that tree.

Second: if above you took advantage of the `.size()` method, write a version without it. If you did not use `.size()` originally, write a version that does.

☐ Test Cases for BST2 Repair

In the challenge following this one, we will write code to detect and repair a potentially invalid `BST2`. Before you start that, here is a related challenge: what *test cases* would you create to ensure that your solution detects and correctly fixes the possible error cases? For this challenge, a *test case* is a `BST` that you send to `bst2Repair(BST2)`.

☐ BST2: Repair

Given a potentially invalid `BST2`, create standalone function `bst2Repair(BST2)` to detect whether it is invalid. If so, fix it and return `true` (if not, return `false`). Potential problems include incorrectly placed nodes, as well as incorrect pointers (`.parent`, `.left`, `.right`) that create loops, etc.

Chapter 15 – Trees, Part II

Breadth-First Search

Previously we have talked about traversing a binary search tree. Whether we used pre-order, in-order, or post-order, we traversed from the root of the tree all the way to a leaf node, before backtracing. This is an example of **depth-first-search (DFS)**, in which we (starting at the root) explore as far as possible along each branch before exploring adjacent paths.

Can you think of a scenario in which DFS is not the best way to traverse a binary tree? Let's say we have a generic binary tree (not a BST) with 300 nodes, and each node contains a single upper-case letter. How would we find the 'P' that was closest to the root node? To solve this problem, Depth-First Search would not be a great choice. What if we wanted to find *all* the instances of the letter 'P'? In that case, we need to visit every node anyway, so DFS is a reasonable choice.

To find the closest 'P', a better strategy would be, as sage Jerry Seinfeld advised, "go for the miracle parking spot, then concentric circles." With **breadth-first search (BFS)**, we would first start looking at the root node itself, then proceed to every possible node that is only one step further away, then advance to every node that is one step further, etc. (like concentric circles, but in a tree).

Breadth-first, used in conjunction with a Queue data structure, is a good way to advance search evenly away from the starting point. Remember, once we examine a given node, we must then check all other nodes of similar distance from the origin, before we check that given node's children. The Queue can help us remember a node, from the moment we examine *its parent* until the time we check *it*.

We will encounter BFS later with graphs; for now breadth-first is an important new way to iterate trees.

☐ BST: Values for Layer

Jeff has divided his workgroup into a perfectly balanced hierarchy, to the extent that his organizational chart looks just like a binary tree! To learn how things are going "in the trenches", he wants to have a meeting with all the line managers, but not include their bosses. Given a BST and a layer number (starting at zero for the root), return an array containing all the values at that layer in the BST. If a BST is a *full* tree, what percentage of nodes are leaves? What percentage are 'first-level managers'?

☐ BST: Layer Arrays

Given a BST, return a two-dimensional array containing all values in the BST. The outer array represents each layer (starting at zero for the root), and the inner array for each layer represents the values at that layer in the BST.

Chapter 16 – Tries

Adding to our growing knowledge base of reference-based data structures (lists, trees), in the next two chapters we will learn about **tries** and **graphs**.

Trie Data Structure

The *trie* data structure (initially pronounced "tree" as the middle syllable of *retrieval*, but now universally pronounced "*try*" to avoid confusion) is useful in scenarios usually reserved for a hash, but it is best known for its power to predict – particularly auto-complete. Let's examine the trie *conceptually*.

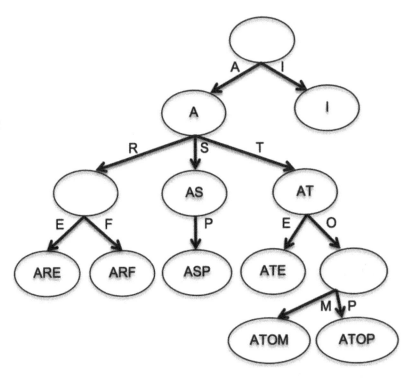

As shown in the diagram, a trie is a set of connected nodes. The root node represents the empty string ""; from that node, there can be many pointers to other nodes. Each pointer+node represents the addition of a letter to that sequence. If the sequence of letters adds up to a word, then the word is stored within the node as well. If not, it still exists in the trie if it is needed for another, longer word (like the 'R' node below the top-level 'A'). Because each node represents a unique word, two parent nodes can never point to the same child node – although 'ATE' and 'ARE' are both in our trie, the 'AR' node and the 'AT' node point to different children for an additional 'E'.

Nodes are added only when they are needed to store a word – the diagram above represents the words "a", "are", "arf", "as", "asp", "at", "ate", "atom", "atop" and "I". If we were to add the word "asps", a pointer representing "s" would extend from the "ASP" node to a new node containing "ASPS". If we add the word "ar", a node already exists at the appropriate location, so "AR" would be stored into the node.

Codewise, a `TrieSet` object is quite similar to a basic binary tree object: it contains a single attribute – a pointer to the root node – plus the instance methods. Each `TrieNode` object contains an optional node value, plus an array of pointers. This array is initially empty but can hold as many pointers as there are letters in the alphabet. If we choose to lower-case all the strings that we hold in our `TrieSet`, then each node's array could contain as many as 26 pointers. Again, each pointer+node represents the addition of a specific letter to the sequence of letters from the root up to that node.

To add a word to our trie, we iterate each letter, following the appropriate pointer for that letter. If the node's array has no pointer there, we create a node, write it to the array location and proceed. When we reach the last letter, we save the word in the node, signifying that it is *terminal*, not intermediate.

Chapter 16 – Tries

After walking through a trie in both concept and code, hopefully you see how tries might enable one to predict the word, given the first few letters! Implement the following challenges to create a `TrieSet`:

☐ Trie: Insert

After building simple `TrieSet` and `TrieNode` constructors, create an `add` method to insert a string to the set. For our purposes, assume that input strings will be letters only – no numerals or punctuation. Also, you can convert inputs to lowercase before storing them. Return `false` if word has already been stored (after all, it's a `TrieSet` not a `TrieMultiSet`!), or `true` if insertion is successful. Tries are treelike (not a purely linear one like a linked list), so recursion at the node level is a reasonable choice.

☐ Trie: Contains

Create a `TrieSet` method to check whether a given string is present within the set. Again, you can assume that all inputs are letters-only; you can also convert all strings to lowercase. Return `true` if word is found, `false` if not.

☐ Trie: First

Tries are reasonable substitutes for Hashes, yet they retain order! Build a method to return trie's first value. *First* means *lowest-alphabetically*, not earliest-added. N.B.: `"Todd"` comes before `"toddy"`.

☐ Trie: Last

Return its *last* value. `"Kelvin"` comes after `"kelp"`.

☐ Trie: Remove

Construct a method in `TrieSet` class that removes a given string from our set. As earlier, safely assume that all input strings will contain only letters (not numerals or punctuation). Also, lowercase all strings before storing or checking for them. When removing trie values, remember that in some cases you need to remove a terminal `TrieNode`. You may potentially need to remove certain ancestor intermediate nodes. Make sure to return `true` on a successful removal, `false` if string not found.

Second: Incorporate punctuation and case-sensitivity across the `TrieSet` class. Suggestion: the 95 typeable characters on a keyboard have consecutive charCode values, starting with [space].

Chapter 16 – Tries

Today, finish `TrieSet`. Auto-complete is used by search engines and mobile devices.

☐ Trie: Size

Return the number of values added to the `TrieSet`. There are two valid ways to implement this method – can you come up with both? In which usage cases would you prefer one over the other?

☐ Trie: Next

Given a string that might not be in the trie, return the contained string that is immediately subsequent. Hashes don't do well with this, but tries can! Return `null` if there is no subsequent string.

☐ Trie: Auto Complete

Assume your trie is populated with a wide array of valid words. Given string (presumably what user typed so far), use your trie to rapidly return an array of words beginning with that string.

Second: augment `autoComplete(str)` to accept `maxResults`, and return at most that many.

Chapter 16 – Tries

Trie MultiSet

We mentioned it earlier, so let's build `TrieMultiSet`. Remember, multiset is identical to set, except it tracks number of instances along with value. Implement the following that build a `TrieMultiSet`:

☐ Trie MultiSet: Insert

For this exercise, `Insert` increments count, adds nodes as needed and always succeeds.

☐ Trie MultiSet: Size

`Size` should return total (multi) count.

☐ Trie MultiSet: Remove

`Remove` should decrement count and eliminate nodes, returning previous count (0 if not found).

☐ Trie MultiSet: Contains

`Contains` should return count (0 if not found).

Note: `First` / `Last` / `Next` are unchanged when moving from `Set` to `MultiSet`.

☐ Trie MultiSet: Auto Complete

Given an entire dictionary and a short initial string fragment, autocomplete might return a huge number of results. Let's use the `count` aspect of each `TrieMultiNode` to denote the frequency of that word, and use this to prioritize the return results from `autoComplete`, so that most frequent words are listed first. In addition to the string fragment, accept `maxResults`, and return at most that many results.

Trie Map

We can expand a `TrieSet` to a `trieMap` by associating an additional value to each stored string.

☐ Trie Map: Insert

`Insert` should accept a key and a value, and should return the preexisting value (if key already existed) or `null` if key is new.

☐ Trie Map: Contains

`Contains` should return the value for the given key (`null` if key is not found).

☐ Trie Map: Remove

`Remove` deletes the given key (and value), returning `true` if key was found, else `false`.

☐ Trie Map: Size

`Size` is unchanged from `TrieSet`.

☐ Trie Map: First

`First` returns an object containing the key-value pair for the alphabetically-lowest key.

☐ Trie Map: Last

Conversely, `Last` returns the final key-value.

☐ Trie Map: Next

Given a key that may not be present, `next(key)` returns the subsequent key-value.

Chapter 17 – Graphs

One reason Amazon is an amazing company is because it can, overnight, deliver (almost) anything, from anywhere, to anywhere. How is that possible at *any* price, let alone a reasonable one? Amazon has made huge investments in *logistics*. This means storing goods at centers around the world, but also being incredibly efficient at getting those goods from suppliers, and to customers. Optimizing their transportation needs is a **graph theory** problem easily worth many hundreds of millions of dollars every year to Amazon, likely $1Billion or more.

Large software projects such as Office, Android or World of Warcraft have highly complex processes required to build these products. From synchronizing source code, to compiling and linking source code, to substituting localized text strings for more than 100 non-English languages, to creating installable packages, to automatically installing and testing a daily build, to automatically releasing it to the large team of engineers *only if the builds and tests pass* – there are hundreds of steps that can be automated, with numerous interdependencies. Constructing a dependency chains for large software projects that works at all – let alone optimizing it – is an enormous graph theory problem. Looking more deeply into just one of these steps – compiling and linking an iOS application: these tools could not *begin* to interpret source code without significant use of dependency analysis, rooted in graph theory.

Every network problem is a graph problem as well. Is there enough Internet backbone bandwidth for future needs? Although our roads and bridges might be adequate for average demands, can we forecast how they will fare during events such as local NFL games or university graduations? The modern industrial company deals with complicated dependency chains (graphs) when they manage their materials and their manufacturing lines. Social network companies such as Facebook, LinkedIn, Twitter consider their knowledge of the interconnections between us to be their core asset. *Org charts* that show teams and leadership relationships are graphs. Even our understanding of how the human brain works (a neural network) is modeled as a complex and enormous graph. Graphs are extremely important, if for no other reason than that our world is increasingly a *connected* one.

What is a graph? How do we process and manage them in computing? Why are there different ways to represent them? Where and when is each method appropriate?

A graph is any collection of nodes that can be connected. Singly linked lists and binary trees, for example, are graphs. When we look at a graph on a computer screen or on paper, the actual shape of that graph does not matter – what matters are the connections between nodes. The number of connections out of or into each node need not be limited to just one or two: it is possible for every node to be connected to every other. Also, the connections between nodes may or may not have *direction* (the 'arrows' between nodes may not have 'arrowheads'). Connections also may or may not have a *weight* that we choose to store within it. For example, if downtown intersections A and B are nodes, for the connection between them we could use its weight to signify the distance between them, or the time needed to travel between them, or the cost in fuel+toll. Hopefully you are starting to see how programs like Google Maps might store a city transportation grid! There are two common ways graphs are represented in data structures. Before we go into those, we need to define a few common terms.

Chapter 17 – Graphs

Graph Terms

These terms are not necessarily essential to understand graph theory or how networks operate. They are mainly only important if you intend to work with others who have some level of 'classical' training in graph theory, or when you dive into additional materials in this area.

Important:
Graph: a collection of nodes that may or may not have connections between them.
Vertex: what we have called a node; a *vertex* is where connections meet (plural: *vertices*).
Edge: what we have called a connection; an *edge* runs between two vertices (nodes).

Walk: a *walk* is any route from a vertex through edges to subsequent vertices.
Circuit: a *circuit* is a path (every vertex) that ends where it started; also *connected* or *closed path*.

Directed: in a *directed* graph, edges have a direction from one vertex to another.
Undirected: in an *undirected* graph, edges do not have direction: they are two-way.
Degree: the number of edges to/from a vertex, if undirected (*in-degree* and *out-degree*, if directed).

Acyclic: *acyclic* graphs contain only one way to travel between two vertices.
Cyclic: *cyclic* graphs can contain multiple ways of getting from one node to another.

Order: a graph's *order* is the number of vertices in the graph (inexplicably, usually called **n**, not v).
Size: a graph's *size* is the number of edges in that graph (inexplicably, usually **m**, not e).

Root: a designated vertex, for 'rooted graphs' and potentially, directed graphs.

Other terms you might hear:
Cycle, Path, Tour: various types of walks; conflicting interpretations are used, so look for clarification.
Component: a maximal subset of vertices on a circuit (maximal means all that *can* be included *are* included). A graph may be made up of more than one component; these do not intersect.

Chapter 17 – Graphs

Representing Graphs

We've told you to think about a graph much the same as you might think about a BST: some collection of nodes with pointers between them. That is a fine starting point, and good when drawing them on whiteboards, but graphs are almost never actually represented in source code that way. Why not?

The problem with graphs, compared to linked lists or binary trees, is that they are *unpredictable*. Graph vertices can point wherever they want. Vertices can have any number of outbound connections, including zero. They can have any number of inbound connections, including 0. They can form cycles, and cycles-within-cycles. A vertex could even point to itself! For this reason, a graph doesn't have a clearly-designated *head* node, as lists and trees do. Also, it isn't just *nodes* (vertices) that have values, as we are used to. The *connections between them* have values too – those "arrows" between nodes have *thicknesses* that can vary. Some graphs have *bidirectional* connections that we wouldn't think of as arrows or pointers. Further, graphs need not be entirely connected: there can be entire sections wholly disconnected from the rest, or loner vertices with no inbound or outbound edges at all. Compared to graphs, even doubly linked lists and unbalanced binary trees are well-behaved and (gasp!) *boring*. So, what *is* the right way to reduce a graph into a data structure in source code?

Graphs are most commonly represented in three different ways. These include *edge list*, *adjacency map* and *adjacency list* concepts. We will build simple versions of each, later this chapter. Despite their differences, each graph data structure does two things: *manage vertices*, and *manage edges*.

You can think of vertices in the same way that you have thought of nodes in a linked list: each is located in a particular place in the structure and has a value that can be set to ... well ... anything. As mentioned before, we can't just store the "head node", because a graph's vertices may not be interconnected. We need to maintain a list of them. With this in mind, in addition to the graph constructor function, we would expect a graph to have a `this.vertList` that contains our vertices, as well as the following functions to manage vertices:

```
addVertex(val) // returns vertId        getVertexValue(vertId)
removeVertex(vertId)                    setVertexValue(vertId, val)
```

Furthermore, we'd expect to see the following functions, to manage edges:

```
addEdge(vertId1, vertId2, val)          getEdgeValue(vertId1, vertId2)
removeEdge(vertId1, vertId2)            setEdgeValue(vertId1, vertId2, val)
```

Graph representations may not have a dedicated list of edges – this is one place where our graph data structures differ in their approaches. Also, notice that edges can attach a value – more on that later.

First, though, let's dive into one way to represent graphs.

Chapter 17 – Graphs

Edge List

Our first data structure, **Edge List**, has a basic approach. Like other representations, it has a vertex list. Mirroring that, it has a simple list of all graph edges, represented by IDs for source and destination nodes, plus optional weight. For now, omit weight from list entries. An edge list representing the following graph would be: `[[A,C],[A,E],[B,A],[B,C],[C,B],[D,B],[D,E],[E,D]]`. With only edge lists, can we know whether a given vertex exists?

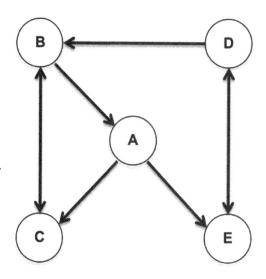

☐ Edge List Exercise 1

Create edge lists for the following graphs A, B and C.

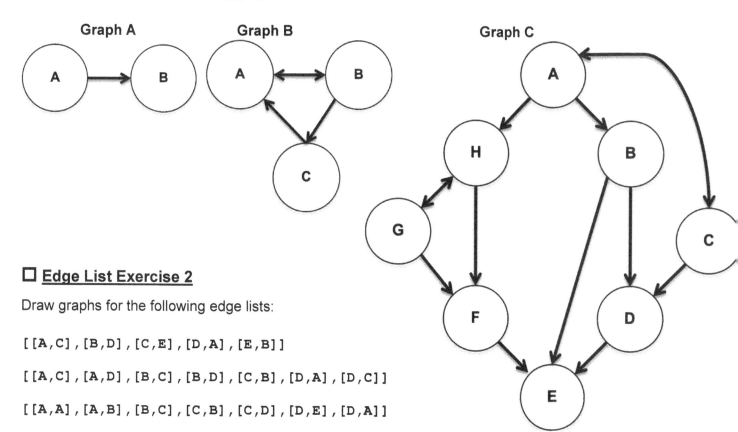

☐ Edge List Exercise 2

Draw graphs for the following edge lists:

`[[A,C],[B,D],[C,E],[D,A],[E,B]]`

`[[A,C],[A,D],[B,C],[B,D],[C,B],[D,A],[D,C]]`

`[[A,A],[A,B],[B,C],[C,B],[C,D],[D,E],[D,A]]`

Now, onward to the next graph representation!

Chapter 17 – Graphs

Adjacency Map

Our next graph representation organizes information more efficiently. To find whether vertices are neighbors, we might iterate the entire edge list. If instead, vertices store edge information to *every* other, we can directly map *all* adjacencies: this is the **Adjacency Map**.

Adjacency map:
[[0,-1, 1,-1, 1],
  [1, 0, 1,-1,-1],
  [-1, 1, 0,-1,-1],
  [-1, 1,-1, 0, 1],
  [-1,-1,-1, 1, 0]]

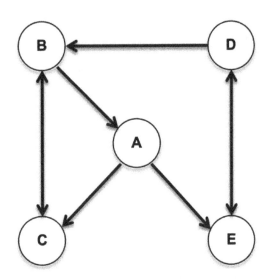

Adjacency maps are two-dimensional arrays. Outer array rows represent a vertex's outward connections; cells represent all possible destinations. If an edge exists, the cell stores that edge's *weight* (additional info mentioned earlier, such as length or cost to traverse that edge). If we are allowed to move from given node directly back to itself, this weight would be **0**. Otherwise, and for any other cells representing "you can't get to that destination from this origin", cells are given a value which is recognizable as an *invalid* cost (in this case, specifically **-1**). In *unweighted* graphs, valid edges are commonly given a weight of **1**.

☐ Adjacency Map Exercise 1

Build adjacency maps for the following graphs. As above, treat vertex A as [0], B as [1], C as [2]. As is a default for adjacency maps, in these maps represent "source == destination" with a weight of **0**.

☐ Adjacency Map Exercise 2

Draw graphs for the following maps:

[[0,-1, 1, 1],
 [-1, 0, 1, 1],
 [1,-1, 0,-1],
 [-1, 1, 1, 0]]

[[1, 1,-1,-1,-1],
 [-1, 0, 1,-1,-1],
 [-1, 1, 0, 1,-1],
 [1,-1,-1, 0, 1],
 [-1,-1, 1,-1, 0]]

[[0,-1, 1,-1,-1],
 [-1, 0,-1, 1,-1],
 [-1,-1, 0,-1, 1],
 [1,-1,-1, 0,-1],
 [-1, 1,-1,-1, 0]]

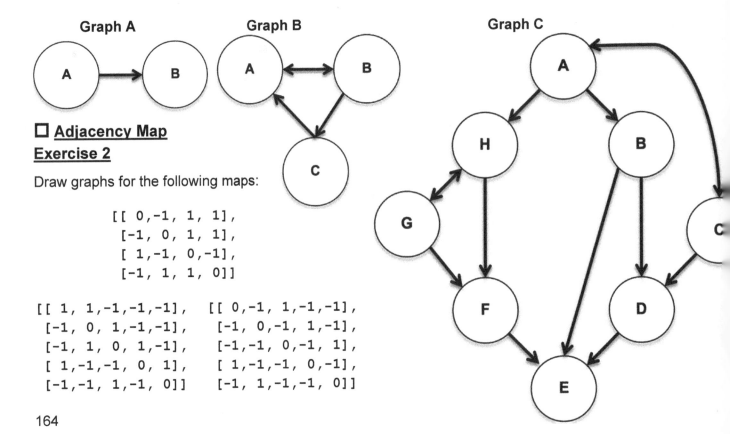

164

Next, our final graph representation….

Chapter 17 – Graphs

Adjacency List

With adjacency maps, spot-checking whether arbitrary vertex A directly connects to vertex B is a simple array lookup. Likewise, to determine vertex A's neighbors, we take an entire row from our map and extract the subset of cells that indicate edges. Unfortunately, adjacency maps don't scale well for memory, as the number of vertices grows: `O(v²)`, where `v` is vertices. Edge lists, however, are `O(e)`, where `e` is edges. For *dense* graphs (with high edge-to-vertex ratio), memory usage is comparable, but for *sparse* graphs (low edge-to-vertex ratio), this difference is significant. An ideal graph representation for *sparse* graphs would have the faster edge- and neighbor-checking of adjacency maps, with the smaller memory consumption of edge lists. These are characteristics of the **Adjacency List**.

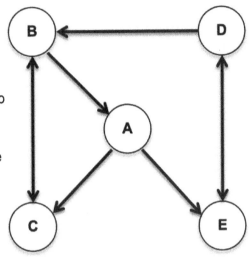

Like adjacency maps, adjacency lists are two-dimensional arrays. Each row represents the outward connections for a vertex, but *only valid edges* are stored. An adjacency list for graph above is smaller than an adjacency map, but retains the fast (indexed) lookup: `[[C,E],[A,C],[B],[B,E],[D]]`.

☐ Adjacency List Exercise 1

Create adjacency lists for the following graphs. As earlier, make vertex A `[0]`, make B `[1]`, C `[2]`, etc.

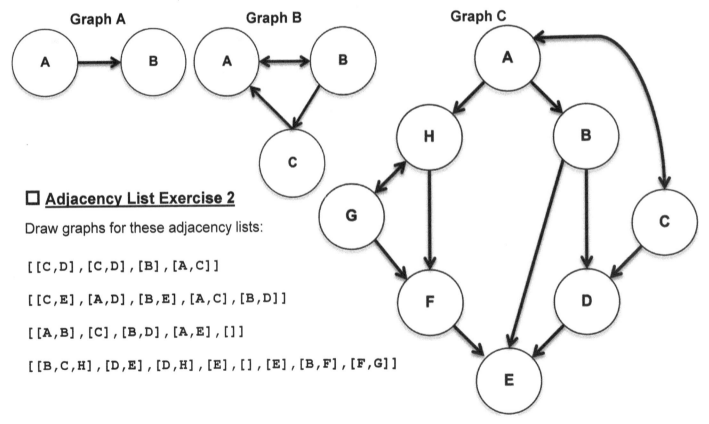

☐ Adjacency List Exercise 2

Draw graphs for these adjacency lists:

`[[C,D],[C,D],[B],[A,C]]`

`[[C,E],[A,D],[B,E],[A,C],[B,D]]`

`[[A,B],[C],[B,D],[A,E],[]]`

`[[B,C,H],[D,E],[D,H],[E],[],[E],[B,F],[F,G]]`

Chapter 17 – Graphs

Directed and Undirected Graphs

The graphs examined so far had 'arrowheads' on every edge: each connection between vertices had *direction*. This is appropriate where an opposing edge may not exist (or might have different weight). Twitter, for example, is a *directed graph*: more than 1 million people follow `@karaswisher`; she follows ~1300 in turn. Conversely, LinkedIn is *undirected*, with directionless edges. For these, it is easier to create two connections than to store one and constantly check both sides (if adequate memory exists).

Edges Have Weight

Upfront we mentioned that additional data can be attached to each edge. Did that seem odd? Edges are not all equal, just as distances between all intersections are not necessarily equal. Shipping costs are not universally identical. The traffic present on our roads varies across the map. This is why we attach a value or some other metadata to each edge. Use this value however you wish – if you attach *distance* to an edge, your graph will be able to compute <u>shortest distance</u> between nodes. If you attach *time* to an edge, your graph will be well-equipped to handle <u>quickest trip</u> calculations. But if you are interested in <u>fewest turns</u>, stick with a basic graph without edge weights – just vertices and edges.

☐ Edge List Implementation

Now you build them! Using the descriptions that we have given you, create a class that uses the Edge List paradigm to represent a graph. Your `ELGraph` class should have the following methods:

```
addVertex(value)                        // return vertID
removeVertex(vertID)                    // true:removed. false:unfound
getVertexValue(vertID)                  // return value
setVertexValue(vertID, value)           // true:set. false:unfound
addEdge(vertID1, vertID2, value)        // true:added. false:unfound
removeEdges(vertID)                     // delete all edges to/from vert
removeEdge(vertID1, vertID2)            // true:removed. false:unfound
getEdgeValue(vertID1, vertID2)          // return value
setEdgeValue(vertID1, vertID2, value)   // true:set. false:unfound
adjacent(vertID1, vertID2)              // true:vert1->vert2. false:not
neighbors(vertID)                       // return [adjacent vertIDs]
```

☐ Adjacency Map Implementation

Using the descriptions that we have given you, create a class that uses the Adjacency Map paradigm to represent a graph. Your `AMGraph` class should have the same methods that your `ELGraph` class does.

☐ Adjacency List Implementation

Using the descriptions that we have given you, create a class that uses the Adjacency List paradigm to represent a graph. `ALGraph` should have the same methods as `ELGraph` and `AMGraph`.

Chapter 17 – Graphs

Depth-first and *breadth-first* iteration can be used in graphs, so long as one knows when to apply each.

Depth-First Search

With depth-first iteration, we continue along a chosen path until it ends before exploring alternate paths. If we are iterating a *BST*, we know that a path ends when child pointers are `NULL`, and we recurse until we get there. For graphs, we'll need a different way, since graphs can have loops. Rather than using recursion (which uses a *call* stack) to handle backtracing through all the possibilities, we will use a stack of our own; as we discover new possible vertices, we add them to our stack. To prevent our iterating into infinite loops, we will mark each vertex when we visit it.

We start the Depth-First Search (DFS) process on a graph by marking the source vertex as *visited*, then pushing it onto our stack. Then we enter the main loop, which continues until the stack is empty. The loop begins by popping the next vertex from our stack. Is this the vertex we are looking for? If so, we exit our loop by immediately `return`ing with success. Otherwise, we retrieve the neighbors for this vertex. For those neighbors that have not yet been visited, we push them onto our stack and restart the loop, when we again pop a vertex from our stack. Eventually, if we have not found our vertex, we will stop finding unvisited vertices and the stack will be emptied. If we exit our loop, then we have iterated the graph without finding our target vertex, so we return an appropriate failure (such as `false` or `[]`). In short, DFS dives deep immediately rather than methodically advancing along all paths.

☐ Someone on the Inside

Everybody knows that it is easier to get a job at a company when you know someone that already works there – you can learn the culture, what technologies they use, what teams are hiring, etc. – all before making official contact! Using graph operations, determine whether you know someone "on the inside" at your target company, and if so, who. You are given an undirected graph (representing your social network), your own vertex ID, and an array of vertex IDs for those working at the company.

Second: often you *won't* know anyone "on the inside" at your target. If so, find one of your contacts that does, returning vertex IDs for contact and insider. Can you optimize the performance of your solution?

☐ Vertex Is Reachable

Given a generalized graph and two vertex IDs, return whether a path exists from first to second vertex.

Second: on success, return array of vertex IDs representing one possible path. If none exist, return `[]`.

☐ All Paths

Given a graph, as well as IDs for source and destination vertices, return an array of all possible paths from source to destination. A path cannot revisit a vertex. If no path exists, return an empty array.

Chapter 17 – Graphs

Breadth-First Search

If depth-first search is *impulsive* – choosing a path and "not looking back" until the string of possibilities is disproved – then breadth-first search (BFS) is *methodical* and almost *cautious*. With BFS, we visit vertices based on how close they are to the source. In an interconnected graph, this is similar to ripples spreading on a pond. When is breadth-first useful, compared to depth-first?

Say we want to find shortest path from vertex D to vertex J. With DFS, we would determine all possible paths, then compare lengths. The last path DFS explores might turn out to be shortest. BFS, however, guarantees to explore options from closest, outward. As soon as we find a valid path, we know it is optimal – maybe *one of many*, but nonetheless optimal. BFS is ideal for *find shortest path* problems.

In another example, our graph resembles a mostly complete binary tree structure. A number of the vertices contain a specific value, and we are searching for any of them, starting from a 'root' vertex. (From what we know so far, either BFS or DFS are reasonable choices.) Further, we know that *all the vertices we seek are leaves*. Now, DFS is a *clear* choice. Here's why: if graph resembles complete BST, with BFS we won't reach leaf vertices until after traversing *all* intermediate vertices (guaranteed to be 50% of graph), whereas with DFS we get to leaf vertices as soon as possible. In worst case, both approaches still check the entire graph, but in best case DFS finds a target almost immediately. DFS also wins in average case: based on number of targets, this linearly scales between best and worst.

What enables BFS to work outward evenly, compared to DFS? Hint: something in the algorithm is inherently more *fair* than the DFS algorithm. In *DFS*, we use a Stack to store the possibilities that we want to explore. When one path is exhausted, we next explore the path *most recently discovered*. This takes DFS "down toward the leaves" and keeps it there, rather than evenly expanding our ripples on the pond. It would be more *fair* to explore paths from first-discovered to last-discovered. So, which data structure should we use? *Queues* are 'fair' data structures and used in BFS for this reason. In fact, this is usually the <u>only</u> change needed, to convert a DFS algorithm to a BFS one!

☐ Shortest Path

Given an unweighted graph as well as IDs for source and destination vertices, find a path that requires minimal fewest edges. Return this path as an array of vertex IDs, or `[]` if no path exists.

☐ Gimme Three Steps

Given undirected graph and ID for start vertex, return IDs for vertices three or fewer edges away.

☐ Easy to Get There

Given directed graph, return `[vertID]` for vertices with more incoming edges than outgoing edges.

Chapter 17 – Graphs

You built graph representations, solved shortest-path problems, maybe even visited oracleofbacon.org or 6degreesofvincegill.com. Now what? Let's talk about graphs with and without *cycles*.

In graphs, unlike binary trees, a vertex can have inbound edges from multiple source vertices. Does this create a cycle? Not necessarily! A graph does not necessarily have a single 'ancestor' vertex from where all paths originate. What if node A had two children B and C, and they both pointed to the same vertex D – is *that* a cycle? Again, not necessarily. Recall: some (most) graphs are *directed*, meaning edges have direction. The existence of paths ABD and ACD does not create a cycle (unless graph is *undirected*: ABD would imply DBA, which along with ACD creates a cycle.) A cycle is a path that starts and ends with the same vertex, not revisiting any intervening vertices. **Cyclic graphs**, then, *might* have cycles, whereas **acyclic graphs** are guaranteed to have none. What does this give us?

For one, undirected graphs that contain *as many edges as vertices* must be cyclic (although if there are fewer edges, this doesn't prove it is acyclic). Counting edges is one way to "fail-fast" when determining if a graph is cyclic. On the *directed* graph side, all acyclic graphs must have at least one vertex without inbound edges, as well as at least one vertex with no outbound edges – if the graph does not contain both, we know it is cyclic (although again, the existence of these vertices doesn't prove it is acyclic).

Directed Acyclic Graphs

A directed acyclic graph (DAG) is a special subset of graph that has been much studied. DAGs are used to represent dependency chains – for source code compiler tools, manufacturing process schedule optimization, hardware circuit design, spreadsheet calculations, and many others. Primarily, we care whether a graph is a DAG because this allows us to apply certain optimizations. Many of these optimizations are based on Topological Sorting (also called TopoSort), the process of reducing a directed acyclic graph to an array of vertices, arranged so that every edge moves forward in the array.

☐ Graph: Is DAG

Given a graph, determine whether it is a Directed Acyclic Graph.

☐ DAG to Array

Given a DAG, *TopoSort* its vertices (create array of vertex IDs so each edge moves forward in array). Combine with previous solution to return the vertex array if graph is DAG, or [] if not.

☐ Weekend Challenge: Word Ladder

Given two words, list intermediate words that change a letter at a time, transforming one into other. Use www-01.sil.org/linguistics/wordlists/english/wordlist/wordsEn.txt. Return a chain of valid intermediate words that connect the two given words.

Second: Return only the minimal-length chain. If there is more than one, return the first.

Third: Return all the minimal-length word chains found (not just the first one).

Fourth: return the minimal-length chain with the highest Scrabble letter score!

Chapter 18 – Bit Arithmetic

Numerical Systems

As humans, we have been raised from a young age to have a specific attitude toward the number 'ten'. This is rooted in the fact that as a species we have ten fingers, ten toes. As a result, there are ten numerals in the modern symbolic representation of numbers (0-9). But how would our world look if from the beginning our species had only eight fingers? Or what if we had *sixteen* fingers? Or what if we, like computers, primarily thought about only "on" and "off" – the equivalent of having only two numerals to choose from? Our writing would look different, although the actual quantities would be the same.

Numerical systems by nature are simply different ways that symbols can represent a quantity. A certain quantity can be represented by different symbols. Whether we say "quarante-deux" or "forty-two" or `0x2A` or **42**, the amount is the same. So, why can't we just stay with the *decimal* (ten-based) system that is 'native' and natural to humans?

Computers don't think that way, that's why. Computer architecture from the beginning has evolved from a foundation based on binary digital logic, where signals are either ON or OFF. They live in a world of two numerals, not ten numerals – almost as if they count using two fingers, rather than ten fingers. Each of these 0/1 numerals is called a *bit*. If you can only use 0's and 1's then a number like 42 (decimal) becomes `0b0101010` (binary). This would make for very long and tedious numbers indeed, except that we have combined these groups of 2, to create number systems that they are closer to the 10-based system that is natural to us.

Chapter 18 – Bit Arithmetic

Octal System

There is a number system called 'octal' that uses 8 numerals, grouping three bits together into one numeral that goes from 0 to 7. After counting up to 7, we start using an additional digit, just like in our usual decimal system we start using the "tens" digit when counting beyond 9. The indicator that we are using octal is the prefix '0o', so the number 8 (decimal) will appear in octal as 0o10. In decimal notation, each numeral has a jump in value of 10x as we move from the 'ones' digit to the 'tens' digit, or from the 'tens' digit to the 'hundreds' digit. Similarly, in octal each digit represents a jump of 8x. A number like 0o4213, then, is $(4 \times 8^3) + (2 \times 8^2) + (1 \times 8^1) + (3 \times 8^0) = 2187$ (decimal). You won't need to deal with octal numbers much – if anything, you will deal with either base-2 or base-16 – but it gives a good introduction to the idea that computers don't have ten fingers and hence don't agree with our completely arbitrary decision to think about numbers as having exactly 10 numerals.

☐ Decimal to Octal Practice

For practice, convert the following from decimal to octal representation. Example: 31 becomes 0o37.
13   6   25   8   45   10   -9   64   255

☐ Octal to Decimal Practice

For practice, convert the following from octal to decimal. Example: 0o47 becomes 39.
0o610   0o5   0o26   0o47   0o302   0o0   -0o12   0o76   0o101

☐ Decimal to Octal String

Create a function `dec2OctStr(value)` that converts a number into a string representing that number in octal notation. For this challenge, do not use the (very convenient) `toString` function.

☐ Octal String to Value

Create a function `octStr2Val(str)` that accepts a string representing an integer in octal notation, and returns the value. For this challenge, do not use the (very convenient) `parseInt` function.

Chapter 18 – Bit Arithmetic

Octal represents groups of three bits, and since three is an odd number, it isn't the very best way to represent how a computer natively thinks about numbers. It is much more common for us to represent numbers in groups of four bits (hexadecimal) or simply one bit at a time (binary).

Hexadecimal System

For a second, imagine that each of us have had eight fingers on each hand, since birth. As a result, when we created our numeral system, we created more than just 0-9 numerals. Instead, we created enough numerals to represent every quantity that was "less than two hands" worth. In our hypothetical world, that means there are extra numerals after 9 that represent *in a single character* the amounts up to "two hands worth". That system is hexadecimal (16-based), and hexadecimal numbers are prefixed by `0x` ("zero-X"), just as octal numbers are prefixed by `0o` ("zero-Oh"). The extra numerals `0xA`, `0xB`, `0xC`, `0xD`, `0xE`, `0xF` are equivalent to 10, 11, 12, 13, 14, 15. Each additional digit in hexadecimal is a multiplication by 16, so the number `0x10` is equivalent to 16. The number `0x2A` is equivalent to 42.

☐ Decimal to Hexadecimal

For practice, convert the following from decimal to hexadecimal. Example: 31 becomes `0x1F`.
13   6   25   8   45   10   -9   64   255   238

☐ Hexadecimal to Decimal

For practice, convert the following from hexadecimal to decimal. Example: `0x47` becomes 71.
0xDB   0x5   0x20C   0x4F   0xB2   0x0   -0x12   0x7E   0x101

☐ Decimal to Hexadecimal String

Create a function `dec2HexStr(value)` that converts a number into a string representing that number in hexadecimal notation. For this challenge, do not use the (very convenient) `toString` function. For example, given the value `108`, the function should return `"0x6C"`.

☐ Hexadecimal String to Value

Create a function `hexStr2Val(str)` that accepts a string representing an int in hexadecimal notation, and returns the value. For this challenge, do not use the (very convenient) `parseInt` function. For example, given the string `"0x1D2"`, the function should return `466`.

Chapter 18 – Bit Arithmetic

There are 10 kinds of people in this world. Those that understand binary, and those that don't.

Binary System

If "hex" numbers make sense to you, then good job – you are starting to think like a computer. If you *really* want to get geeky, you'll need to understand binary as well. In binary, each additional digit is an additional power of 2, so a number like 0b1111111 = $(1 \times 2^7) + (1 \times 2^6) + (1 \times 2^5) + (1 \times 2^4) + (1 \times 2^3) + (1 \times 2^2) + (1 \times 2^1) + (1 \times 2^0)$ = 255, or 0xFF. Each four bits of binary translate into a single hex digit, so translation should be fast. 0x3 = 0b0011, 0x8 = 0b1000, 0xB = 0b1011, 0xE = 0x1110.

☐ Decimal to Binary

For practice, convert the following from decimal to binary. Example: 117 becomes 0b1110101.
13   6   25   8   45   10   -9   64   255   128   35   0   198

☐ Binary to Decimal

For practice, convert the following from binary to decimal. Example: 0b100111 becomes 39.
0b10100101   0b111   0b1111000   0b110110   0b000   0b11
  -0b1010   0b100110   0b1010101010   0b111001   0b100101

☐ Decimal to Binary String

Create a function `dec2BinStr(value)` that converts a number into a string representing that number in binary notation. For this challenge, do not use the (very convenient) `toString` function. For example, given the value 35, the function should return `"0b100011"`.

☐ Binary String to Value

Create a function `binStr2Val(str)` that accepts a string representing an int in binary notation, and returns the value. For this challenge, do not use the (very convenient) `parseInt` function. For example, given the string `"0b1010101"`, the function should return 85.

Ready for a bit of a break from bits? Here is a completely unrelated (*difficult!*) challenge, if you wish:

☐ Reorder Word Fragments

You are given an array of equal-length strings containing lowercase alphabetical characters or '?'. Reorder the words so that from word to word, each letter is in alphabetical order (first letters are in order, second letters are in order, etc). The '?' can represent any letter needed to satisfy this. Return the array in this order, with ? converted into the alphabetically earliest possible letter. Return `null` if the ordering is impossible. Given `["XD?E","BDE?","?A?E"]`, return `["AAAE","BDEE","XDEE"]`. For `["BQX?","XD?E"]`, return NULL because first letters require a different order than second letters allow.

Second: Ensure you minimize every word. For `["S?","?Q"]`, return `["AQ","SQ"]` not `["SA","SQ"]`.

Chapter 18 – Bit Arithmetic

Bitwise Operators, Part 1

Most math operators don't know or care about a number system. Addition is addition, whether "10 + 11 = 21" or "0b1010 + 0b1011 = 0b10101". Ditto subtraction, multiplication, division, negation, comparison and equality. Other operators make sense only if we think of numbers in binary representation. To best understand these *bitwise operators*, we must first consider three logical operators (AND, OR, NOT). These operators work on Boolean values, which are essentially one-bit values (true = 1, false = 0).

- **&&** (logical AND) operates on two booleans. It returns `true` only if both are `true`, else `false`.
- **||** (logical OR) operates on two booleans, returning `true` if either is `true`, otherwise `false`.
- **!** (logical NOT) operates on a single boolean value, inverting `true` to `false` and vice versa.

Bitwise operators are equivalent to logical operators, except they work one-bit-at-a-time across entire numbers. Some bitwise operators accept two numbers, and others work on a single number.

- The **bitwise AND** operator is **&**. It operates on two numbers and compares them, one bit at a time (their least-significant bits, their second-least-significant bits, etc). If both bits are 1, then that same bit in the result is set to 1, otherwise that bit is set to 0. It does this for every bit in the two operands. Example: `0b10101010 & 0b01100110 = 0b00100010`.
- The **bitwise OR** operator is **|**. It operates on two numbers and compares them, one bit at a time (least-significant bits, second-least-significant bits, etc). If either are 1, then that bit in the result is set to 1, otherwise it is set to 0. It does this for every bit in the two operands. Example: `0b10101010 | 0b01100110 = 11101110`.
- The **bitwise NOT** operator is **~**. It operates on one number, examining one bit at a time in isolation. Each bit in the original is inverted in the result. Each 1 becomes 0; each 0 becomes 1. Example: `~0b10101010 = 0b01010101`.

Note: JavaScript stores numbers as 64-bit (floating-point) values, but its bitwise operators operate on 32-bit integers. So, before any bitwise operation begins, values are converted to 32-bit integer format.

For the expressions below, indicate the results in binary, hexadecimal and decimal notations:

☐ Bitwise AND

`0b010101 & 0b0110111`   `57 & 87`   `0b01101001 & 0b00011000`   `0xBABE & 0xBEEF`

☐ Bitwise OR

`0b010101 | 0b0110111`   `57 | 87`   `0b01101001 | 0b00011000`   `0xBABE | 0xBEEF`

☐ Bitwise NOT

`~0b010101`   `~0b0110111`   `~5787`   `~0b01101001`   `~0b00011000`   `~0xBABE` `~0xBEEF`

Chapter 18 – Bit Arthmetic

Bitwise Operators, Part 2

After **&** (bitwise AND), **|** (bitwise OR), and **~** (bitwise NOT), here are other important bitwise operators.
- The **bitwise XOR** (exclusive or) operator is **^**. It operates on two numbers and compares them, one bit at a time. If the bits are different than each other, then that bit in the result is set to 1, otherwise it is set to 0. It does this for each bit in the two operands. Example: `0b10101010 ^ 0b01100110 = 0b11001100`.
- The **bitwise LSL** (shift left) operator is **<<**. It operates on two numbers and shifts the bits in the first number to the left; the second number indicates the number of places by which to shift the number. Numbers are treated as 32-bit integers; with each shift the most-significant bit (bit 31) is lost, and a value of 0 shifts into the least-significant binary digit (bit 0). Example: `0b1111011100000000111000011001010 << 3 = 0b1011100000000111000011001010000`.
- The **bitwise LSR** (logical shift right) operator is **>>>** (yes, three > symbols not two). It operates on two numbers, shifting the first number to the right by the number of bits indicated by the second number. Numbers are treated as 32-bit ints; with each shift the number loses its least-significant bit (bit 0), and 0 shifts into the most-significant binary digit (bit 31). Example: `0b11111000011100001101010 >>> 3 = 0b00011111100001110000011001`.
Important Note: JavaScript's **ASR** (arithmetic shift right) operator **>>** is identical to **>>>** in every way *except* that when shifting right, the most-significant binary digit (bit 31) is used to fill in the new leftmost digits, instead of a zero being used. For our purposes, >>> is much more useful than >>. Example: `0b11111000011100001101010 >> 3 = 0b11111111100001110000011001`.

For the operations below, indicate the results in binary, hexadecimal and decimal notations:

☐ Bitwise XOR

```
0b010101 ^ 0b0110111        57 ^ 87         0b01101001 ^ 0b00011000
     0x0BADCACA ^ 0xD00DAD      0xCAFED00D ^ 0xDECAF      123 ^ 124
```

☐ Bitwise LSL

```
0b010101 << 7               57 << 8         0b01101001 << 0b00000111
     0xF00D << 0xA     0x000BABEE << 0b1      42 << 0xA
```

☐ Bitwise LSR

```
0b0101010101 >>> 7          157 >>> 3       0b10110100101010011 >>> 15
       0b00011000 >>> 2     0xDEADBEEF >>> 0xA    0xCAFEBABE >>> 0b11
```

☐ Count in Binary

Given integer representing the number of bits, recursively print strings that count, in binary representation, from 0 up to the max number representable by that number of bits.

Chapter 18 – Bit Arthmetic

Bit Shifting and Masking

To save space, you can encode numbers into large containers, by shifting values into different sections of the container. Example: left-shift `0x1CED` by sixteen (`<< 16`) to `0x1CED0000`, leaving space for another 16-bit num. Combine these using `|`, like so: `(0x1CED << 16) | 0xF00D == 0x1CEDF00D`.

Sometimes bits in a number represent 32 independent ON/OFF states (such as the Yes/No votes of 32 people, or the current settings of 32 light switches in your house). This can be much more convenient than storing each of the 32 values individually, as long as we can manipulate each bit separately.

Thinking about our bitwise operators, every bit can be set by using a combination of `|` and `<<`. To set bits 17 and 18 but keep the rest of the variable untouched, we could `val |= (0x3 << 17)`. Those bits might have previously been 0 or 1, but now they are 1 (because any value **OR 1** becomes 1).

On the flip side, we may want to clear a certain bit. In that case, we take advantage of the fact that any value **AND 0** becomes 0. If we don't want to affect the rest of the variable when we clear that bit, then we must **AND** it with a very specific *bit mask*. This bit mask should have a value of all-ones, except for the one bit we want cleared. The `~` operator flips every bit value, making bit masks easy to create. To clear bit 12, but keep the rest of the variable untouched, we could `val &= ~(1 << 12)`. The `(1 << 12)` creates a *positive mask* so to speak, and the `~` turns it into a negative mask. Our variable might previously have had a 0 or a 1 at bit 12, but now it is 0.

Using what we've learned earlier, solve these bit-related challenges today:

☐ Count Set Bits

Given integer, return how many bits are set to 1. For an input of `1023` (`0x3FF`), return `10`. Given the value `8192` (`0x2000`), return `1`.
Second: can you make it `O(s)`, where `s` is the number of *set* bits?

☐ Reverse Bits

Given a 32-bit unsigned integer, reverse its bits and return this value. If you are given the value `0b01100110011001101111000011110000`, then your function should return the value `0b00001111000011110110011001100110`.

☐ Encode Bytes to 32

Given four values between 0-255, encode them into a 32-bit integer. First should map to most significant 8 bits. Given `[0xF0, 0xC3, 0x96, 0x59]`, return `4039349849` (`0xF0C39659`).

☐ Decode 32 to Bytes

Given 32-bit integer, return a set of values for the four bytes in the integer. Given `306542763` (which in hex is `0x124578AB`), return `[0x12, 0x45, 0x78, 0xAB]`.

☐ Byte Array

With encode/decode you've written above, create a `ByteArray` data structure to store 8-bit values encoded into 32-bit ints to save space. Build `set(index, value)` and `get(index)`.

Chapter 18 – Bit Arthmetic

☐ Encode Bit Num

Given bit val, bit number, and 32-bit val, mask bit into 32-bit val and return new val. For `(1,22,1)` return `0x400001`; for `(0,3,0x18)` return `0x10`.

☐ Decode Bit Num

Given bit number and 32-bit value, return val of referenced bit number. For `(30,0x4FFFFFFF)`, return 1. For `(3,0x4FFFFFF7)`, return 0.

☐ Bit Array

With encode/decode functions you've written above, create a `BitArray` class that stores 1-bit values encoded into 32-bit integers. Include methods `set(index,val)` and `get(index)`.

☐ Radix Sort2

Implement RadixSort, based on powers of two instead of digit numerals 0-9. Sort by lowest significant bit, then next least significant bit, etc. What is the big-O runtime to sort 32-bit integers?

☐ Sprinklers

The Rockefeller country estate is watered by a 28-head sprinkler system. Create a function to return a 28-bit number; a landscape microcontroller calls the function each minute to determine which heads to enable. Only one sprinkler can run at a time; each runs 20 minutes a day. Four global variables alter system behavior, in increasing priority: `RAIN_SENS` is a precipitation meter – if true, disable all heads. `SENS_OVERRIDE`, if true, disables the precipitation meter. While `SYS_TEST` is true, cycle through all 28 sprinklers for 1 minute each. Finally, if `SYS_DISABLE` is true, turn off all sprinklers.

☐ LED Encoding

Classic LEDs have seven segments that are individually turned on or off to produce the desired letter or numeral, arranged as in diagram at right. Each segment's on/off state will be determined by a different bit in a container byte (bits numbered at right). Value `0x7B` signifies that segments `[0,1,3,4,5,6]` would be enabled, which would display numeral '6'. Build function `LED2Numeral(ledByte)` that accepts a byte representing the states of LED segments in one base-10 numeral, returning the numerical value of that base-10 numeral (i.e. 0-9). Given the input 36 (`0x24`, segments 2 & 5), return 1.

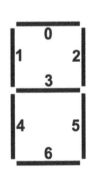

Second: create function `Int2LED(value)` that accepts a 16-bit integer value and translates it into the values needed to produce the corresponding LED readout in base-10. The function should return an array of five bytes: each byte representing one of the numerals from *least-significant* to *most-significant*. Using our examples above, `LEDBytes(85210) == [0,36,93,107,127]`.

☐ Where's the Bug? (bitwise operators version)

```
// How many bugs can you find?
function numSetBits(num) {    // count num of set bits in a 64-bit val
   while (num) { bitCount = bitCount + num && 0x1; num = num >> 1; }
   return bitCount;
}
```

Chapter 19 – Trees, Part III

AVL Trees

Remember that a binary search tree's performance is linked to how balanced it is. If a tree is unbalanced and deep, then there is a chance that the value we seek is down in the depths of the tree, far beyond the average expected height. But what if our BST could somehow keep itself balanced? How would it do this, and how expensive would it be? Soviet mathematicians Georgy Adelson-Velsky and Evgenii Landis responded to this problem by inventing the first self-balancing tree: named after their surname initials, we call it the **AVL tree**.

The rules of an AVL tree are simple: for every node, the heights of its two child subtrees must differ by at most one. If an insertion or removal changes the tree so that this rule is no longer valid (in other words, an insertion or removal makes the tree *unbalanced*), the tree must 'rotate' its shape to become balanced again. To optimize the AVL tree for the fact that it will constantly check its balance at various locations, each node contains (and maintains) a *balance factor* (1 if its left subtree is one node deeper than its right subtree, -2 if the right subtree is deeper by two, 0 if both sides are even, etc). For today, let's just measure and detect these situations; tomorrow we will address them.

```
function AVLTree() {
   var head = null;

   this.add = function(value) {}
   this.remove = function(value){}
   // Assume these exist and
   // correctly update node.balance

   this.height = function() {
      // ...write this code today
   }
   this.isBalanced = function(){
      // ...write this code today
   }
}

function AVLNode(value) {
   this.val = value;

   this.balance = 0;
   this.left = null;
   this.right = null;

   this.height = function() {
      // ...write this code today
   }
   this.isBalanced = function() {
      // ...write this code today
   }
}
```

☐ AVL: Height

Create `height()` methods for both the `AVLTree` and `AVLNode` classes.

☐ AVL: Is Balanced

Given an AVL tree whose nodes have up-to-date `.balance` values, create the `isBalanced()` methods for both `AVLTree` & `AVLNode`.

Chapter 19 – Trees, Part III

AVL trees are a type of *self-balancing tree* (we touch on other variants later). The motivation for staying balanced is efficiency: unbalanced trees do not add/remove/find as quickly. However, keeping balanced might be expensive; if we aren't careful, the costs eclipse the benefits. How can we minimize costs?

1. Minimize the cost of checking a tree's cost. This implies that we:
    a. Store a value in each node, rather than recomputing height/balance each time;
    b. Store *balance*, not height, to avoid checking children when testing for balance;
    c. Check the tree's balance only at appropriate times;
    d. Check the tree's balance only at necessary tree locations.
2. Minimize the cost of maintaining the tree's balance indices, implying that we:
    a. Only update the balance indices when we add/remove values (or rebalance);
    b. Update balance indices for *only nodes affected* by the add/remove, so that we minimize the number of nodes whose balance need rechecking (see 1c).
3. Minimize the cost of rebalancing the tree, when this is needed. This implies that we:
    a. Minimize the number of nodes changed during a rebalance, so that in turn we
    b. Need to update *balance* for only a small number of nodes (see 2b), in order to minimize the number of nodes whose balance needs rechecking (see 1c).

What does 1b mean? `AVLNode.isBalanced()` is inexpensive if we maintain `.balance` – it's a quick attribute check. If instead we store `.height`, `isBalanced()` requires checking and comparing heights of both children. This makes *updating* balance more tricky but contributes to a successful item 1 in our list. Method `height()` is less critical, but `.balance` tells us which way to branch as we dive to the deepest leaf. It isn't $O(1)$, but it is $O(N \log N)$, which is good enough.

Let's explore 2a and 2b. Remember those methods that yesterday we glossed over, *assuming* they already existed? We will create them today. Write `add(value)` and `remove(value)` methods for the `AVLTree` class. When you do so, remember to keep the `.balance` attribute up-to-date for each node.

```
function AVLTree() {
    var head = null;
    // assume isBalanced() works fine
    this.isBalanced = function() {}

    // ...write these today
    this.add = function(value) {}
    this.remove = function(value) {}
}
```

```
function AVLNode(value) {
    this.val = value;
    this.balance = 0;
    this.left = null;
    this.right = null;

    // assume isBalanced() works fine
    this.isBalanced = function() {}
}
```

☐ AVL: Remove

Create `remove(value)` for the `AVLTree` class. Update `.balance` for any affected nodes, but don't worry about rebalancing the tree.

☐ AVL: Add

Create `add(value)` for the `AVLTree` class. Update `.balance` for any affected nodes, but don't worry about rebalancing the tree.

Chapter 19 – Trees, Part III

Let's review the challenges we face, if we want an AVL tree to have high performance:

1. Minimize the cost of <u>checking</u> a tree's cost. This implies that we:
   a. Store a value in each node, rather than recomputing height/balance each time;
   b. Store *balance,* not height, to avoid checking children when testing for balance;
   c. Check the tree's balance only at appropriate times;
   d. Check the tree's balance only at necessary tree locations.
2. Minimize the cost of <u>maintaining</u> the tree's balance indices, implying that we:
   a. Only update the balance indices when we add/remove values (or rebalance);
   b. Update balance indices for *only nodes affected* by the add/remove, so that we minimize the number of nodes whose balance need rechecking (see 1c).
3. Minimize the cost of <u>rebalancing</u> the tree, when this is needed. This implies that we:
   a. Minimize the number of nodes changed during a rebalance, so that in turn we
   b. Need to update *balance* for only a small number of nodes (see 2b), in order to minimize the number of nodes whose balance needs rechecking (see 1c).

For 2a and 2b, as you discovered yesterday, we minimize the cost of updating balance indices by only updating the balance of nodes being inserted/removed and their ancestors upward (*not* the entire tree). When an ancestor node's balance is unaffected, we need not continue checking upward.

What about our other major implication: rebalancing? We handle this with an operation called *rotation*.

Rotation

The benefit of AVL trees over other BSTs is that AVL trees automatically keep themselves relatively balanced. When an AVL tree discovers an imbalance (if any node's left subtree height and right subtree height differ by more than one), it fixes that condition by *rotating* that node.

Think of rotation as a clockwise (Rotate Right) or counter-clockwise (Rotate Left) shift of both the node in question as well as its "tall" child node. Child is promoted above parent, reducing overall tree height.

Consider a large BST where in the midst of the tree, node A has a `.right` child: node B. Following an insertion somewhere below B, node A's right subtree height is now two greater than its left subtree height. We should *Rotate-Left* node A. This will change the height for A and B, but how are all the other nodes affected? It would be expensive to move lots of nodes around whenever we do a rotation.

Fortunately, this isn't the case. Think about where the rest of the nodes in the tree *end up*, when we do a rotation. To start with, nodes above this rotation do not move, nor do those in other parts of the tree. As a result, we only need to worry about A's and B's children. Those children have values that are either
   a) less than A's (conveniently located under `A.left`), or
   b) greater than/equal to B's (conveniently located under `B.right`), or
   c) between A and B (*currently* conveniently located under `B.left`).

Chapter 19 – Trees, Part III

When we `rotateLeft` node A, it becomes the `.left` of node B. Let's put their groups of children in place. Child nodes less than A (the entire `A.left` subtree) should stay where they are. Nodes greater than B (the `B.right` subtree) should also stay put. However, nodes *in between* might pose a problem. They can't stay where they are (under `B.left`), because that's where A has moved. What to do?

Let's reason through this. Nodes in question have values less than B, so they go to B's *left* somewhere. They have values greater than A, so they go to A's *right* somewhere. After promoting B, `A.right` is available! Subtree previously located at `B.left` can move to `A.right`. *Voila!* Rotate-Left is complete.

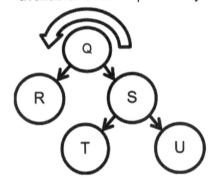

Calling `rotateLeft(Q)` on first tree converts it to the second one. Cool! In most (not all) cases, one rotation corrects an imbalance. Drawing diagrams, you may discover *corner cases* where rotation does not succeed.

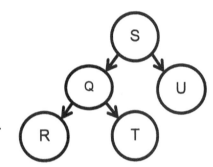

Revisiting the first tree: what if a tall `T` subtree causes our imbalance? After `rotateLeft`, `T` shifts from `S.left` to `Q.right` but does not move toward root; imbalance remains. Our objective was to pull a 'tall grandchild' toward root.

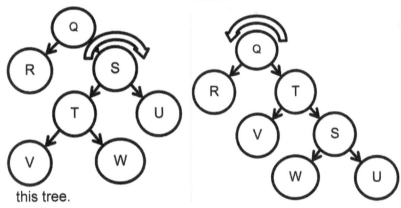

Note the next graph. If `.left` of a tall right child causes imbalance, we can't just `rotateLeft(Q)`. We must `rotateRight(S)` to transform it into

this tree.

Then, `rotateLeft(Q)` transforms middle tree into (shallower) final tree.

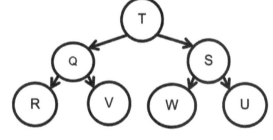

☐ AVL: Rotate Left

Create `rotateLeft(node)` method in the `AVLTree` class. First counter-rotate the child if needed, and as always update `.balance` attributes appropriately and inexpensively.

☐ AVL: Rotate Right

Create a `rotateRight(node)` method for `AVLTree`. Counter-rotate the 'tall child' first, if needed, and keep all `.balance` attributes appropriately and inexpensively up-to-date.

Chapter 19 – Trees, Part III

Let's review how nodes move, on our previous Right-Left Rotation. If `.left` of a tall right child causes imbalance (specifically T), then before we `RotateLeft(Q)` we `RotateRight(S)`, transforming first tree into second tree. Then, `RotateLeft(Q)` transforms second tree into (shallower) third tree.

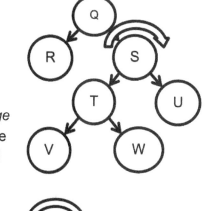

*Note: in this example, the heights of **child** nodes (R, V, W, U) don't change during the rotation process*; the heights of all nodes in those subtrees are unaffected, all the way down to the leaves. Heightwise, the only affected nodes are red, black, and green – as well as their parent chain. For this reason, when fixing heights after a rotation we must follow any change upward to the parent, in case that parent's height changed as well. In what scenario should we *not* continue to notify upward? Specifically, if after *adding* some value we see a node's `.balance` change (say, from 1) *to 0*, then that node's height did not change, and hence its parent chain is unaffected. Similarly, if after *removing* some value we see a node's `.balance` change from 0 to some other value, then that node's height did not change (try drawing a few on paper!). If a node's height didn't change, there's no need to check its parent nodes. This significantly optimizes our Update Balance Indices process.

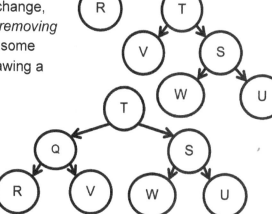

Now that we can 1) add and remove while updating `.balance`, as well as 2) rotate to bring trees back into balance, we are equipped to create the most powerful `AVLTree` methods: *balanced add / remove*.

☐ AVL: Balanced Add

Using all you learned this chapter, create a `balancedAdd(value)` method for `AVLTree` class. Ensure that by the time it returns, our value is added, the tree is balanced, and all node attributes are updated and accurate.

☐ AVL: Balanced Remove

Build `balancedRemove(value)` for our `AVLTree` class. Ensure that when method returns (`true` if removed, `false` if not found), the value is removed, tree is balanced, and all node attributes are updated and accurate.

☐ AVL: Rebalance

Similar to `repair()` on regular `BST`s, create `rebalance()` for `AVLTree`s. Just as `repair()` is not really needed (since we expect `BST`s to insert and delete nodes correctly and never become invalid), similarly we could argue that `rebalance()` is unneeded since an `AVLTree` will continually keep itself balanced. Nonetheless, quickly build this, using other methods you've already created.

Chapter 19 – Trees, Part III

There are other types of self-balancing tree as well. One example is the Red-Black Tree.

Red-Black Trees

A Red-Black Tree is based on our normal Binary Search Tree, plus these rules:
1. A boolean within each node designates it as currently *red* or *black*.
2. The root node is black.
3. The `null` underneath each leaf node is considered black.
4. If a node is red, then both its children must be black.
5. Every path from node to descendent `null` contains the same number of black nodes. The uniform number of black nodes in paths from root to leaves is the tree's **black-height**.

As with the `AVLTree`, search methods in an `RBTree` (such as `contains`) are identical to those of a `BST`. The `add` and `remove` properties, however, are more interesting. To add a value to an `RBTree`, we create an `RBNode` (these default to Red) and insert it at the appropriate place in the tree. If the Red-Black rules are not violated, we are done. Otherwise, we either "repaint" certain nodes or we rebalance (and then repaint) certain nodes as necessary.

☐ RBTree and RBNode Class Definitions

Create the simplest possible class definitions of `RBTree` and `RBNode`.

☐ Red-Black Tree: Contains

Create a `contains(value)` method for `RBTree`. Is this function interesting?

☐ Red-Black Tree: Add

Create the `add(val)` method on the `RBTree` class. As needed, repaint and/or rebalance; this is a self-balancing method.

☐ Red-Black Tree: Remove

Create the `RBTree`'s `remove(val)` method. As needed, repaint and/or rebalance nodes; this is a self-balancing method.

☐ Short-Answer Questions on AVL and Red-Black Trees

- Self-balancing seems like a lot of work. When are costs *justified*? When are they *not justified*?
- Between AVL trees and Red-Black trees, which incurs more rebalancing cost?
- How would shapes of AVL trees and Red-Black trees generally differ (if at all)?
- What are the performance differences between these trees?
- When would you choose AVL tree over Red-Black, and vice-versa?
- Between AVL, Red-Black and binary search trees, which `height()` implementation would generally be fastest, given a large diverse data set? What is its big-O for runtime?

Chapter 19 – Trees, Part III

Another type of self-optimizing tree does not automatically *balance* itself. Instead, it *optimizes* for how it is being used. This data structure, the **Splay Tree**, is flexible and adaptable to many scenarios.

Splay Trees

Splay Trees, like the AVL and Red-Black Trees, are based on generic Binary Search Trees, plus additional rules. Here are the additional rules that enable the Splay Tree to optimize itself:
1. When a value is added, the new node becomes the root of the tree;
2. On a search, the last node accessed (whether the *found* node or not!) becomes the root;
3. When a value is deleted, the *parent* of the removed node moves to become the root.
4. To promote nodes to root position, the tree uses a rotation operation called a Splay.

When a node is Splayed, we effectively perform a series of tree rotations until the node is moved to the root position. If the node is currently the left child of a left child, or if the node is currently the right child of a right child, then the 'grandparent' node is rotated twice. Otherwise the 'parent' node is rotated once, and then the 'grandparent' node once. This two-rotation cycle repeats as necessary. One last single rotation might be needed to move the node into the root position.

☐ Splay Tree Class Definitions

Create the simplest possible `SplayTree` class definition. Do you need a `SplayNode`?

☐ Splay Tree: Add

Create the `add(value)` method on the `SplayTree` class, splaying the new node.

☐ Splay Tree: Contains

Create a `contains(value)` method for `SplayTree`, splaying as needed.

☐ Splay Tree: Remove

Create a `remove(value)` method for `SplayTree`, splaying as needed.

☐ Short-Answer Questions on Splay and Self-Balancing Trees

- How would shapes of Splay, AVL, Red-Black and BST trees generally differ (if at all)?
- What are the performance differences between Splay trees and BSTs?
- When would you choose Splay trees over AVL or Red-Black?
- Compare the likely performance of `height()` across Splay, Red-Black and BST.
- For the most recently accessed item in a Splay Tree, what is the big-O to remove it?

Chapter 19 – Trees, Part III

☐ Black Belt Exam

Today is an advanced belt exam in Algorithms, leading to the extremely rare, very-much-coveted Black Belt in advanced Algorithms & Data Structures.

Good luck! Remember our superb suggestions, great guidance, tremendous tips and prescient pearls of wonderful wisdom!

Chapter 20 – Spatial, Logic, Estimation

Many challenges in this section are drawn from technical interviews at various companies. Note that a significant number of them don't actually require coding. Stay sharp!

Spatial Problems

These problems test mathematical thinking without overtly requiring more advanced algorithms or data structures. Remember your basic geometry for surface area, circumference, and symmetry!

☐ Minding the Gap

Given two points on a two-dimensional plane, return the distance between them.
Second: what if the points are in 3-D space?

☐ Sketching the Circle

Draw a circle on screen, given screen dimensions, circle's center and radius, all in pixels. You can call `setPixel(x,y)` to draw a single point.
Second: Once you've calculated the first 1/8 of the circle, can you quickly draw the rest?

☐ Describing the Rectangle (or, 'Get Rect')

How would you best represent a two-dimensional rectangle, if you were passing one as a parameter?

☐ Detecting the Overlap

Write a function to determine whether two rectangles overlap. Design an elegant function interface.

☐ Checking the Connectedness Count

You are given an array containing a number of rectangles. Determine whether each rect intersects with at least one other.
Second: Determine whether all rectangles interconnect into one interconnected section. If rect A connects to rects B and C, plus rects B and D connect, then ABCD are interconnected. If AB are separate from CD, then ABCD do *not* interconnect: they create 2 (not 1) sections.

☐ Admiring the Skyline

You are given array of building objects; your job is to calculate the skyline. Buildings consist of `[start,height,width]`; a skyline is an array of `[start,height]` elements. Given the array `[[2,3,4],[5,1,7]]`, return `[[0,0],[2,3],[6,1],[12,0]]`.

☐ Calling the Big One

You are given an array, containing non-negative integers that correspond to a height (on the Y-axis) for that index (on the X-axis). In essence, this array of integers represents the same type of skyline shape that you worked with in the previous challenge. Return the size of the largest rectangle that can be drawn within that shape. Note that the lines outlining the shape of the input are all vertical and horizontal; there are no diagonals.

Chapter 20 – Spatial Problems, Logic Puzzles, Estimation

Logic (Thought) Problems

Logic, or thought, puzzles don't fit cleanly into previous chapters, because they are not *coding* problems. However, they have been asked in technical interviews to assess reasoning ability, so we pose them to you here. With each, just as with estimation challenges, consider the information and assets you have and make the best use of them. Many companies are moving away from brainteaser puzzles, so don't worry if these questions are 'not your thing'. Just have fun with them!

A common class of thought problems involves identical objects whose weights vary slightly. Unless stated, assume "scales of justice" that compare two quantities (rather than a scale with a readout).

☐ Finding the Fraud

Given 64 apparently identical coins, one of which is heavy, how many weighings do you need (in the *worst-case*), to determine the bad coin? How low can you get the *average* number of weighings?
Second: what if it is possible that there is NO bad coin? Does that change your calculus?

☐ Revealing the Wrong

Given twelve apparently identical coins, one of which is *either light or heavy*, how many weighings do you in order to identify the bad coin – as well as whether it is light or heavy?
Second: what if it is possible that there is NO bad coin? Does that change your calculus?
Third: extrapolating, what is the maximum number of coins you can handle with five weighings?

☐ Querying the Quarters

You have a *digital* scale that gives very precise readouts; it can handle up to 90 grams. Six vendors have each given you large stacks of apparently identical quarters. One vendor is dishonest: evidently his entire coin stack is counterfeit. Each counterfeit quarter weighs 6 grams instead of the usual 5.67g. *If you know* that one pile consists of heavy quarters, determine *which* one, in only a single weighing.

☐ Lighting the Way

Three light switches are located outside a room, where we cannot see which lamps they control. Andy figured a way to set the switches to determine the mapping after a single trip into the room. Can you?

☐ Making the Train

A family of four must cross a bridge to reach a midnight train on the other side. The rickety bridge only holds two; they can only cross with their one flashlight. The youngest can cross in 1 minute; the next can cross in 2; the parent in 6; the grandparent needs 12. Can they make their train in 20 minutes?

☐ Escaping the Hunt

Fiona Fox wants Dunn the Duck for lunch. Now Dunn is in the center of a circular pond. Fiona cannot enter the water; she must run around it. To fly away and escape, Dunn must reach the edge before Fiona reaches him. Fiona runs four times as fast as Dunn swims. Is Dunn *done*, or can he escape?

Chapter 20 – Spatial Problems, Logic Puzzles, Estimation

☐ Surviving the Train

While hiking, Minh and Crazy Brian find a narrow train tunnel running north-south. At Crazy Brian's urging, they go in. At exactly 2/3 through this tunnel (closer to the north end than the south end), they hear a train nearing! Crazy Brian runs *toward* the train, *just* exiting the tunnel as it enters. Minh runs the other way, also barely escaping the tunnel as the train passes. Both Minh and Crazy Brian ran 10mph. How fast was the train? Also, did the train enter at the north end or the south end of this tunnel?

☐ Racing the Balls

Two identical-length tracks are each wide enough for a rolling marble. Starting at the same moment, marbles accelerate downward, diverge (one upward, one downward), reconverge at a point lower than where they diverged, and continue onward, both finishing. Do the marbles finish at the same time?

☐ Crossing the River

Traveling with a fox, a hen and a sack of corn, you reach a river with rowboat. The boat can only fit you and one other. If left alone, hen eats corn; likewise fox eats hen. Can you get everything across? How?

☐ Burning the String

You have two pieces of string, and evidently both will take precisely 60.0 seconds to burn – although they burn at unpredictable rates during that time. Can you use these to measure 45.0 seconds exactly?

☐ Outfoxing the Fox

Fiona Fox is hungry again. She has trapped Reggie Rabbit inside a circular pen. Reggie can run exactly as fast as Fiona. Can Fiona catch Reggie? What is Reggie's best strategy to survive?

☐ Swapping the Lockers

You are at a high school with lockers numbered 1-100. First open them all. Then, for all locker numbers divisible by <u>two</u>, toggle the locker door (if open, close it; if closed, open it). Then, toggle all that are divisible by <u>three</u>. Then, toggle those divisible by <u>four</u>.... Repeat this process for successive integers until, finally, you toggle the one and only locker (#100) that is divisible by <u>one hundred</u>. How many lockers are open at this point? Which ones? Why?

☐ Combining the Numbers

You are given five numbers. Using any combination of the four common arithmetic operators (+ - * /), but keeping these numbers in the order they were given, combine the first four to make a total of the fifth. For example, given `(3, 10, 2, 40, 100)`, one solution is `(3*10*2)+40`, which equals `100`.

Chapter 20 – Spatial Problems, Logic Puzzles, Estimation

Can you accurately answer the next 3 questions in a total of 15 seconds or less?[1]

☐ Pricing the Movie

A movie plus popcorn costs $11. Movie costs $10 more than popcorn. How much does popcorn cost?

☐ Building the Widgets

If 5 machines build 5 widgets in 5 hours, how long will 100 machines take to build 100 widgets?

☐ Padding the Pond

A large pond has a patch of lily pads in the center. Each day the patch doubles in size. The entire pond is covered in 48 days. How many days does it take to cover half the pond?

The following is a system design problem, not a logic puzzle. However, it still requires logical analysis. As with most design problems, there's no lack of input information – but which are actually important?

☐ Elevating the Passengers

Design the operating software for an elevator system that serves a 20-story office building. Each of the four elevators contain buttons for floors 1-20, for passengers to press when they enter the elevator, indicating where they want to travel. The north elevator receives more sunlight than the other elevators. Near the elevator doors on each floor there are Up and Down buttons to call an elevator going that direction. The lobby at floor 1 has a marble floor. Elevators can handle 1000 kilograms of weight, and 100 persons work on each floor. The busiest times for elevator travel are between 7:30am and 8:15am, and between 4:30pm and 6:30pm. Office workers are, for the most part, patient – except for old man Surrey who always complains about 'slow creaky elevators'. The building owner, Bo, has a Spaniel named 'Spike', and this dog weighs exactly 10.0 pounds. The doors to the elevators remain open for 10 seconds at a time, and the elevator cars take an average of 1 second/floor to ascend and descend. Spike likes the south elevator, which has transparent glass walls. Bo thinks Spike is just about perfect[2].

What data structures might you use to manage this elevator system?
More importantly, can you produce a state diagram representing the logic that governs the elevators?

---

[1] When using these exact questions, the <u>faster</u> you answer, the <u>less likely</u> you will answer all correctly. Changing the wording to make the questions slightly *more* confusing actually *increased* the number of people that got all three correct, by slightly slowing readers down. So be careful not to work *too* fast!

[2] Spike may or may not *actually* be just about perfect.

Chapter 20 – Spatial Problems, Logic Puzzles, Estimation

Estimation

Estimation problems assess your ability to break problems into smaller pieces to be solved separately. In some cases they measure judgment. Don't get hung up on a precise answer. Remember: each part of your answer is only accurate to an order of magnitude. Use numbers that make mental math easier. Here's a general process for estimation problems. Break the problem into pieces that you can estimate more accurately, then chain them together. Often the trick is the mental math to get the units right.

Example question: *"How tall would a stack of credit cards with every possible credit card number be?"* Example answer: "Well, 16 digits makes 10^{16} different numbers. I'm told that one digit is a checksum ☺, so that makes 10^{15} possibilities." (If the questioner says ignore the checksum, then stick with 10^{16}.) "Let's assume we will stack about 25 cards in an inch, which makes 100 cards in 4 inches. That means we have 4×10^{13} inches in our stack. Dividing by 12 inches in a foot (a little more than 10) would make maybe 3.5×10^{12} feet, and dividing by 5280 feet/mile (a little more than 5000) makes about 6×10^8 – 600 million miles! Whoa, that's, like, more than three *round-trips* between the Earth and the Sun!!"

☐ Piano Tuners

How many piano tuners are there in the U.S.?

☐ Basketballs in a 747

How many basketballs fit into a 747? With your answer, state which parts of the plane are used.

☐ Kindergarten Teachers

How many kindergarten teachers work in the state of Washington?

☐ Weight of a Ferry

What is the weight of the Bainbridge Island ferry? Full or empty?

☐ Hot Diggity

How many hot dogs made from an adult cow?

☐ Beachfront Property in Colorado

How much would the ocean rise, if all ice melted?

☐ Earth's Circumference

What is the circumference of the earth?

☐ Gas Stations

How many gas stations are there in this state?

☐ Line 'Em Up

How many golf balls would you require, to completely encircle the Earth at the equator?

☐ Building Capacity

How many people work in that 72-story office building over there, would you say?

☐ Painting a Room

To paint this room, how many cans of paint would we need? Just guess, why don't you….

☐ Blades of Grass

How many blades of grass would you estimate there are, in your state?

☐ Lottery Stack

The Powerball lottery contains seven numbers, each number between 1 and 60. How tall would a stack of every possible ticket be?

Chapter 21 – Optimization

Earlier we discussed what *good* software looks like. Valid answers were bug-free, resilient to erroneous or malicious inputs, easily deployed and managed in production, compatible in older and diverse environments, diagnosable upon problems, well-documented, escorted by other services, easily localized into world languages, etc. *Good* software implies dozens of things, but particularly that it is ready for you, and it runs the tasks needed rapidly and efficiently. How can we analyze software performance and tune it, when necessary? The following section applies to software we've identified as performance-critical. If it isn't, then you shouldn't submit it to this type of scrutiny.

The Performance Journey

Software performance can be really difficult to get right. Just as there are many facets of what can slow down a piece of software, there are many avenues that you can pursue to improve it. Probably the most important first step, though, it simply to quantify the existing performance of that code. What are the important Metrics That Matter? Is it a server module, where *throughput* is king? Is it a client feature, where customers are most likely to value *responsiveness*? Choose the right metrics, then measure, *measure*, **measure**. Measure all the time – when adding new features, changing things, or fixing bugs. There's no telling when a well-intentioned bug fix will undo an important set of performance tuning.

Using this performance system, *set performance goals*. These should be explicit and well-understood before anyone goes off on some crazy performance overhaul. Goals are specific and quantifiable, and once you reach them, you don't need to (and usually *should not*) optimize further. Code is often most understandable when first written; any optimization takes us away from that easily-understood state.

Before starting optimization, compare your goals with your current state. Get a feel for how far away you are. If you need a small improvement, go with more tactical, low-risk, high-confidence tweaks. If you need a big improvement, you're likely going to need to pull all the levers you can find.

There are many different altitudes at which you can engage in performance optimization. Design level, algorithm level, code tuning, and more. Design changes are the most disruptive. Naturally, the best time to make a design-level course correction is before (much) code has been written. Don't be afraid to work on paper to demonstrate that the system really *can* scale the way your design intends. A back of the envelope sketch to double-check things might save multiple person-years of work down the line.

Let's work through three challenges/solutions. Each includes a sequence of small improvements, along with narration to take you through the optimization thought process. You will benefit most if you create fully coded solutions for each step along the way, before referring to the next page.

☐ Closest Three-Sum (Series)

Given an assorted array of numbers, plus a `target` number, return the three array elements whose sum is closest to `target`. For example, given `([1,8,5,10,2,4,3],6)`, return `[1,2,3]`.

Chapter 21 – Optimization

☐ Closest Three-Sum (Series) – continued

How did you test your solution? Before optimizing, ensure your code works. Did you try inputs with less than three elements? Do you ensure array elements can only appear once in the *result trio*? The inputs ([1,4,6,7],3) should return [1,4,6], *not* [1,1,1]. If you have correctness confidence, continue.

Next, examine your solution's performance, and characterize it with Big-O. How much space does it require? What about run-time performance? Did you make unnecessary assumptions? Below we list one possible answer to this challenge. What is your analysis of this solution?

```
// Calculate sums, determine which are closest to target, and return them.
function closestThreeSum1(arr, target) {
  var sums = [];
  for (var idx1 = 0; idx1 < arr.length; idx1++)
  {
    sums[idx1] = [];
    for (var idx2 = 0; idx2 < arr.length; idx2++)
    {
      sums[idx1][idx2] = [];
      for (var idx3 = 0; idx3 < arr.length; idx3++)
      {
        sums[idx1][idx2][idx3] = arr[idx1] + arr[idx2] + arr[idx3];
      }
    }
  }
  var bestSum = Number.MAX_VALUE;
  var bestNums = [];
  for (var idx1 = 0; idx1 < arr.length; idx1++) {
    for (var idx2 = 0; idx2 < arr.length; idx2++) {
      for (var idx3 = 0; idx3 < arr.length; idx3++) {
        if ((target - sums[idx1][idx2][idx3]) < bestSum)
        {
          bestSum = target - sums[idx1][idx2][idx3];
          bestNums[0] = arr[idx1];
          bestNums[1] = arr[idx2];
          bestNums[2] = arr[idx3];
        }
      }
    }
  }
  return bestNums;
}
```

Chapter 21 – Optimization

☐ Closest Three-Sum (Series) – continued

We hope you share our opinion that `closestThreeSum1` is ... unfortunate. It has a number of significant problems. First, it does not actually work because of the absence of two `Math.abs()` calls. Can you identify where these should be? Also, it is susceptible to crash if sent incorrect inputs. We must fix those before considering any optimization. At that point, what are our performance goals?

Let's say our goals are to return a correct answer for 2000-element arrays in 10 milliseconds (ms), and to successfully scale to handle 1,000,000-element arrays in less than an hour. The previous code, after being fixed, fails on both accounts. It returns the answer for 300-element array in 386ms, and it crashes Chrome when trying to handle a 515-element array (solves 514-element array in 1963ms). We're a long way from those goals! What are the major problems leading to this abysmal outcome? At a glance they might be: memory consumption and (*two different sets of*) nested loops. Which should we tackle first?

Memory consumption is often our worst culprit. To quantify its impact, let's eliminate the second nested set of loops altogether. We could continue to create a large three-dimensional array, but instead of calculating the answer after-the-fact, we could keep track of the best-so-far as we go (there would be little need to create the large array at that point, but stay with me). This only improves performance by about 5%. If we eliminate the array, performance is much better: 65ms for 300 elements, and 300ms for 514 elements! Plus, we scale further: for 2000 elements, we require 17828ms. Code is below:

```
function closestThreeSum2(arr, target) {
   if (arr === undefined || target === undefined) { return; }
   if (arr.length === undefined || arr.length < 3) { return; }
   var bestSum = Number.MAX_VALUE;
   var bestNums = [];

   for (var idx1 = 0; idx1 < arr.length; idx1++) {
      for (var idx2 = 0; idx2 < arr.length; idx2++) {
         for (var idx3 = 0; idx3 < arr.length; idx3++) {
            var sum = Math.abs(arr[idx1] + arr[idx2] + arr[idx3] - target);
            if (sum < bestSum) {
               bestSum = sum;
               bestNums[0] = arr[idx1];
               bestNums[1] = arr[idx2];
               bestNums[2] = arr[idx3];
            }
         }
      }
   }
   return bestNums;
}
```

If our goal is 10ms (not 17000) for a 2000-element array, then we still have work to do!

Chapter 21 – Optimization

☐ Closest Three-Sum (Series) – continued

Actually, the solution above is still incorrect. It will put a single array element into the solution multiple times. We need to adjust our FOR loops so that this does not occur. Related, the `idx1` outer loop does not need to extend out to `arr.length`, since `idx2` and `idx3` will always be after it. Those could be:

```
for (var idx1 = 0; idx1 < arr.length - 2; idx1++) {
   for (var idx2 = idx1 + 1; idx2 < arr.length - 1; idx2++) {
      for (var idx3 = idx2 + 1; idx3 < arr.length; idx3++) {
```

Also, must we continue if we find a combination that matches our target exactly? No, in that case let's fast-finish. This would result in our having the following code. What is your assessment now?

```
function closestThreeSum4(arr, target) {
   if (arr === undefined || target === undefined) { return; }
   if (arr.length === undefined || arr.length < 3) { return; }
   var bestSum = Number.MAX_VALUE;
   var bestNums = [];

   for (var idx1 = 0; idx1 < arr.length - 2; idx1++) {
      for (var idx2 = idx1 + 1; idx2 < arr.length - 1; idx2++) {
         for (var idx3 = idx2 + 1; idx3 < arr.length; idx3++) {
            var sum = Math.abs(arr[idx1] + arr[idx2] + arr[idx3] - target);
            if (sum < bestSum) {
               bestNums[0] = arr[idx1];
               bestNums[1] = arr[idx2];
               bestNums[2] = arr[idx3];
               if (sum === 0) { return bestNums; }
               bestSum = sum;
            }
         }
      }
   }
   return bestNums;
}
```

The FOR loop adjustment improves our 2000-element performance to 2.989 seconds (from 17). The fast-return is harder to quantify, but for integer arrays it usually returns in *much* less than a millisecond (0.008ms in some tests). If the values are not integers, however, our performance is unchanged unless we change `(sum === 0)` to something like `(sum < 0.0001)`. Let's say we really do want to find the very best match, so must leave this as-is. We must focus on bringing the 2.989-seconds number down. What about a totally different approach? Think about this before going on to the next page.

Chapter 21 – Optimization

☐ Closest Three-Sum (Series) – continued

If we are already operating at $O(n^3)$, then there is little harm in sorting the input array (unless this is forbidden by the interviewer). If the array is sorted, does that help?

If array is sorted, the sum will increase as we progress through each loop. For our innermost loop, once `sum` exceeds `target`, we won't get any closer, so we should break out of that particular inner loop. What performance gain would you expect from this optimization? Are there drawbacks? Code is below:

```
function closestThreeSum5s(arr, target) {
   if (arr === undefined || target === undefined) { return; }
   if (arr.length === undefined || arr.length < 3) { return; }
   var bestSum = Number.MAX_VALUE;
   var bestNums = [];

   selectionSort(arr);
   for (var idx1 = 0; idx1 < arr.length - 2; idx1++) {
      for (var idx2 = idx1 + 1; idx2 < arr.length - 1; idx2++) {
         for (var idx3 = idx2 + 1; idx3 < arr.length; idx3++) {
            var sum = arr[idx1] + arr[idx2] + arr[idx3] - target;
            var absSum = Math.abs(sum);
            if (absSum < bestSum) {
               bestNums[0] = arr[idx1];
               bestNums[1] = arr[idx2];
               bestNums[2] = arr[idx3];
               if (absSum === 0) { return bestNums; }
               bestSum = absSum;
            }
            else {
               if (sum > 0) { break; }
            }
         }
      }
   }
   return bestNums;
}
```

What would you change about the above? At this speed, it would take four years to handle a million-element array – not exactly the speed we want. What about performance on our 2000-element goal?

Good news and bad news. For floating-point values, we get almost 2x speedup! However, for 2000-integer arrays, performance moves from <0.01ms to 6ms – a 600x slowdown! Not good, right?

Chapter 21 – Optimization

☐ Closest Three-Sum (Series) – continued

Don't be distracted by attempts to lure your focus away from your performance goals. This is still good, assuming our goals remain 1) correctly handle 2000-element arrays in 10ms, and 2) correctly handle 1-million-element arrays in 60 minutes. Nonetheless, it is good to understand the cause of the slowdown. Even if the first three elements yield a fast-finish result, we have a guaranteed cost of sorting the array (6 ms to `selectionSort` 2000 elements). Substituting `quickSort` for `selectionSort` eliminates about 2 ms, giving us 1650 ms for 2000 floats, or 4 ms for 2000 integers. Not bad, but not there yet.

What else would take advantage of the fact that the array is sorted? Techniques like *binary-search* can find a value much faster than linear iteration. Could we do that with `idx3`? The code below uses binary-search to narrow in on an ideal `idx3` value, moving on when `low` and `high` bookends come together.

```
function closestThreeSum6q(arr, target) {
  if (arr === undefined || target === undefined) { return; }
  if (arr.length === undefined || arr.length < 3) { return; }
  var bestSum = Number.MAX_VALUE;
  var bestNums = [];

  quickSort(arr);
  for (var idx1 = 0; idx1 < arr.length - 2; idx1++) {
    for (var idx2 = idx1 + 1; idx2 < arr.length - 1; idx2++) {
      var high = arr.length - 1;
      var low = idx2 + 1;
      while (high >= low) {
        var idx3 = Math.floor((high + low) / 2);
        var candidateSum = arr[idx1] + arr[idx2] + arr[idx3] - target;
        var absDiff = Math.abs(candidateSum);
        if (absDiff < bestSum) {
          bestNums[0] = arr[idx1];
          bestNums[1] = arr[idx2];
          bestNums[2] = arr[idx3];
          if (absDiff === 0) { return bestNums; }
          bestSum = absDiff;
        }
        if (candidateSum > 0) { high = idx3 - 1; }
        else { low = idx3 + 1; }
      }
    }
  }
  return bestNums;
}
```

Theoretically, this takes us from **O(n^3)** to **O(n^2logn)**, which is a 100x win if we have 2000 elements....

Chapter 21 – Optimization

☐ Closest Three-Sum (Series) – continued

This makes a big difference! For 2000 floats, we now run in 71ms, which starts to approach our 10ms goal. Integers run in 0.225ms, which is fantastic. Unfortunately, extrapolating to 1 million elements, we still require more than 10 hours to run: we need more perf wins. How about the `Math.floor` call? Aren't those expensive? We get a 10% speedup by instead using >>> (`closestThreeSum7q`, not shown), but that won't give us an order-of-magnitude improvement. We need a better way to scale up.

Rather than code tuning, our answer lies in another algorithmic breakthrough. Have `idx2` and `idx3` count toward each other as follows: start `idx2` at `idx1+1`; start `idx3` at `arr.length-1`. If the three-way sum is too small, move `idx2` up by one, otherwise move `idx3` down by one. For each `idx2`, there are very few `idx3` values worth considering. This reduces the `idx2|idx3` inner loops from O(NlogN) to O(2N) – a big win, and perhaps enough to meet our goals! The code would look like this:

```
function closestThreeSum8q(arr, target) {
   if (arr === undefined || target === undefined) { return; }
   if (arr.length === undefined || arr.length < 3) { return; }
   var bestSum = Number.MAX_VALUE;
   var bestNums = [];

   quickSort(arr);
   for (var idx1 = 0; idx1 < arr.length - 2; idx1++) {
      var idx2 = idx1 + 1;
      var idx3 = arr.length - 1;
      while (idx2 < idx3) {
         var candidateSum = arr[idx1] + arr[idx2] + arr[idx3] - target;
         var absDiff = Math.abs(candidateSum);
         if (absDiff < bestSum) {
            bestNums[0] = arr[idx1];
            bestNums[1] = arr[idx2];
            bestNums[2] = arr[idx3];
            if (absDiff === 0) { return bestNums; }
            bestSum = absDiff;
         }
         if (candidateSum > 0) { idx2++; } else { idx3--; }
      }
   }
   return bestNums;
}
```

What do you predict? Could a simple change like this really make a noticeable change?

Chapter 21 – Optimization

☐ Closest Three-Sum (Series) – continued

Success! For a 2000-element array of floats, `closestThreeSum8q` handles them in 5.46ms (down from 62). For integers, our performance is up to 4.3ms, but this is still within range. This actually suggests performance of straight-up $O(n^2)$, which suggests that we would handle a million-element array in 1350 seconds, or only 22 minutes. Could this be the case? Yes – in less than 24 minutes, our function returns. From `closestThreeSum1` to this one, we sped the 500-element case by 5000x. For `closestThreeSum2`, a million-element array would take 70 years. The `8q` function makes it 5.46ms.

Bottom line: Algorithm choice is truly crucial when optimizing software. This is particularly the case in your most central, highly-frequented inner-loop code locations. Here, a tiny win can be magnified into significant savings. The Big-O decision does and should overshadow other decisions here. Once you have achieved the right order of magnitude to meet your goals, identifying additional ways to cut your runtime in half can give huge gains even if your Big-O doesn't change. People will still notice.

The next challenge explores two axes simultaneously – improving performance, and adding features. Enhancements range from algorithm to data structure to plain old logic. We hope you enjoy the ride.

☐ N Queens (Series)

Recall this challenge from earlier material on recursion. Chessboards are square, with 8 rows of 8 squares each. Queens are one type of chess piece, and in a single move they can travel any number of squares in either of the horizontal directions (along a *row*), or either of the vertical directions (along a *file* or *column*), or either of the diagonal directions (staying on the same color). A piece is considered *under threat* from a queen if it is situated in a square where that queen can directly move.

☐ Is Chess Move Safe

`isChessMoveSafe(intendedMove,queenArr)` returns `true` if square is threatened, else `false`. Accepts location object to check, and current locations of an array of opposing queens.

☐ N Queens

Create `nQueens(numQns,xSize,ySize)` using previous work such as `isChessMoveSafe`, returning all arrangements of N unthreatened queens on X-by-Y rectangular board. `eightQueens() == nQueens(8,8,8)`.

As with earlier challenges, it behooves you to solve it on your own before moving on to the next page. Refresh your memory by revisiting the Recursion material, if needed.

Chapter 21 – Optimization

☐ N Queens (Series) – continued

Again, it benefits you most if you have already created a solution before reading on. If not, do so now. Did the previous performance journey change how you viewed this one? For this challenge, we start with a most ridiculous implementation. Do your best to spot the fix or optimization before we get to it!

```
function isChessMoveSafe1(intendedMove, queenArr) {
   var xCoord = 0, yCoord = 1;
   var safe = true;
   for (var qNum = 0; qNum < queenArr.length; qNum++) {
      for (var row = 0; row < 8; row++) {
         if ((intendedMove[xCoord] == row)
         && (intendedMove[yCoord] == queenArr[qNum][yCoord])) { safe=false;}
      }
      for (var col = 0; col < 8; col++) {
         if ((intendedMove[xCoord] == queenArr[qNum][xCoord])
         && (intendedMove[yCoord] == col)) { safe = false; }
      }
      for (var lDiag = -7; lDiag <= 7; lDiag++) {
         if ((  intendedMove[xCoord]   - intendedMove[yCoord] == lDiag)
         && (queenArr[qNum][xCoord]  - queenArr[qNum][yCoord] == lDiag))
         { safe = false; }
      }
      for (var rDiag = 0; rDiag <= 14; rDiag++) {
         if ((  intendedMove[xCoord]   + intendedMove[yCoord] == rDiag)
         && (queenArr[qNum][xCoord]  + queenArr[qNum][yCoord] == rDiag))
         { safe = false; }
      }
   }
   return safe;
}
function queens1(nQueensLeft,results,queensSoFar) {
   if (results === undefined)    { results = [];    }
   if (queensSoFar === undefined) { queensSoFar = [];  }
   if (nQueensLeft) {
      for (var row = 0; row < 8; row++) {
         for (var col = 0; col < 8; col++) {
            if (isChessMoveSafe1([row, col], queensSoFar)) {
               var newQueen = [row,col];
               queens1(nQueensLeft-1,results,queensSoFar.concat([newQueen]));
            }
         }
      }
   } else { results.push(queensSoFar); }
}
```

Chapter 21 – Optimization

☐ N Queens (Series) – continued

First, we're sorry about the previous page's code. It is a bit below Dojo standards, in performance but also in correctness. Perhaps you spot the bugs already, but first let's talk about what this code is *trying* to do. This is a typical recursive approach for the Eight Queens problem. To identify a location, we use a two-element array. Using a technique known as dynamic programming, the `queens1` function calls itself, building up an array of queens in safe locations. When all the required queens are placed, it adds the `queensSoFar` array to the final `results` array, and then it backtraces in order to continue.

Good idea, but unfortunately the code is dreadful. To determine all the ways of placing just 5 queens on an 8x8 board, it took more than 30 seconds – and it returned the wrong answer (do you see why?). There are duplicates in the results returned, because regardless of where we may have put the previous queen, we always start at the top row when suggesting the next set of safe squares. This may be the right thing if we are creating an `allSafeChessSquares` function, but here we don't want that. So, our first change will be to address a *defect*: once we put down a queen, *don't allow subsequent queens to be placed on earlier rows*.

The following code at least functions correctly:

```
function queens2(nQueensLeft,results,queensSoFar) {
   if (results === undefined)       { results = [];     }
   if (queensSoFar === undefined) { queensSoFar = []; }
   if (nQueensLeft) {
      var row = 0;
      if (queensSoFar.length) {
         row = queensSoFar[queensSoFar.length - 1][0];
      }
      for ( ; row < 8; row++) {
         for (var col = 0; col < 8; col++) {
            if (isChessMoveSafe1([row, col], queensSoFar)) {
               queens2(nQueensLeft-1,
                       results,
                       queensSoFar.concat([[row,col]])
               );
            }
         }
      }
   }
   else { results.push(queensSoFar); }
}
```

What else is hiding in here that we should address? Let's measure performance. How do you think this version will compare to the previous one? The previous one took about 30 seconds to find ways to place 5 queens on an 8x8 board.

Chapter 21 – Optimization

☐ N Queens (Series) – continued

The new version `queens2` only took 310 milliseconds (ms) to correctly return the 46736 possible ways of placing 5 queens on an 8x8 board. Now that we have code that actually runs correctly, let's crank it all the way up to 8 queens. The `queens2` version, when run with 8 queens on an 8x8 board, requires 720 milliseconds to return the correct 92 solutions. By the way, you may be wondering how we make these timing measurements. Our initial profiling code looks like the following:

```
function timeQueens1(num) {
   var start, end;
   var results = [];
   start = Date.now();
   results = queens1(num); // or queens2, etc.
   end = Date.now();
   console.log("Found %d solns in %f millisec", results.length, end-start);
}
```

So, how *about* that `queens2` function? It runs a lot faster, yes? It does, but not fast enough. There are a couple of things that leap out; let's handle them. One, we "check for undefined" in every recursive call. Let's move that out of our main recursion path into a wrapper function. Two, when adding a queen to our `queensSoFar` collection, we don't resume on the *next* row, we resume on the *same* row. Those squares will never be fruitful, so it's wasted time. If you haven't seen `FOR` loops with blank initialization sections, those *are* legal, if uncommon. Also, the *double-[* within `queensSoFar.concat` is intentional. Without them, `concat` will think we want to append those two elements to `queensSoFar`, instead of appending the array itself. After making those fixes, let's try the following updated `queens3`:

```
function queens3(nQueensLeft,results,queensSoFar) {
   if (nQueensLeft) {
      var row = 0;
      if (queensSoFar.length) {
         row = queensSoFar[queensSoFar.length - 1][0] + 1;
      }
      for ( ; row < 8; row++) {
         for (var col = 0; col < 8; col++) {
            if (isChessMoveSafe1([row, col], queensSoFar)) {
               queens3(nQueensLeft - 1, results,
                       queensSoFar.concat([[row,col]]));
            }
         }
      }
   } else { results.push(queensSoFar); }
}
```

What do you predict? Remember, the previous version correctly ran 8 queens in 720 ms.

Chapter 21 – Optimization

☐ N Queens (Series) – continued

`Queens3` is our best attempt so far, without question. It correctly runs 8 queens in 262 milliseconds! Something is still rotten in the state of our code, however. Earlier on, did you happen to raise an eyebrow at our `isChessMoveSafe` function? Honestly, it's about as inefficient as possible.

Here's a much-improved final version of `isChessMoveSafe`:

```
function isChessMoveSafe(intendedMove, queenArr) {
   if (  !(intendedMove instanceof Array)
      || !(queenArr     instanceof Array)) { return false; }

   for (var qNum = 0; qNum < queenArr.length; qNum++) {
      if (                     intendedMove[0]==queenArr[qNum][0]
         ||                    intendedMove[1]==queenArr[qNum][1]
         || intendedMove[0]+intendedMove[1]==queenArr[qNum][0]+queenArr[qNum][1]
         || intendedMove[0]-intendedMove[1]==queenArr[qNum][0]-queenArr[qNum][1]
         )
         { return false; }
   }
   return true;
}
```

Oh my, much better. Instead of 168 array reads, this has 12. Previously 62 compares, now is 4. Our 30 adds and 30 subtracts became 2 adds and 2 subtracts. Best of all, we have a fast-fail: the numbers cited are *worst-case*. This function is called <u>constantly</u>. We should expect significant speedup, yes?

Our `queens4` function is essentially unchanged, other than calling the above improved subroutine:

```
function queens4(nQueensLeft,results,queensSoFar) {
   if (nQueensLeft) {
      var row = 0;
      if (queensSoFar.length)
      { row = queensSoFar[queensSoFar.length - 1][0] + 1; }
      for ( ; row < 8; row++) {
         for (var col = 0; col < 8; col++) {
            if (isChessMoveSafe([row, col], queensSoFar)) {
               queens4(nQueensLeft-1,results,queensSoFar.concat([[row,col]]))
            }
         }
      }
   } else { results.push(queensSoFar); }
}
```

What next? Will our performance improve? Have we introduced bugs?

Chapter 21 – Optimization

☐ N Queens (Series) – continued

So far so good with our performance journey. The `queens4` function (powered by `isChessMoveSafe`) runs in 62 millisec, a *major* (12x) improvement from our initial 720 ms version (and that doesn't count our original version that ran in 30 secs and didn't even work right). Where do we go from here – are we done? No! The original challenge asked us to extended our code out as far as we could, to faster times and larger boards. If we don't yet see how to tune this code further, then we can at least extend it from hard-coded 8-by-8 dimensions to arbitrary X-by-Y dimensions. As we get faster, the larger boards can be a better barometer for measuring our progress. Let's refactor `queens` to handle any board size:

```
function queens5(nQueensLeft, xSize, ySize, results, queensSoFar)
{
   if (nQueensLeft) {
      var row = 0;
      if (queensSoFar.length) {
         row = queensSoFar[queensSoFar.length - 1][0] + 1;
      }
      for ( ; row < ySize; row++) {
         for (var col = 0; col < xSize; col++) {
            if (isChessMoveSafe([row, col], queensSoFar)) {
               queens5( nQueensLeft - 1, xSize, ySize, results,
                     queensSoFar.concat([[row,col]]));
            }
         }
      }
   }
   else { results.push(queensSoFar); }
}
```

One additional thing. We will start using `performance.now()` instead of `Date.now()` in our timings. The `Date` object is useful, but the newer `performance` object is intended for exactly this sort of high-precision timing, and at this point it is available on all important browser versions. So, now if we measure performance, will we see a big win? What is our expected result?

Chapter 21 – Optimization

☐ N Queens (Series) – continued

As expected, performance is *unchanged* between `queens4` and `queens5` – we only extended our game board to arbitrary sizes. However, now we can measure larger boards. 8x8: 56ms; 9x9: 402ms; 10x10: 3362ms; 11x11: 30383ms. As you profile your code, you may see ups and downs. Shut down programs to clear memory, making your test environment slightly more consistent. In the end, though, these readings will always have variability. A time-honored convention is to take multiple readings (perhaps 5), throw out the best and worst, and average the rest. The timings below do exactly that.

Now what? It would be good to retrieve a set of *next safe squares*, instead of continually asking about each different square – essentially, `allSafeChessSquares`. My first version, `nextChessSquares1` (not included), did not include our earlier bug fix, so after placing queens in lower rows, it subsequently offered first-row queens. Oops! While there, I added error checking to our wrapper function, in case someone asks for 10 queens on a 9x9 board, etc. Here are latest fixed versions of everything involved:

```
function nextChessSquares2(queenArr, x, y) {
   var safeSquares = [];
   var row = (queenArr.length) ? queenArr[queenArr.length - 1][0] + 1 : 0;
   for ( ; row < y; row++) {
      for (var col = 0; col < x; col++) {
         if (isChessMoveSafe([row,col], queenArr))
         { safeSquares.push([row,col]); }
      }
   }
   return safeSquares;
}

function queens6(nQueensLeft, x, y, results, queensSoFar) {
   if (nQueensLeft) {
      var candidates = nextChessSquares2(queensSoFar, x, y);
      for (var candNum = 0; candNum < candidates.length; candNum++) {
         queens6( nQueensLeft - 1, x, y, results
                  queensSoFar.concat([candidates[candNum]]));
      }
   } else { results.push(queensSoFar); }
}

function nQueens2(num, x, y) {
   var results = [];
   if (num <= x && num <= y) { queens6(num, x, y, results, []); }
   return results;
}
```

Queens6 looks good, but `nextChessSquares2` and `nQueens2` are nothing new. Let's measure.

Chapter 21 – Optimization

☐ N Queens (Series) – continued

The measurements for `queens6` are the same as those for `queens5`. Remember that we created `nextChessSquares` function to streamline the process of identifying candidates for the next queen? Within it, we just used the standard `isChessMoveSafe`, which is why performance has not yet improved. We can optimize the checking of a square further, and that should help a lot, since this is done continuously. First, we eliminate the function call by putting `isChessMoveSafe` code _inline_ – into our `nextChessSquares` function itself. That by itself may not do a lot, but we can further eliminate one of the four checks as well: remember, we don't have to do a row check any longer, since we will always start exploring on the row following the previous queen. That is, all queens are placed in successive rows on our board. With that, here is the tuned-up `nextChessSquares` function:

```
function nextChessSquares3(queenArr, x, y) {
   var safeSquares = [];
   var row = (queenArr.length) ? queenArr[queenArr.length - 1][0] + 1 : 0;
   for ( ; row < y; row++) {
      for (var col = 0; col < x; col++) {
         for (var qNum = 0; qNum < queenArr.length; qNum++) {
            var qY = queenArr[qNum][0];
            var qX = queenArr[qNum][1];
            if ( qX == col
               || qX - qY == col - row
               || qX + qY == col + row)
            { break; }
         }
         if (qNum == queenArr.length) { safeSquares.push([row,col]); }
      }
   }
   return safeSquares;
}
```

Any predictions? This will be faster, presumably, but will it be a big win?

Chapter 21 – Optimization

☐ N Queens (Series) – continued

Well, the gain is measurable, but it isn't a *big* win – maybe 5% better (which is never bad). Our timings are as follows: 52.8ms for 8x8, 378.7 ms for 9x9, 3159 ms for 10x10, and 29234 ms for 11x11. At this point we need a new approach. What about memory usage? Generally smaller is faster. Can we make things smaller? There are no obvious ways that jump out at us, on that. Well, what things are taking up memory? Our location arrays take up space. Also, our candidate location chains are coming and going all the time. Even if our memory needs stay constant, we could always try to reduce ongoing memory churn. Memory operators can be expensive, particularly in problems like this with big backtrace results.

The change seems like a reasonable one, because we do see the `candidates` array constantly growing and shrinking, as recursion/backtracing happens. We should not continually deallocate and reallocate that array; let's keep it more stable. If we want to `push` and `pop` it, that means we can't add it 'live' to the results array, though. We'll need to make a shallow copy each time we add a new final result. That is a very good tradeoff, since we `push`/`pop` candidates constantly, and only occasionally add a new final `result` solution.

```
function queens8(nQueensLeft, x, y, results, queensSoFar) {
   if (nQueensLeft) {
      var candidates = nextChessSquares3(queensSoFar, x, y);
      for (var candNum = 0; candNum < candidates.length; candNum++)
         queensSoFar.push(candidates[candNum]);
         queensTest(nQueensLeft - 1, x, y, results, queensSoFar);
         queensSoFar.pop();
      }
   }
   else {
      results.push(Array.from(queensSoFar));
   }
}
```

One additional note: I just read a post talking about the fastest way to make a copy of an array. I expected that `Array.from` would be the winner. Actually, it *isn't* – doing it by hand is much better! So, we'll change the one-liner (commented out below) to this chunk of code instead:

```
// results.push(Array.from(queensSoFar));

var result = [];
for (var idx = 0; idx < queensSoFar.length; idx++) {
   result[idx] = queensSoFar[idx];
}
results.push(result);
```

Let's do a check-in on performance to see how far we've come.

Chapter 21 – Optimization

☐ N Queens (Series) – continued

Our *eliminate memory churn* fixes worked brilliantly. Our timings have experienced the first significant downtick in a while. We measure 14.4ms for 8x8, 98.1 ms for 9x9, 825 ms for 10x10, and 7387 ms for 11x11. This is almost a 4x improvement, which is massive! Also, measuring separately, doing an array copy by hand *is* much faster than using a built-in. This saved us an entire second, on the 11x11.

Where now? Are we empty of ideas – is this as good as it gets? Believe it or not, there are three more `queens` improvements out there to show us additional tuning!

You know how we significantly reduced our time, by making sure to start exploring next queen locations *after* previous one? That eliminated lots of dead ends (and false duplicates). What about the flip side? It would not make sense, for example, to place a queen on the last row if we still have *two* queens to place after it! So, just as we can constrain the starting row for each candidate queen, we can also constrain the ending row. If we have three queens remaining, then we can't put one of them any lower than the third-to-last row (it can't go in the second-to-last row, because then where would the subsequent queens be placed? Again, every successive queen must move forward to a next row).

Here's the code. Can it really make a difference?

```
function queens9(nQueensLeft, x, y, results, queensSoFar) {
   if (nQueensLeft) {
      var candidates = nextChessSquares3(queensSoFar, x, y -nQueensLeft +1);
      for (var candNum = 0; candNum < candidates.length; candNum++) {
         queensSoFar.push(candidates[candNum]);
         queens9(nQueensLeft - 1, x, y, results, queensSoFar);
         queensSoFar.pop();
      }
   }
   else {
      var result = [];
      for (var idx = 0; idx < queensSoFar.length; idx++) {
         result[idx] = queensSoFar[idx];
      }
      results.push(result);
   }
}
```

Let's see if this helps. At this point, unless it makes the code really confusing we want the improvement – we will take all the performance and scale-up wins we can get.

Chapter 21 – Optimization

☐ N Queens (Series) – continued

Are you kidding? This optimization's *huge*: 0.67ms for 8x8, 2.26ms for 9x9, 10.5ms for 10x10, 45.3ms for 11x11. How about larger? 254ms for 12x12, 1434ms for 13x13 and 8838ms for 14x14. Nice!

15x15 takes a very long time, then crashes. Why? Our code now generates *lots* of data, quickly. We don't waste time looking at unfruitful squares. We are hitting memory limits. Let's address that. It may make our code less readable, but if you made it this far, you deserve the end of the story!

Let's compress our location data: that huge array of final results and `queensSoFar` fragments. Even a small fix might get us to 15x15. Let's bit-encode the X and Y coordinates into a number (not an array). We'll encode/decode when we write/read them (`readability--`, but performance might be worth it):

```
function nextChessSquares4(queenArr, x, y) {
   var safeSquares = [];
   var row = (queenArr.length) ? ((queenArr[queenArr.length-1] >>8) +1) : 0;
   for ( ; row < y; row++) {
      for (var col = 0; col < x; col++) {
         for (var qNum = 0; qNum < queenArr.length; qNum++) {
            var qY = queenArr[qNum] >> 8;
            var qX = queenArr[qNum] & 0x0ff;
            if (qX == col || qX-qY == col-row || qX+qY == col+row)
            { break; }
         }
         if (qNum == queenArr.length) { safeSquares.push((row << 8) + col); }
      }
   }
   return safeSquares;
}
function queens10(nQueensLeft, x, y, results, queensSoFar) {
   if (nQueensLeft) {
      var candidates = nextChessSquares4(queensSoFar, x, y -nQueensLeft +1);
      for (var candNum = 0; candNum < candidates.length; candNum++) {
         queensSoFar.push(candidates[candNum]);
         queens10(nQueensLeft - 1, x, y, results, queensSoFar);
         queensSoFar.pop();
      }
   }
   else {
      var result = [];
      for (var idx = 0; idx < queensSoFar.length; idx++)
      { result[idx] = queensSoFar[idx]; }
      results.push(result);
   }
}
```

Chapter 21 – Optimization

☐ N Queens (Series) – continued

This optimization is nice as well: 20-30%! Also, as expected it reduces our memory usage (that's why it runs faster), allowing us to reach 15x15, in 41 seconds! Congratulations. Here are timings: 0.53ms for 8x8, 1.35ms for 9x9, 6.62ms for 10x10, 32.5ms for 11x11, 169ms for 12x12, 1019ms for 13x13, 6320ms for 14x14, and 41329ms for 15x15. Yes, at 16x16 we crash, but this is still a huge success.

We have one last trick up our sleeve. Has it already occurred to you? Every arrangement can be mirrored from left-to-right. So, how about if we try only the first-queen possibilities of the *left* side, and then just "reflect" (quick copy) all the complete results to the other side as well! Basically, this just means we take a complete result and reflect the X coordinate across the board's midline. On an 8x8 board, column 0 would become column 7. Column 4 would become 3. Look at the code for more.

```
function nextChessSquares5(queenArr, x, y) {
   var safeSquares = [];
   var row =(queenArr.length) ? ((queenArr[queenArr.length - 1] >>8) +1) :0;
   for ( ; row < y; row++) {
      var highestCol = (row == 0) ? x/2 : x;
      for (var col = 0; col < highestCol; col++) {
         for (var qNum = 0; qNum < queenArr.length; qNum++) {
            var qY = queenArr[qNum] >> 8;
            var qX = queenArr[qNum] & 0x0ff;
            if (qX == col || qX - qY == col - row || qX + qY == col + row)
            { break; }
         }
         if (qNum == queenArr.length) { safeSquares.push((row << 8) + col); }
      }
   }
   return safeSquares;
}
```

This is one side of it. Let's also look at the `queens11` function that consumes it.

Chapter 21 – Optimization

☐ N Queens (Series) – continued

```
function queens11(nQueensLeft, x, y, results, queensSoFar) {
   if (nQueensLeft) {
      var candidates = nextChessSquares5(queensSoFar,x,y-nQueensLeft+1);
      for (var candNum = 0; candNum < candidates.length; candNum++) {
         queensSoFar.push(candidates[candNum]);
         queens11(nQueensLeft - 1, x, y, results, queensSoFar);
         queensSoFar.pop();
      }
   }
   else {
      var result = [];
      var result2 = [];
      for (var idx = 0; idx < queensSoFar.length; idx++) {
         result[idx] = queensSoFar[idx];
         var xCoord = queensSoFar[idx] & 0x0ff;
         xCoord = (x - 1 - xCoord);
         result2[idx] = queensSoFar[idx] & (~0x0ff) | xCoord;
      }
      results.push(result);
      if (queensSoFar[0] < (x - 1)/2) { results.push(result2); }
   }
}
```

Bottom line: this halves our runtime *yet again*. We've successfully taken initial measurements down by 1500x or more. Here are final timings: 0.214ms for 8x8, 0.83ms for 9x9, 3.44ms for 10x10, 20.2ms for 11x11, 93.5ms for 12x12, 582ms for 13x13, 3283ms for 14x14, and 23459ms for 15x15.

There you have it, a play-by-play performance journey that took initially dysfunctional code and, after fixing it, improved performance by (depending on the size of the board) a factor of 20,000x. Not bad!

Chapter 21 – Optimization

Code Tuning

You've chosen a good design; your algorithm choice is sound; you are keeping all the different pipes (network, storage, memory, CPU, power) fully-utilized and at approximately equal levels; you've applied all the appropriate compiler optimization and server configuration settings; somehow it isn't enough to give your software the performance it needs. What now?

Code tuning is becoming a bit of a lost art, except in larger products where all the obvious levers have already been pulled. In the old days, grey-bearded gurus would hand-code assembly-language inner-loop routines because compilers were not yet as good as a human could be. This is no longer the case, but you can still make a major difference in performance with some important choices in how you code something. Pay attention to what functions you use and how much data you have. Is your data space growing fast? Large-but-relatively-unchanging is better than almost-as-large-but-highly-variable. In these cases, rewriting a chunk of code might make a noticeable difference. When data sets get large, the software maxim of "smaller is faster" really sets in. In these cases, you need to pay special attention to your data structure choice. Algorithms ("work smarter") can save CPU and battery, whereas data structures ("work smaller") help with everything else: RAM, storage, network, etc. When you are running out of RAM, you'll do almost anything to generate more (or consume less!). Stay tuned....

The next journey is largely algorithmic, based on a question from the earliest chapters. Have fun!

☐ Is Number Prime (Series)

Given number, return whether it is prime. Prime numbers are only evenly divisible by themselves and 1.

Before moving on, quickly write a naïve `isNumberPrime`, and *then* optimize it.

☐ Counting Primes

Build on the `isNumberPrime(num)` function at left to count the primes that are equal or less than given integer.

Second: add the ability to profile this function, measuring progress as we optimize `isNumberPrime`.

OK, hopefully you've spent good quality time with pencil, paper, marker, whiteboard. From our side, here is a naïve implementation we came up with on very short order. No guarantees!

What do you see? Is it a starting point?

```
function isPrime(num) {
    for(var count=1; count<=num; count++) {
        if (num/count == parseInt(num/count))
        { return false; }
    }
    return true;
}
```

Chapter 21 – Optimization

☐ Is Number Prime (Series) – continued

For the record: no, the previous source is a *piece*, but not a *piece of code*. It doesn't work; it considers *nothing* prime (some people are just impossible to please). Fixing it, now we have the following. This should be much better, but again, no guarantees!

```
function isPrime0(num)
{                                              // start at 2 not 1
   for (var count = 2; count < num; count++) {  // < num, not <= num
      if (num / count == parseInt(num / count)) {
         return false;
      }
   }
   return true;
}
```

Hopefully `isPrime0` will work as a starting point. Also, below is some code to quantify our improvements. Using a function pointer enables me to quickly measure new routines.

```
function countPrimesUpTo(limit, primeFn)
{
   var count = 0;
   var start = performance.now();

   for (var num = 0; num <= limit; num++) {
      if (primeFn(num)) {
         count++;
      }
   }
   var end = performance.now();
   return "The function " + primeFn.name + "()"
        + " found " + count + " primes"
        + " in " + (end - start) + " msec.";
}
```

```
countPrimesUpTo(1000000,isPrime0);  // Here's how we'll use the profiler.
```

What do you think about this implementation? How similar is it to yours? What might you expect the run-time performance to be, if we counted primes up to *1 million*? Because the larger the number, the greater number of possible divisors we must check, the complexity of this function as `num` grows is *O(n²)*. The fact that we *count* all of them compounds the problem, so we should expect *O(n³)* behavior.

On this machine, `isPrime0` returned that there are 78500 primes under 1 Million, and it did so in 501.5 seconds. That will be our baseline. Do you note anything about `isPrime0`? Does it do all that it should? Specifically, *where's the bug*?

Chapter 21 – Optimization

☐ Is Number Prime (Series) – continued

The `isPrime0` function is fine – unless you expect it to return *correct* answers for *all inputs*. (-:

Specifically, now we are considering *too many* numbers to be prime. (That kind of degrades the whole *prime* label, if you get what I mean. We need that club to be more exclusive.) Negative numbers cannot be prime. Fractional numbers are not prime. Also, the numbers 0 and 1 are by definition not prime. So, as it turns out, we cannot consider `isPrime0` our baseline; we are still on the hunt for a function that returns <u>correct outputs</u>. Let's fix it and see how far we get. Here's `isPrime1` (of many, to be sure):

```
// Fixes bugs: num = 1, 0, negatives, non-integers
function isPrime1(num)
{
   if (num < 2 || num != parseInt(num)) { return false; }

   for (var count = 2; count < num; count++) {
      if (num / count == parseInt(num / count)) {
         return false;
      }
   }
   return true;
}
```

Unlike `isPrime0`, this one is correct. Non-integers, or anything below 2 is considered non-prime. Counting primes to 1 Million, it returned 78498 primes (correct!) in 476.3 seconds. We have a baseline! Sadly, for our $O(n^3)$ behavior, counting primes to *100* Million would take 100*100*100 longer: **15 yrs**.

How can we make it faster? It is already fairly basic; it only calls `parseInt` – actually a good target. `ParseInt` exists to convert various inputs to integers – floats but also strings or even arrays. If expect only floats, we can use a less expensive function. Instead of `parseInt`, let's try using `Math.floor`.

```
// Uses Math.floor() instead of parseInt().
function isPrime2(num)
{
   if (num < 2 || num != Math.floor(num)) { return false; }

   for (var count = 2; count < num; count++) {
      if (num / count == Math.floor(num / count)) {
         return false;
      }
   }
   return true;
}
```

Chapter 21 – Optimization

☐ Is Number Prime (Series) – continued

Before we go further, it is important to set our *performance goals*. Don't go optimizing unless you have some sort of goal in mind. Here it is: 1) we want to count the primes up to *100 Million, in 60 seconds*; 2) we also want to be able to count primes up to *1 Billion* but we're not sure how long that should take.

So how did `isPrime2` fare when measured? A lot better than `isPrime1`! Specifically counting primes to 1 Million took 147.7 seconds, which is an improvement of more than 3x over previous baseline. Nice! Now what? Would it be possible to eliminate the function call altogether? What do you recommend?

As it turns out, there is an even less expensive way to check whether something is an integer. Do you remember the modulus operator %? Consider what `num` might be after executing `num = num % 1`. Basically, it returns the less-than-one fractional component of the number. Certainly, any primitive operator (such as + - * / % & | ^ ~) will be much faster than any function call.

Let's make this quick change and measure the improvement.

```
// Uses % instead of Math.floor().
function isPrime3(num)
{
   if (num < 2 || num % 1) { return false; }

   for (var count = 2; count < num; count++) {
      if (num % count == 0) {
         return false;
      }
   }
   return true;
}
```

What improvement do you expect? In a way, it depends on how bad you think `Math.floor` is.... The function `isPrime3` completes counting 1 million primes in 111.1 seconds. That's a nice 25% cut. As before, you will see plenty of variability in your own measurements, and a good practice is to create as stable and reproducible an environment as you can, make 5 or 7 measurements, throw out the best and worst measurements, and average the rest. This is what I did for this chapter's measurements.

That seems like as much as we can squeeze out of the actual math operation. What else is there? Well, let's think through all the values of `count` that we are dividing against `num`. The values are 2, 3, 4, 5, 6, ... wait a minute! 4 and 6 aren't going to matter. The value 2 is the only *even* one we really care about. We can eliminate all the rest of the even numbers from our `FOR` loop! We should expect this to cut our run-time basically in half. On the next page is the updated code, and following that we mention how it impacted the performance. What do you expect?

Chapter 21 – Optimization

☐ Is Number Prime (Series) – continued

Here is updated code. Note how we immediately exit on special cases – the very definition of *fail-fast*.

```
// Only check odd factors (after checking 2).
function isPrime4(num)
{
   if (num % 2 == 0 && num > 2) { return false; }
   if (num < 2       || num % 1) { return false; }

   for (var count = 3; count < num; count += 2) {
      if (num % count == 0) {
         return false;
      }
   }
   return true;
}
```

The `isPrime4` function counts 1 Million primes in 60.7 seconds: not quite a 2x speedup, but close. So far we have a 7.5x acceleration from our `isPrime1` baseline of 476 seconds. This is good, but what else can we do to reduce the number of unnecessary divisors?

Think about various *prime* factors of a compound number. How large could these prime factors be? Prime factors, when multiplied by other prime factors, equal a compound number. A number like 36 has (multiple) prime factors of 2 and 3. We would immediately discover this number is not prime, upon checking 2, but that doesn't help us understand how far toward a number we need to check divisors, before having confidence that the number is prime (what if our 36 were 37 instead?). Perhaps we need to check factors up to a specific fraction of the given number?

Maybe a different example. To think more clearly about this first-prime-to-number ratio, let's pick a number with only two prime factors. How about 65 – prime factors are 5 and 13. When we get to the 5, we again have discovered that it is not prime. A little better, but again we haven't learned anything – it's not as if we will always hit all the primes for a number once we get to 10% of the number. There are numbers smaller than 65 that have first-primes bigger than 5, it seems. What are they? Well, if we want the first-prime to be larger, then we need the second-prime to be smaller. How about trying numbers with prime factors *really close together* – a square: 49. Squares give us first-prime factors that are as far from zero as possible (if they were any bigger, they would exceed the second-prime).

This guides our next optimization! Just as we try only odd divisors (after trying 2), we also need to try divisors *only as high as the number's square root*. For 97, we need not try prime factors higher than **9**.

But will this make a real difference in performance? What would a good implementation be?

Chapter 21 – Optimization

☐ Is Number Prime (Series) – continued

Here's an implementation of `isPrime5` that tries divisors up to the number's square-root.

```
// Only check factors up to sqrt(num).
function isPrime5(num)
{
   if (num % 2 == 0 && num > 2) { return false; }
   if (num < 2       || num % 1) { return false; }

   for (var count = 3; count <= Math.sqrt(num); count += 2) {
      if (num % count == 0) { return false; }
   }
   return true;
}
```

How is performance? Fabulous! To count primes under 1 million, `isPrime5` uses 130.4 millisecs (ms)! Compared to `isPrime4`, it's a 500x speedup for that benchmark. Also, it means we can count higher. How about 50 million instead of 1 million? This successfully runs and completes in 30.7 seconds.

Gee, how do we get much better than that? Maybe we don't. Something important to note here is that you should always *have reasonable performance goals in mind before you start optimizations*. Then stop optimizing when you reach them. Without these goals, how will you ever know when you *should be done* with it? (I realize some of you may feel I *should be done* with this journey, but I'll continue.)

If, like us, you are a purist and want to profile your code using single-pass measurements with just a single large value, we can help. Here is a set of progressively larger prime numbers, as well as a set of roughly correlated compound numbers that require significant calculation to prove as non-prime:

```
var bigPrimes = [         99991,            999983,          9999991,
                       99999989,         999999937,       9999999967,
                    99999999977,       999999999989,     9999999999971,
                 99999999999973,    999999999999989,  9007199254740881 ];

var bigCompounds = [      99221,            995779,          9922331,
                       99799811,         999634589,       9999399973,
                    99999515333,       999966000289,     9999919930081,
                 99999919999487,    999998950017311,  9007197807561043 ];
```

What is our next step? Maybe we can unroll our inner loop a little, to skip a few more obvious values – not unlike what we are doing when we `count += 2` each time (skipping the even values). Could we do that for multiples of three as well? Maybe, but would that make a noticeable difference?

Chapter 21 – Optimization

☐ Is Number Prime (Series) – continued

Turns out it does help, considerably. Compared to `isPrime5`, our new function `isPrime5a` executes in about 2/3 the time. From the changes we made to our inner loop, this makes sense.

```
function isPrime5a(num)
{
   if (num % 2 == 0 && num > 2) { return false; }
   if (num % 3 == 0 && num > 3) { return false; }
   if (num < 2      || num % 1) { return false; }

   for (var count = 5; count <= Math.sqrt(num); count += 4) {
      if (num % count == 0) { return false; }
      count += 2;
      if (num % count == 0) { return false; }
   }
   return true;
}
```

So now we are counting primes to 1 million in about 84.1 millisecs, and to 100 Million in about 46 secs. This is great – we are passing our first performance goal!

Side note: a single run of `isPrime5a(9007199254740881)` – our biggest prime – completes in 270ms. Our baseline `isPrime1` scales linearly, needing 2.5 minutes for **9999999967** (1,000,000x faster). We can extrapolate what `isPrime1` needs for **9007199254740881**: a whopping 4.4 years!

Let's say that the business team identified an exciting new opportunity for our product if we can optimize it even more than before. Our performance goals are now threefold:
1) Count primes to 100 Million in 60 seconds, *first time* (with 'cold cache'),
2) Count primes to 1 Billion on standard laptop without crashing, and
3) (new) Count primes to 100 Million in *1 second thereafter* (with 'warm cache').

These are very aggressive goals – remember when we were counting primes to **1** Million in 476 secs?

Our `isPrime5a` function has been good to us so far. Let's set it loose counting primes toward 1 Billion, shall we? Good news: after 17 minutes or so, it eventually gets to 1 Billion without error. So, we've **met our new performance goal #2** as well!

Goal #3 is going to be tough. What is a reasonable step toward that goal? We already calculate primes quickly; the only way faster would be to *not* calculate at all … ah! Perhaps we won't calculate: we'll *remember* them. Yes, a caching strategy. Just as we did earlier with Fancy Fibonacci, let's save previous results when asked if a number is prime.

The next page should have a reasonable implementation of our caching scheme, but before you turn to it, *create this yourself*. It's for your own good, you know.

Chapter 21 – Optimization

☐ Is Number Prime (Series) – continued

We are now up to `isPrime6` – and if this one doesn't speed things up, then we don't know what will. What are the issues, if any, with this implementation?

```
// Cache previous results.
var prevResults = [false, false, true];
function isPrime6(num)
{
   if (num < 0 || num % 1) { return false; }

   if (prevResults[num] === undefined) {
      if (num % 2 == 0) { prevResults[num] = false; }
      else {
         for (var count = 3; count <= Math.sqrt(num); count += 2) {
            if (num % count == 0) {
               prevResults[num] = false;
               break;
            }
         }
         if (count > Math.sqrt(num)) { prevResults[num] = true; }
      }
   }
   return prevResults[num];
}
```

Looks like this version will be a real memory hog, that's the main issue. As a result, though, it should work really well for subsequent requests. In fact, this is exactly the case. It counts primes under 1 Million in 0.189 seconds! Furthermore, it counts primes to 100 million with cold cache in less than 90 seconds, and second time in just 0.653 seconds! So, we have now **met performance goal #3**. We still need to get the "cold cache" version down to 60 second for 100 Million. While we're here let's see whether `isPrime6` can scale to 1 Billion.

Unfortunately, we don't get there. At something like 117 million, we run out of memory and crash (with the "Aw, Snap!" screen in Chrome, for example). Ugh. Why is this, and what do we do now?

Chapter 21 – Optimization

☐ Is Number Prime (Series) – continued

Let's continue going after goal #1 before starting in on the scalability goal (#2). How else can we make this process faster? How about an extension of our (don't check evens) idea? What if we *only* check prime numbers as the factors: only check whether the number is divisible by 2, 3, 5, 7, 11, 13, etc. As the numbers get larger, this should save a lot of time. How would you know whether a number is prime, without calling yourself to find out, though? (-: I think we would specifically cache an array of only the primes, so we can oh-so-quickly breeze through them to check whether to add to our prime list. This won't necessarily scale any higher, but it should be a good bit faster! Let's code it first, then measure it.

```
// Only check PRIME factors (up to sqrt). Cache primes for this.
// Try cache first, before checking for negative / fractional.
var prevResults = [false, false, true];
var primes = [2];
function isPrime7(num)
{
   if (prevResults[num] === undefined) {
      if (num < 0 || num % 1) { return false; }

      while (prevResults.length <= num) {
         var next = prevResults.length;
         var rootNext = Math.sqrt(next);
         for (var primeIdx = 0; primes[primeIdx] <= rootNext; primeIdx++) {
            if (next % primes[primeIdx] == 0) {
               prevResults.push(false);
               break;
            }
         }
         if (primes[primeIdx] > rootNext) {
            prevResults.push(true);
            primes.push(next);
         }
      }
   }
   return prevResults[num];
}
```

So how did `isPrime7` do? Did it meet our performance goals? Yes, it met some! First, we counted to 100 Million primes in only 33.91 sec, cold cache. With warm cache, we ran in 0.685 sec for subsequent 100 Million requests! So, we have goals #1 and #3 taken care of, nicely. We've really come far!

About goal #2... how far *can* `isPrime7` count, anyway? Not a lot farther, as it turns out. It counts to 122 Million without problem (getting there in 40sec), but 123 Million causes an "Aw, Snap!" So there.

Chapter 21 – Optimization

☐ Is Number Prime (Series) – continued

We've met our #1 and #3 performance goals. The only one remaining is scalability, so we must figure out how to jettison memory usage without sacrificing the big speed that we've won. Let's assess.

Currently we are caching previous results – a boolean for every positive integer. To count to 1 Billion, we'll need a Boolean for each of those. In JavaScript, a Boolean consumes 4 bytes, so if this algorithm did get all the way to 1 Billion, the `prevResults` array would consume 4GB of memory – whoa. Also, what about the cached `primes` array? At 100 Million, this is an array of 5.76 Million elements. These are numbers, hence eight bytes, but at 46 MB it still looks pretty svelte compared to `prevResults`. What if we tossed the whole `prevResults` array and relied only on `primes[]`, working solo? Here's the code:

```
// Cache primes ONLY (not prevResults[]). Mem usage dramatically reduced.
var primes = [2];
var highestCheck = 2;
function isPrime8(num)
{
   if (num < 2 || num % 1) { return false;       }
   if (num % 2 == 0)       { return (num == 2); }

   var checkStart = Math.min(num, highestCheck) | 1;
   for (var check = checkStart; check <= num; check += 2) {
      var rootCheck = Math.sqrt(check);
      for (var primeIdx = 0; primes[primeIdx] <= rootCheck; primeIdx++) {
         if (check % primes[primeIdx] == 0) { break; }
      }
      if (primes[primeIdx] > rootCheck) {
         if (check > highestCheck) { primes.push(check); }
         if (check == num) {
            highestCheck = Math.max(highestCheck, num);
            return true;
         }
      }
   }
   highestCheck = Math.max(highestCheck, num);
   return false;
}
```

What do you think? Will we still see the gains we earned? Form a view, then join me on the next page.

Chapter 21 – Optimization

☐ Is Number Prime (Series) – continued

The `isPrime8` implementation is fascinating. It was able to count primes to 100 Million in about 50 seconds, first time (*cold* scenario). However, as we might expect from removing a direct-result cache, the *warm* scenario did lose some of the previous gains. Specifically, a second-time count to 100 Million required about 25.6 sec, rather than about 700 ms with `isPrime7`. On the flip side, it scales. *It scales!* It counted past 500 Million (it's still going as I type this!). I'll need to update this when it does in fact cross 1 Billion, but I trust that this will certainly occur. (Yep, it did.)

To win the warm scenario, we'll need to hold on to some flavor of our `prevResults` array. We also need to reduce our size though, and the direct result cache is by far our largest size component. This suggests that we go right at the big memory consumer and figure out even a small improvement.

To really squeeze space, we could convert a boolean array into a `BitArray`. Here, we put 32 bits into the space usually filled by 1 boolean; this would *dramatically* reduce our cache's size. Let's give it a try.

```
function BitArray(numBits)
{
   var arr = [];
   for (var i=0; i<(numBits/32); i++)
   {
      arr[i] = 0;
   }
   this.numBits = numBits;

   this.set = function(bitIdx) {
      if( bitIdx < 0 || bitIdx % 1)
      { return; }
      if (bitIdx >= this.numBits) {
         var idx=(this.numBits+31)/32
         for(;idx<(numBits/32);idx++)
         { arr[idx] = 0; }
         this.numBits = bitIdx + 1;
      }
      var bitNum = bitIdx & 0b11111;
      var arrIdx = bitIdx >>> 5;
      arr[arrIdx] |= (1 << bitNum);
   }
```

```
   this.read = function(bitIdx)
   {
      if(bitIdx<0 || bitIdx % 1
      || bitIdx >= this.numBits)
      { return; }
      var bitNum = bitIdx & 0b11111;
      var arrIdx = bitIdx >>> 5;
      return(arr[arrIdx]>>bitNum) &1;
   }
   this.clear = function(bitIdx) {
      if (bitIdx < 0 || bitIdx % 1)
      { return; }
      if (bitIdx >= this.numBits) {
         var idx=(this.numBits+31)/32
         for(;idx<(numBits/32);idx++)
         { arr[idx] = 0; }
         this.numBits = bitIdx + 1;
      }
      var bitNum = bitIdx & 0b11111;
      var arrIdx = bitIdx >>> 5;
      arr[arrIdx] &= ~(1 << bitNum);
   }
}
```

Chapter 21 – Optimization

☐ Is Number Prime (Series) – continued

```
// prevResults to BitArray: 30x smaller
// than bool arr. Otherwise is isPrime7.
var primes = [2];
var baPrimes = new BitArray(3);
baPrimes.clear(0);
baPrimes.clear(1);
baPrimes.set(2);
function isPrime9(num) {
   var result = baPrimes.read(num);
   if (result !== undefined)
   { return result; }
   if (num < 0|| num % 1)
   { return false; }
   while (num >= baPrimes.numBits) {
      var next = baPrimes.numBits;
      var rootNext = Math.sqrt(next);
      for ( var primeIdx = 0;
          primes[primeIdx] <= rootNext;
          primeIdx++) {
         if (next%primes[primeIdx] ==0) {
            baPrimes.clear(next);
            break;
         }
      }
      if (primes[primeIdx] > rootNext) {
         primes.push(next);
         baPrimes.set(next);
      }
   }
   return baPrimes.read(num);
}
```

There simply is no better way to finish off a performance journey than with a geeky bit-encoded data representation. Essentially, `isPrime9` performs as `isPrime7` does, but without an oversized memory footprint.

The results are fabulous. First, scalability: `isPrime9` runs to 1 Billion and keeps going! On my Mac, it almost reaches 2 Billion: *much better* than the requirement.

On the other goals, during our first-time counting primes to 100 Million, `isPrime9` consumed about 30.5 sec. This is well ahead of our goal of 60 secs (and *destroys* `isPrime1`'s expected 15 yrs). Great!

Even better, the second-time count ("warm cache"), ran in 0.964 sec. It feels awesome to *barely* meet your performance goals, as you know you didn't add unnecessary optimization (which can convolute code).

What do you think about our final code? Is it as readable as the first version? Might an intern innocently 'fix' a bug and break an important feature by mistake? *Yes* – that is a reasonable worry. Like racehorses, high-performance code can be brittle. Always measure, and watch for regressions!

Optimization Review

Software performance is a rich area, with multiple engagement levels. Most importantly, always measure code you want to remain high-performance. Set goals. Once you achieve them, don't let further optimization become a black hole. A few simple calculations upfront can tip you off that certain designs cannot perform as required. Always best to fix *designs* early, but don't optimize *code* earlier than you must. Algorithm choice is critical – easily 30,000x or more, as data get large. Pay attention to highly-used code, where tiny wins are magnified. Detailed code tuning can play a role. Simple tweaks to central routines are good, but defer changes that impact readability and debuggability until absolutely needed. Get creative, be wise, and as with any aspect of your life, *keep your eyes on the goals!*

Index of Challenges

CAPITALIZED TITLES are chapters
☐ Titles are algorithm challenges. Feel free to check them off when you've completed them!

Check with your instructor/mentor for access to solutions.

CHAPTER 1 – FUNDAMENTALS — 16
- ☐ Setting and Swapping — 16
- ☐ Print -52 to 1066 — 16
- ☐ Don't Worry, Be Happy — 16
- ☐ Multiples of Three – but Not All — 16
- ☐ Printing Integers with While — 16
- ☐ You Say It's Your Birthday — 16
- ☐ Leap Year — 16
- ☐ Print and Count — 16
- ☐ Multiples of Six — 16
- ☐ Counting, the Dojo Way — 16
- ☐ What Do You Know? — 16
- ☐ Whoa, That Sucker's Huge… — 16
- ☐ Countdown by Fours — 16
- ☐ Flexible Countdown — 16
- ☐ The Final Countdown — 16
- ☐ Countdown — 20
- ☐ Print and Return — 20
- ☐ First Plus Length — 20
- ☐ Values Greater than Second — 20
- ☐ Values Greater than Second, Generalized — 20
- ☐ This Length, That Value — 20
- ☐ Fit the First Value — 20
- ☐ Fahrenheit to Celsius — 20
- ☐ Celsius to Fahrenheit — 20
- ☐ Biggie Size — 22
- ☐ Print Low, Return High — 22
- ☐ Print One, Return Another — 22
- ☐ Double Vision — 22
- ☐ Count Positives — 22
- ☐ Evens and Odds — 22
- ☐ Increment the Seconds — 22
- ☐ Previous Lengths — 22
- ☐ Add Seven to Most — 22
- ☐ Reverse Array — 22
- ☐ Outlook: Negative — 22
- ☐ Always Hungry — 22
- ☐ Swap Toward the Center — 22
- ☐ Scale the Array — 22
- ☐ Only Keep the Last Few — 24
- ☐ Math Help — 24
- ☐ Poor Kenny — 24

- ☐ What *Really* Happened? — 24
- ☐ Soaring IQ — 24
- ☐ Letter Grade — 24
- ☐ More Accurate Grades — 24
- ☐ Short Answer Questions: Fundamentals — 26
- ☐ Weekend Challenge: Fundamentals — 26

CHAPTER 2 – FUNDAMENTALS, PART II — 28

- ☐ Sigma — 28
- ☐ Factorial — 28
- ☐ Star Art — 28
- ☐ Character Art — 28
- ☐ Threes and Fives — 29
- ☐ Generate Coin Change — 29
- ☐ Messy Math Mashup — 29
- ☐ Twelve-Bar Blues — 30
- ☐ Fibonacci — 30
- ☐ Sum to One Digit — 30
- ☐ Clock Hand Angles — 30
- ☐ Is Prime — 30
- ☐ Rockin' the Dojo Sweatshirt — 31
- ☐ Clock Hand Angles, Revisited — 31
- ☐ Extract-o-matic — 32
- ☐ Most Significant Digit — 32
- ☐ Gaming Fun(damentals) — 33
- ☐ Statistics Until Doubles — 33
- ☐ Claire is Where? — 33
- ☐ Date, on a Deserted Island — 34
- ☐ Short Answer Questions: Fundamentals, Part II — 35
- ☐ Weekend Challenge: Fundamentals, Part II — 35

CHAPTER 3 – ARRAYS — 37

- ☐ Array: Push Front — 38
- ☐ Array: Insert At — 38
- ☐ Array: Pop Front — 38
- ☐ Array: Remove At — 38
- ☐ Array: Swap Pairs — 38
- ☐ Array: Remove Duplicates — 38
- ☐ Array: Min to Front — 39
- ☐ Array: Reverse — 40
- ☐ Array: Rotate — 40
- ☐ Array: Filter Range — 40
- ☐ Array: Concat — 40
- ☐ Skyline Heights — 40
- ☐ Array: Remove Negatives — 42
- ☐ Array: Second-to-Last — 42
- ☐ Array: Nth-to-Last — 42
- ☐ Array: Second-Largest — 42
- ☐ Array: Nth-Largest — 42
- ☐ Credit Card Validation — 42

- ☐ Array: Shuffle — 43
- ☐ Array: Remove Range — 43
- ☐ Intermediate Sums — 43
- ☐ Double Trouble — 43
- ☐ Zip It — 43
- ☐ Short Answer Questions: Arrays — 44
- ☐ Weekend Challenge: Arrays — 44

CHAPTER 4 – STRINGS AND ASSOCIATIVE ARRAYS — 49
- ☐ Remove Blanks — 50
- ☐ String: Get Digits — 50
- ☐ Acronyms — 50
- ☐ Count Non-Spaces — 50
- ☐ Remove Shorter Strings — 50
- ☐ String: Reverse — 51
- ☐ Remove Even-Length Strings — 51
- ☐ Integer to Roman Numerals — 51
- ☐ Roman Numerals to Integer — 51
- ☐ Parens Valid — 52
- ☐ Braces Valid — 52
- ☐ String: Is Palindrome — 52
- ☐ Longest Palindrome — 52
- ☐ Is Word Alphabetical — 53
- ☐ D Gets Jiggy — 53
- ☐ Common Suffix — 53
- ☐ Book Index — 53
- ☐ Drop the Mike — 53
- ☐ Coin Change with Object — 54
- ☐ Max/Min/Average with Object — 54
- ☐ Zip Arrays into Map — 55
- ☐ Invert Hash — 55
- ☐ Associative Array: Number of Values (without .Length) — 55
- ☐ String.concat — 56
- ☐ String.slice — 56
- ☐ String.trim — 56
- ☐ String.split — 56
- ☐ String.search — 56
- ☐ Short Answer Questions: Strings and Associative Arrays — 57
- ☐ Weekend Challenge: Strings and Associative Arrays — 57

CHAPTER 5 – LINKED LISTS — 59
- ☐ List: Add Front — 60
- ☐ List: Contains — 60
- ☐ List: Remove Front — 60
- ☐ List: Front — 60
- ☐ SList: Length — 61
- ☐ SList: Display — 61
- ☐ SList: Max — 61
- ☐ SList: Min — 61
- ☐ SList: Average — 61

- ☐ SList: Back — 62
- ☐ SList: Remove Back — 62
- ☐ SList: Add Back — 62
- ☐ SList: Move Min to Front — 62
- ☐ SList: Move Max to Back — 62
- ☐ SList: Prepend Val — 63
- ☐ SList: Append Val — 63
- ☐ Create SList (prompt) — 63
- ☐ SList: Remove Val — 63
- ☐ SList: Split on Value — 64
- ☐ SList: Remove Negatives — 64
- ☐ SList: Concat — 64
- ☐ SList: Partition — 64
- ☐ SList: Second to Last Value — 65
- ☐ SList: Delete Given Node — 65
- ☐ SList: Copy — 65
- ☐ SList: Filter — 65
- ☐ SList: Second Largest Value — 66
- ☐ Zip SLists — 66
- ☐ Dedupe SList — 66
- ☐ Dedupe SList Without Buffer — 66
- ☐ Short Answer Questions: Objects, Classes and Linked Lists — 68
- ☐ Weekend Challenge: Linked Lists — 68

THE "BUGGY 13" (#1)   70

CHAPTER 6 – QUEUES AND STACKS   72
- ☐ SLQueue: Enqueue — 73
- ☐ SLQueue: Front — 73
- ☐ SLQueue: Is Empty — 73
- ☐ SLQueue: Compare Queues — 73
- ☐ SLQueue: Dequeue — 73
- ☐ SLQueue: Contains — 73
- ☐ SLQueue: Size — 73
- ☐ SLQueue: Remove Minimums — 73
- ☐ SLQueue: Interleave Queue — 73
- ☐ ArrStack: Push — 74
- ☐ ArrStack: Top — 74
- ☐ ArrStack: Is Empty — 74
- ☐ ArrStack: Pop — 74
- ☐ ArrStack: Contains — 74
- ☐ ArrStack: Size — 74
- ☐ SLStack: Push — 74
- ☐ SLStack: Top — 74
- ☐ SLStack: Is Empty — 74
- ☐ SLStack: Pop — 74
- ☐ SLStack: Contains — 74
- ☐ SLStack: Size — 74
- ☐ Compare Stacks — 74
- ☐ Stack: Copy — 75

- ☐ Create Queue Using Two Stacks — 75
- ☐ Queue: Is Palindrome — 75
- ☐ Stack / Queue Code-Sharing — 75
- ☐ Deque: Implementation — 75
- ☐ Stack: Remove Stack Min — 75
- ☐ CirQueue: Front — 76
- ☐ CirQueue: Is Empty — 76
- ☐ CirQueue: Is Full — 76
- ☐ CirQueue: Size — 76
- ☐ CirQueue: Enqueue — 76
- ☐ CirQueue: Dequeue — 76
- ☐ CirQueue: Contains — 76
- ☐ CirQueue: Grow — 76
- ☐ Reorder Absolute Queue — 77
- ☐ Stack: Partition — 77
- ☐ Stack: Is Sorted — 77
- ☐ Stack: Switch Pairs — 77
- ☐ Stack: Mirror — 77
- ☐ Weak Finger — 77
- ☐ Short Answer Questions: Queues and Stacks — 78
- ☐ Weekend Challenge: Stacks and Queues — 79

CHAPTER 7 – ARRAYS, PART II — 80

- ☐ Array: Average (Warmup) — 80
- ☐ Balance Point — 80
- ☐ Balance Index — 80
- ☐ Taco Truck — 80
- ☐ Array: Binary Search — 81
- ☐ Min of Sorted-Rotated — 81
- ☐ String: Binary Search — 81
- ☐ Array: Flatten — 82
- ☐ Array: Remove Duplicates — 82
- ☐ Array: Mode — 82
- ☐ Array: Buffer Copy — 82
- ☐ Smarter Sum — 83
- ☐ Faster Factorial — 83
- ☐ Fancy Fibonacci — 83
- ☐ Tricky Tribonacci — 83
- ☐ Median of Sorted Arrays — 84
- ☐ Time to English — 84
- ☐ Missing Value — 84
- ☐ Rain Terraces — 84
- ☐ Last Digit of A to the B — 85
- ☐ Matrix Search — 85
- ☐ Max of Subarray Sums — 85

THE "BUGFUL 13" (#2) — 86

CHAPTER 8 – LINKED LISTS, PART II — 89

- ☐ SList: Reverse — 90
- ☐ SList: Kth-Last Node — 90
- ☐ SList: Is Palindrome — 90
- ☐ SList: Shift Right — 90
- ☐ SList: Sum Numerals — 91
- ☐ SList: Setup Loop — 91
- ☐ SList: Flatten Children — 91
- ☐ SList: Unflatten Children — 91
- ☐ SList: Has Loop — 92
- ☐ SList: Break Loop — 92
- ☐ SList: Loop Start — 92
- ☐ SList: Number of Nodes — 92
- ☐ SList: Swap Pairs — 92
- ☐ Where's the Bug? (SList version) — 93
- ☐ DList Class — 94
- ☐ DList: Prepend Value — 95
- ☐ DList: Kth-to-Last Value — 95
- ☐ DList: Is Valid — 95
- ☐ DList: Palindrome — 95
- ☐ DList: Loop Start — 95
- ☐ DList: Append Value — 95
- ☐ DList: Delete Middle Node — 95
- ☐ DList: Partition — 95
- ☐ DList: Reverse — 95
- ☐ DList: Break Loop — 95
- ☐ DList: Repair — 95
- ☐ Short Answer Questions: DLists — 95

CHAPTER 9 – RECURSION — 96

- ☐ Recursive Sigma — 97
- ☐ Recursive Factorial — 97
- ☐ Flood Fill — 97
- ☐ Recursive Fibonacci — 99
- ☐ Recursive "Tribonacci" — 99
- ☐ Paging Dr. Ackermann — 99
- ☐ Zibonacci — 99
- ☐ Recursive Binary Search — 101
- ☐ Greatest Common Factor — 101
- ☐ Tarai — 101
- ☐ String: In-Order Subsets — 101
- ☐ Recursive List Length — 102
- ☐ Got Any Grapes?!? — 102
- ☐ Collatz-apalooza — 102
- ☐ Telephone Words — 102
- ☐ Rising Squares — 103
- ☐ Binary String Expansion — 103
- ☐ String Anagrams — 103
- ☐ Climbing Stairs — 103
- ☐ Sum of Squares — 104
- ☐ All Valid N Pairs of Parens — 104
- ☐ Towers of Hanoi — 104

- ☐ IP Addresses — 104
- ☐ Uneven Digits — 104
- ☐ Generate All Possible Coin Change — 104
- ☐ Is Chess Move Safe — 105
- ☐ Eight Queens — 105
- ☐ All Safe Chess Squares — 105
- ☐ N Queens — 105
- ☐ Where's the Bug? (recursion version) — 106

CHAPTER 10 – STRINGS, PART II — 107

- ☐ String to Word Array — 107
- ☐ Reverse Word Order — 107
- ☐ Longest Word — 107
- ☐ Unique Words — 107
- ☐ String: Rotate String — 108
- ☐ Censor — 108
- ☐ String: ionIs Rotat (Is Rotation) — 108
- ☐ Bad Characters — 108
- ☐ Genetic Marker — 108
- ☐ Optimal Sequence — 108
- ☐ String: Dedupe — 109
- ☐ Index of First Unique Letter — 109
- ☐ Unique Letters — 109
- ☐ Num to String — 109
- ☐ Num to Text — 109
- ☐ String: Is Permtutaoin (Is Permutation) — 110
- ☐ String: All Permutations — 110
- ☐ String: Is Pangram — 110
- ☐ String: Is Perfect Pangram — 110
- ☐ Best Time to Buy and Sell Stock — 110
- ☐ Are Strings Loosely Interleaved — 111
- ☐ All Loosely Interleaved Strings — 111
- ☐ Make String Palindrome (Remove One) — 111
- ☐ Make String Palindrome (Add One) — 111
- ☐ String Encode — 112
- ☐ String Decode — 112
- ☐ Shortener — 112
- ☐ Weekend Challenge: Strings, Part II (Search with Regex) — 112

THE "BUG-LADEN 13" (#3) — 113

CHAPTER 11 – TREES — 116

- ☐ BST: Add — 117
- ☐ BST: Min — 117
- ☐ BST: Size — 117
- ☐ BST: Contains — 117
- ☐ BST: Max — 117
- ☐ BST: Is Empty — 117
- ☐ BST: Height — 118

- ☐ BST: Is Balanced — 118
- ☐ Array to BST — 118
- ☐ Closest Common Ancestor — 118
- ☐ Traverse BST Pre-Order — 119
- ☐ BST to Array — 119
- ☐ BST: Minimum Height — 119
- ☐ Traverse BST Post-Order — 119
- ☐ BST to List — 119
- ☐ Traverse BST Pre-Order, No Recursion — 119
- ☐ BST: Remove — 120
- ☐ BST: Is Valid — 120
- ☐ BST: Remove All — 120
- ☐ BST: Add Without Dupes — 120
- ☐ Traverse BST Reverse-Order — 120
- ☐ BST: Val Before — 121
- ☐ BTNode: Node Before — 121
- ☐ BST: Val After — 121
- ☐ BTNode: Node After — 121
- ☐ BST: Closest Value — 121
- ☐ Tree Path Contains Sum — 121
- ☐ BST With Parent — 122
- ☐ Sum of BST Root-Leaf Numbers — 122
- ☐ Left-Side Binary Tree — 122
- ☐ Short Answer Questions: Trees — 123

CHAPTER 12 – SORTS — 124

- ☐ Array: Bubble Sort — 125
- ☐ SList: Bubble Sort — 125
- ☐ Array: Selection Sort — 125
- ☐ SList: Selection Sort — 125
- ☐ Multikey Sort — 125
- ☐ Array: Insertion Sort — 126
- ☐ Array: Combine — 126
- ☐ SList: Insertion Sort — 126
- ☐ SList: Combine — 126
- ☐ SList: Merge Sort — 127
- ☐ Array: Partition — 127
- ☐ SList: Partition — 127
- ☐ Array: Quick Sort — 128
- ☐ Array: Merge Sort — 128
- ☐ Array: Partition3 — 128
- ☐ Smarter Sorting — 129
- ☐ Quick Sort 3 — 129
- ☐ Master Invoice List — 129
- ☐ Urban Dictionary Daily Add — 130
- ☐ Pancake Sort — 130
- ☐ Radix Sort — 130
- ☐ Wiggle Sort — 130
- ☐ Belt Sort — 130
- ☐ Median of Unsorted Array — 130

| THE "BUG-INFESTED 13" (#4) | 132 |

CHAPTER 13 – SETS AND PRIORITY QUEUES — 135
- ☐ Interleave Arrays — 135
- ☐ Merge Sorted Arrays — 135
- ☐ Minimal Three-Array Range — 135
- ☐ Intersect Sorted Arrays — 136
- ☐ Intersect Sorted Arrays (dedupe) — 136
- ☐ Union Sorted Arrays — 137
- ☐ Intersection Unsorted Arrays (in-place) — 137
- ☐ Union Sorted Arrays (dedupe) — 137
- ☐ Intersection Unsorted Arrays — 137
- ☐ Union Unsorted Arrays — 137
- ☐ Union Unsorted Arrays (in-place) — 138
- ☐ Subset Sorted Arrays — 138
- ☐ Union Unsorted Arrays (no duplicates) — 138
- ☐ Subset Unsorted Arrays — 138
- ☐ My Very Own Square Root — 138
- ☐ SList: Priority Queue — 139
- ☐ Sequencer — 139
- ☐ Heap: Constructor — 140
- ☐ Heap: Size — 140
- ☐ Heap: Contains — 140
- ☐ Heap: Is Empty — 140
- ☐ Heap: Top — 140
- ☐ Heap: Insert — 140
- ☐ Heap: Extract — 141
- ☐ Heap: Heapify Array — 141
- ☐ Heap Sort — 141
- ☐ Median of Data Stream — 142
- ☐ Queue from Two Stacks — 142
- ☐ Priority Queue from Two Stacks — 142
- ☐ Comparing Stacks/Queues to Other Data Structures — 142
- ☐ Short Answer Questions: Sets and Priority Queues — 143

CHAPTER 14 – HASHES — 144
- ☐ Hash: Add — 145
- ☐ Hash: Is Empty — 145
- ☐ Hash: Find Key — 145
- ☐ Hash: Remove — 146
- ☐ Hash: Grow — 146
- ☐ Hash: Add — 146
- ☐ Hash: Load Factor — 146
- ☐ Hash: Set Size — 146
- ☐ Hash: Select Keys — 146
- ☐ Making Maps into Sets or Multimaps — 147
- ☐ Short Answer Questions: Unordered Data Structures — 149
- ☐ Short Answer Questions: Ordered Data Structures — 149
- ☐ Blue Belt Exam — 150

CHAPTER 15 – TREES, PART II — 151
- ☐ BST: Is Full — 151
- ☐ BST: Is Complete — 151
- ☐ BST Discussion — 151
- ☐ BST: Repair — 152
- ☐ BST: Smallest Difference — 152
- ☐ SList: Smallest Difference — 152
- ☐ BST: Closest Value (again) — 152
- ☐ SList: Closest Value — 152
- ☐ Array: Closest Value — 152
- ☐ DList: Closest Value — 152
- ☐ BST: Partition Around Value — 153
- ☐ BST: Partition Evenly — 153
- ☐ BST: Reverse — 153
- ☐ BST: Kth-Biggest — 154
- ☐ Test Cases for BST2 Repair — 154
- ☐ BST2: Repair — 154
- ☐ BST: Values for Layer — 155
- ☐ BST: Layer Arrays — 155

CHAPTER 16 – TRIES — 156
- ☐ Trie: Insert — 157
- ☐ Trie: Contains — 157
- ☐ Trie: First — 157
- ☐ Trie: Last — 157
- ☐ Trie: Remove — 157
- ☐ Trie: Size — 158
- ☐ Trie: Next — 158
- ☐ Trie: Auto Complete — 158
- ☐ Trie MultiSet: Insert — 159
- ☐ Trie MultiSet: Size — 159
- ☐ Trie MultiSet: Remove — 159
- ☐ Trie MultiSet: Contains — 159
- ☐ Trie MultiSet: Auto Complete — 159
- ☐ Trie Map: Insert — 159
- ☐ Trie Map: Contains — 159
- ☐ Trie Map: Remove — 159
- ☐ Trie Map: Size — 159
- ☐ Trie Map: First — 159
- ☐ Trie Map: Last — 159
- ☐ Trie Map: Next — 159

CHAPTER 17 – GRAPHS — 160
- ☐ Edge List Exercise 1 — 163
- ☐ Edge List Exercise 2 — 163
- ☐ Adjacency Map Exercise 1 — 164
- ☐ Adjacency Map Exercise 2 — 164
- ☐ Adjacency List Exercise 1 — 165
- ☐ Adjacency List Exercise 2 — 165
- ☐ Edge List Implementation — 166

- ☐ Adjacency Map Implementation — 166
- ☐ Adjacency List Implementation — 166
- ☐ Someone on the Inside — 167
- ☐ Vertex Is Reachable — 167
- ☐ All Paths — 167
- ☐ Shortest Path — 168
- ☐ Gimme Three Steps — 168
- ☐ Easy to Get There — 168
- ☐ Graph: Is DAG — 169
- ☐ DAG to Array — 169
- ☐ Weekend Challenge: Word Ladder — 169

CHAPTER 18 – BIT ARITHMETIC — 170

- ☐ Decimal to Octal Practice — 171
- ☐ Octal to Decimal Practice — 171
- ☐ Decimal to Octal String — 171
- ☐ Octal String to Value — 171
- ☐ Decimal to Hexadecimal — 172
- ☐ Hexadecimal to Decimal — 172
- ☐ Decimal to Hexadecimal String — 172
- ☐ Hexadecimal String to Value — 172
- ☐ Decimal to Binary — 173
- ☐ Binary to Decimal — 173
- ☐ Decimal to Binary String — 173
- ☐ Binary String to Value — 173
- ☐ Reorder Word Fragments — 173
- ☐ Bitwise AND — 174
- ☐ Bitwise OR — 174
- ☐ Bitwise NOT — 174
- ☐ Bitwise XOR — 175
- ☐ Bitwise LSL — 175
- ☐ Bitwise LSR — 175
- ☐ Count in Binary — 175
- ☐ Count Set Bits — 176
- ☐ Encode Bytes to 32 — 176
- ☐ Reverse Bits — 176
- ☐ Decode 32 to Bytes — 176
- ☐ Byte Array — 176
- ☐ Encode Bit Num — 177
- ☐ Bit Array — 177
- ☐ Decode Bit Num — 177
- ☐ Radix Sort2 — 177
- ☐ Sprinklers — 177
- ☐ LED Encoding — 177
- ☐ Where's the Bug? (bitwise operators version) — 177

CHAPTER 19 – TREES, PART III — 178

- ☐ AVL: Height — 178
- ☐ AVL: Is Balanced — 178
- ☐ AVL: Remove — 179

- ☐ AVL: Add — 179
- ☐ AVL: Rotate Left — 181
- ☐ AVL: Rotate Right — 181
- ☐ AVL: Balanced Add — 182
- ☐ AVL: Balanced Remove — 182
- ☐ AVL: Rebalance — 182
- ☐ RBTree and RBNode Class Definitions — 183
- ☐ Red-Black Tree: Add — 183
- ☐ Red-Black Tree: Contains — 183
- ☐ Red-Black Tree: Remove — 183
- ☐ Short-Answer Questions on AVL and Red-Black Trees — 183
- ☐ Splay Tree Class Definitions — 184
- ☐ Splay Tree: Add — 184
- ☐ Splay Tree: Contains — 184
- ☐ Splay Tree: Remove — 184
- ☐ Short-Answer Questions on Splay and Self-Balancing Trees — 184
- ☐ Black Belt Exam — 185

CHAPTER 20 – SPATIAL, LOGIC, ESTIMATION — 186

- ☐ Minding the Gap — 186
- ☐ Sketching the Circle — 186
- ☐ Describing the Rectangle (or, 'Get Rect') — 186
- ☐ Detecting the Overlap — 186
- ☐ Checking the Connectedness Count — 186
- ☐ Admiring the Skyline — 186
- ☐ Calling the Big One — 186
- ☐ Finding the Fraud — 187
- ☐ Revealing the Wrong — 187
- ☐ Querying the Quarters — 187
- ☐ Lighting the Way — 187
- ☐ Making the Train — 187
- ☐ Escaping the Hunt — 187
- ☐ Surviving the Train — 188
- ☐ Racing the Balls — 188
- ☐ Crossing the River — 188
- ☐ Burning the String — 188
- ☐ Outfoxing the Fox — 188
- ☐ Swapping the Lockers — 188
- ☐ Combining the Numbers — 188
- ☐ Pricing the Movie — 189
- ☐ Building the Widgets — 189
- ☐ Padding the Pond — 189
- ☐ Elevating the Passengers — 189
- ☐ Piano Tuners — 190
- ☐ Basketballs in a 747 — 190
- ☐ Kindergarten Teachers — 190
- ☐ Weight of a Ferry — 190
- ☐ Hot Diggity — 190
- ☐ Beachfront Property in Colorado — 190
- ☐ Earth's Circumference — 190
- ☐ Gas Stations — 190

☐ Line 'Em Up	190
☐ Building Capacity	190
☐ Painting a Room	190
☐ Blades of Grass	190
☐ Lottery Stack	190

CHAPTER 21 – OPTIMIZATION — **191**

☐ Closest Three-Sum (Series)	191
☐ N Queens (Series)	198
☐ Is Number Prime (Series)	211
☐ Counting Primes	211

Interview Tips

Students sometimes wonder *what language* to use in technical interviews. The answer of course: "whatever language they tell you." What if you don't know what they prefer? Or, what if you are not strong in that language? Don't despair! Most interviewers will say "*Use whatever language makes you most productive….*" (while they are also thinking "*…as long as it is appropriate for this problem….*"). So, don't choose Ruby to solve a graphics firmware problem; don't use Fortran in a web interview. Except for specialized roles, it is safe to write in JavaScript, Java, C# or C++. As you know, this course focuses on JavaScript: it is universal to all web front-ends and has growing server-side usage with Node.js.

Interviewing is an artificial situation. Like anything else, you improve your performance with practice. Even post- bootcamp, *code on whiteboard* and paper, to simulate interviews. Resist the urge to code only at a computer. Once you complete a solution, *then* debug it at a computer. What common errors do you make on whiteboard or paper? Note these and refer back to them over time.

How and what you *communicate to interviewers* is as important as getting the right solution. Remember that they can't read your mind; always *think out loud*. As you mentally run through multiple possibilities, discarding numerous dead-end ideas, it behooves you to provide visibility into your thought process.

Don't jump in and start writing code immediately. Ask *clarifying questions* – the answers might surprise you. Often, interviewers are intentionally vague, to test whether you can extract unstated requirements. Ensuring you understand the intention upfront is important. Ask about extreme inputs, including those that violate expectations (whether intentional or not) – jot these on a corner of the whiteboard to double-check later. *Restate to the interviewer* your understanding of the problem. Write out a few important inputs, with expected outputs. If you think of multiple ways to solve the problem (perhaps even if not), it is enlightening to ask "What should we optimize for?" Really listen to the interviewer's response here.

Sooner or later you must start coding – don't let pre-coding stretch out. A common-sense tip: start coding in the whiteboard's upper left corner; leave room so you avoid lots of arrows (good engineers plan ahead, just sayin'…). Start with the function's signature (name and inputs) and a few lines of input checking, just to *get ink on the board*. If you get stuck, try not to stall – leave a comment or pseudocode and mention that you will come back to this. Keep going; *maintain velocity*. Mid-stream, you may realize there is a much better solution. Don't keep it a secret; your interviewer already knows this. Mention the new idea, but suggest that you keep going in order to finish a solution in the time you have. Once you complete something, *run through your test cases* before declaring a function done.

Remember your **RIOT WALK**! (Recap, inputs/outputs, tests, walkthrough the code.) Do it. Every time.

Again: always *keep your ears open* for interviewer hints and guidance. They want you to succeed!

Good luck!   -mp

Have a question, clarification, correction? Heard a good one lately that you are just dying to pass on? Think you'd like to "stump the chump?" Contact the author at mpuryear@codingdojo.com.
Thanks for your focus and energy!